P9-CCV-312

Books by WILLIAM H. PRITCHARD

Randall Jarrell: A Literary Life   (1990)

Frost: A Literary Life Reconsidered   (1984)

Lives of the Modern Poets   (1980)

Seeing Through Everything: English Writers 1918–1940   (1977)

Wyndham Lewis   (1968)

Randall Jarrell

A Literary Life

Randall Jarrell

A Literary Life

by William H. Pritchard

MICHAEL DI CAPUA BOOKS

FARRAR, STRAUS AND GIROUX

New York

To David, Michael, Willy

I *know* those children. I know all about them.
Where are they?

CONTENTS

ILLUSTRATIONS

Following page 146

ACKNOWLEDGMENTS

My foremost debt is to Mary Jarrell, who, in addition to giving generously of her time in letters and conversations, allowed me to read and quote from letters not included in her published edition of Randall Jarrell's letters. Chapter One is particularly indebted to her for facts about Jarrell's childhood.

Much of my pleasure in this project came from conversations with and letters from people who knew Jarrell at various stages of his life. I should like to thank the following: Herschel and Barbara Baker, Cecile Starr Boyajian, Cleanth Brooks, J. A. Bryant, Jr., Charles Farrell, Sally Fitzgerald, R. W. Flint, Marc Friedlaender, the late B. H. Haggin, Elizabeth Hardwick, Beatrice Hofer, Lyle H. Lanier, Robie Macauley, the late Mary McCarthy, Heather Ross Miller, Elizabeth Petway Moses, Patrick Quinn, Sister Bernetta Quinn, Lucille Sasuly, Karl Shapiro, Eileen Simpson, Zaro Starr, Harold Taylor, Peter Taylor, John Thompson, the late Robert Penn Warren, Robert and Betty Watson, Richard Wilbur, Sara Starr Wolff.

Thanks also to those who entertained queries and provided facts or other services: Robert A. Bateman, William O. Batts, Jr., Christopher Benfey, Philip Booth, Ashley Brown, Frances N. Cheney, George Core, James Dickey, Suzanne Ferguson, Richard Flynn, Brendan Gill, the late David Kalstone, Robert V. Keeley, John Lancaster, Estelle Leontief, Wendy Lesser, A. Walton Litz, William McGuire, Jill Stauffer Maney, Jeffrey Meyers, James Olney, Walter Sullivan, Robert Taylor, Donald White, Hardy and Reba Wilcoxon, Stuart Wright.

Maurice Hungeville kindly turned over to me letters he solicited from Jarrell's former students at the University of North Carolina, Greensboro, some of which are quoted in my final chapter.

I am grateful to the following libraries and institutions as well as to people associated with them: The Robert Frost Library, Amherst College;

Acknowledgments

The Berg Collection, New York Public Library; Houghton Library, Harvard University; The Jackson Library at the University of North Carolina, Greensboro; Chalmers Memorial Library, Kenyon College; The Library of Congress; The Jean and Alexander Heard Library, Vanderbilt University; Princeton University Library; Vassar College Library; Beinecke Library, Yale University.

For reading and criticizing the manuscript I am more than usually indebted to Brad Leithauser and David Sofield. Michael di Capua's efforts on behalf of this book have been many and various, as have my agent's, Gloria Loomis. As always, I thank my wife and first editor, Marietta Pritchard.

A grant from the National Endowment for the Humanities assisted the writing of this book.

Randall Jarrell

A Literary Life

Introduction

IN THE MINDS of a good many readers Randall Jarrell is associated with a single, five-line poem, "The Death of the Ball Turret Gunner," which they once encountered in some anthology of twentieth-century American verse. Others know that he wrote a sharp-tongued novel, *Pictures from an Institution*, which satirizes life at a small college. Still others know him as a fierce, though also loving, critic of his American poetic ancestors and contemporaries. Beyond these bits of identifying data, he is remembered as having met a sudden and violent death, the circumstances of which remain less than clear.

Jarrell died in 1965, when he was struck and killed by a car on a dark highway in Chapel Hill, North Carolina. He was, at the time of his death, a patient in a hospital there, undergoing physical therapy on a wrist he had injured in a suicide attempt some months previously. Until the publication in 1985 of his letters, edited by his second wife, Mary Jarrell, the suicide attempt and the nature of Jarrell's stay at the hospital were matters of rumor or conjecture merely. And uncertainties still surround the chronology of events during the last year of his life, as well as exactly what happened the night he was hit by the car. Did he throw himself into its path, or could he have stumbled? Was he sideswiped by the vehicle, thus spun around and fatally injured? Was he deliberately courting the possibility of death, or was he "merely" reckless—unconscionably or forgivably so, depending on your feelings? Or was he unawares, a poet involved in his own world and oblivious of the larger one?

His contemporaries Robert Lowell and John Berryman, whatever they knew or didn't know about Jarrell's death, were not deterred from writing poems about it. Consider Berryman's tribute in Dream Song 121:

> *He endured fifty years. He was Randall Jarrell*
> *and wrote a-many books & he wrote well.*
> *Peace to the bearded corpse.*
> *His last book was his best. His wives loved him.*
> *He saw in the forest something coming, grim,*
> *but did not change his purpose.*
>
> *Honest & cruel, peace now to his soul.*
> *He never loved his body, being full of dents.*
> *A wrinkled peace to this good man.*

Actually Jarrell "endured" fifty-one years, was without a beard when he died, and scarcely comes across in his letters and general behavior as someone who "never loved his body." (Serious tennis players have at least a degree of romance with their physical being, and Jarrell was a serious tennis player.) But Berryman was right about some things too, foremost that Jarrell "wrote a-many books & he wrote well." It would be unfortunate if we forgot this fact in a preoccupation with the outward—or even the inward—circumstances of his death. Moreover, Jarrell's reputation as a writer is not nearly so firm and preeminent as I think it deserves to be.

Let me specify my reasons for claiming that the full range of his interest as a writer has yet to be explored and appreciated. The most secure aspect of his reputation is without doubt that of the reviewer or critic (some would put more stress on "reviewer"). When his *Complete Poems* was published after his death, Helen Vendler made a formulation that has stuck all too adhesively to Jarrell, saying that he "put his genius into his criticism and his talent into his poetry." My own sense is that this critical genius has been more assented to than explored and that much of his writing about other writers remains fairly unfamiliar territory, scattered as it is over four books. But to accept that his poems are merely talented means that they need not be given the sustained, repeated acts of attention by which their singular virtues become apparent. Instead of such attention, there has been a tendency to dismiss Jarrell's poems, or the bulk of them, with the adjective "sentimental." (A recent column in *The New York Times Book Review* stated flatly that the poems "were sentimental—which must be the ultimate terror of the serious modern poet.")

Jarrell's career as a poet has been the subject of an excellent full-length book by Suzanne Ferguson, as well as, more recently, an excellent shorter "guide" by J. A. Bryant, Jr. But the focus in both books is largely explicatory: little space is given to setting the poems against Jarrell's other writings—his essays, reviews, children's stories, novel, letters—and against the significant events of his life. I think that, if a real case is to be made for the permanent interest and value of this writer, it must not be made on the basis of the poems alone—good as they often are, and undervalued at present as I take them to be. From the amount of negative or unenthusiastic commentary I accord—or don't bother to accord —some of the poems (often early ones, but later ones, too), it will be clear that I am no single-minded admirer of Jarrell's verse. He himself provided an excellent standard of critical behavior in this regard when he wrote to Elizabeth Bishop in 1949 about one of his poetic idols:

> Rilke certainly is monstrously self-indulgent a lot of the time, but the good ones are so good it makes up for it. Really one expects most of a good poet's work to be quite bad—if that isn't so it's the 30th of February; it's amusing to have reviewers complain that some of the poems in a poetry book aren't good, because that applies to every book of verse there ever was.

This salutary remark seems obvious until one realizes that nobody had ever said so before—about a Rilke or a Wordsworth, that is, not just about the latest slim volume by a contemporary poet.

Christopher Ricks has remarked that an introduction is the place to say what one has not done. I have not written a biography that aims to provide a comprehensive, detailed record of places and dates, or to tell a continuous story of its subject's growth from one month to the next. Indeed, I am not convinced that such a book is the one most suited to Jarrell's life. His contemporaries and rivals—Lowell and Berryman, and Delmore Schwartz as well—have had good biographies written of them, but it should be pointed out that these men aided their biographers by leading disorderly lives replete with sensational events—with drunkenness, philandering, and madness, just for a start. By contrast, much of Jarrell's life was uneventful, and until almost the end of it he can look "dull" when compared to his contemporaries. He was most himself when reading, writing, and teaching, activities that often prove unexciting when viewed from the outside.

My overriding purpose in this book is to give the man's writings the detailed attention and quotation they deserve. Yet many of my pages focus on Jarrell's life at its most revealing points: as a child visiting his grandparents in Los Angeles; as an undergraduate at Vanderbilt, a teaching assistant at Kenyon, or a young instructor at the University of Texas; as an enlisted man in the Army Air Force; as literary editor of *The Nation*; as a visiting writer at Princeton; as Poetry Consultant to the Library of Congress. We care more about the life when we begin to care about the writing; so it seems to me natural and useful here—as with my previous books on Frost and on modern poets—to move back and forth between life and the "life" that is created by writing. For example, in the letters Jarrell wrote home to his first wife during the Second World War, we delight in the spectacle of army life made memorable through the energies of words.

When I began to entertain the idea of a book about Jarrell, he seemed a totally sympathetic figure, and an ideal aesthetic critic —not just of poetry, but also of music and painting. A consistently witty, often scathing, prose writer, then, and in addition a poet of, at his best, delicate and sympathetic touch. In both his later poems and his criticism, he appeared to be writing about an America in which I also lived, and he cared about such vulgar subjects as professional football, fast cars, and expressive (sometimes expensive) clothes. He was, so it looked to me, surrounded by people, both men and women, who loved and respected him. After living with Jarrell pretty constantly for the last few years and spending a good many hours talking to those who knew him best, I still find him a sympathetic figure, even a hero. But I have become aware of just how strange a phenomenon he was. The man who, on the basis of his later poems, seemed to have had a happy childhood was in fact deeply at odds with that childhood and with his parents' part—or lack of part—in it. The wonderfully rational, common-sensical quality of his critical judgments coincided with a poetical imagination that explored darkly ambiguous patterns of story and myth, whose realest country was that of the folktale, and for whom Freud was the supreme poet of the inner life. The lover of women and the deep friend of at least two men turned out to have been wrapped up in himself to the point of narcissism. His self-involvement was prodigious: at one point Lowell wrote to Bishop that he and Peter Taylor had agreed that Jarrell was a terror for his friends in public since they were "either corrected, ignored or expected to loudly agree."

He demanded of women nothing less than total immersion in his concerns. That his mother, he felt, did not provide this—that she divided her attention between him and his younger brother—seemed a mark of betrayal. At the same time, his valuation of women was immense. Near the end of his late poem "Woman," he says nothing less than:

> *He who has these*
> *Is secure from the other sorrows of the world.*
> *While you are how am I alone? Your voice*
> *Soothes me to sleep, and finds fault with my dreams.*

Jarrell's letters testify to the importance a number of women in addition to his mother and his two wives had for him. Again, unlike his contemporaries Lowell and Berryman, he was sexually unaggressive; fastidious to the point of prudishness, he very much disapproved even of off-color jokes and innuendos. "His body was a little ghostly in its immunity to soil, entanglements, and rebellion," wrote Lowell, adding—and speaking for himself—"one felt, beside him, too corrupt and companionable." On the evidence of the letters, though, and for all his moral fastidiousness about "improper" subjects ("Me for Queen Victoria, as far as Public Life is concerned," he once said), Jarrell apparently was little prone to questionings and explorations of his own behavior, nor was he plagued—so it appears—with a sense of guilt. When he decided to leave his first wife, Mackie, having fallen in love with the woman who would be his second, he gave the process an air of inevitability, something that was fated to happen. And near the end of his life he spoke in similar terms about his second wife, Mary. After he had been hospitalized for his mental breakdown in March of 1965, he wrote her: "I want to say all over again how sorry I am that things have turned out this way for us—considering our earlier life and families, it just couldn't have turned out differently, I think, short of our both being analyzed and thoroughly changed."

A similar "inevitability" attended his operations as a brutal critic of other poets. He did not say harshly funny things merely about now-forgotten poetasters. There was no modern poet he admired more than Robert Frost, yet when Frost, then in his seventies, published *Steeple Bush*, Jarrell tore into him, declaring that "this poet is now, most of the time, an elder statesman like Baruch or Smuts, full of complacent wisdom and cast-iron whimsy." One way to describe such harshness is to say that—as he himself said of the music critic B. H. Haggin—"he couldn't lie to you if he tried." But one feels also that he was in the grip of his taste, and that its roots lay—in Leslie Fiedler's acute formulation—"in something nearer to madness than to method." He rarely changed his mind about a poet, and as for his own poetry, it would scarcely be an overstatement to say that he learned almost nothing from his contemporaries and did not seek out or listen to their criticism (unlike Lowell, say, who profited so much from Jarrell's own criticism).

I am trying to suggest ways in which Jarrell was something like a natural phenomenon, the laws of whose being did not bear his inspecting them too closely; instead, it seemed best simply to act on their proddings and impulses. As far as his relations with other people, especially his marital relations, were concerned, this lack of self-criticism functioned in part as a way of exculpating himself from the consequences of his actions. But for the writer and critic, following his taste wherever it led him resulted in thirty years of memorable and sustaining work. My object in the pages that follow is to tell a story of that work and of the life in which it occurred —*a* story, not *the* story. Jarrell was wise about the difference between books and life, about how much reading can mean but how little effect on the world, finally, it has. The concluding lines from his poem "The Carnegie Library, Juvenile Division" serve as a motto for this study of their author:

> *We learned from you so much about so many things*
> *But never what we were; and yet you made us that.*
> *We found in you the knowledge for a life*
> *But not the will to use it in our lives*
> *That were always, somehow, so different from the books'.*
> *We learn from you to understand, but not to change.*

9

O N E

Early Life and Writing

J ARRELL'S childhood, divided between Tennessee and California, was an appropriately doubly rooted beginning for a person who throughout his life could never be identified with or understood in terms of a single locale. He would have approved of Philip Larkin's sentiment in "Places, Loved Ones": "No, I have never found / The place where I could say / *This is my proper ground, / Here I shall stay.*" In the fifty-one years of his life, he lived for extended periods in Ohio, Texas, Illinois, Arizona, New York, North Carolina, New Jersey, and the District of Columbia, in addition to Tennessee and California, while spending briefer periods at work or on holiday in Massachusetts, Indiana, Colorado, Austria, Italy, Germany, and England. His speech did not sound particularly Southern, and when asked why he didn't share his parents' Tennessee accent, he would reply that he was born there but learned to talk in California. In his late poem "The Player Piano," a woman who is surely a stand-in for the poet looks at a photograph of her mother and father and remarks, "They both look so *young.* / I'm so much older than they are. Look at them, / Two babies with their baby." Jarrell's parents were comparably young—his father twenty-four, his mother twenty—when he was born in 1914, on May 6, a birthday that later and delightedly he found was also Freud's. His father, Owen, came from a working-class family in rural Shelbyville, Tennessee; his mother, Anna Campbell Jarrell, came from a well-to-do Nashville business family. Prior to Randall's birth, Anna had lost a daughter in infancy; a brother, Charles, was born after the family moved to California in 1915.

In California, Owen Jarrell worked as an assistant to a children's photographer in Los Angeles and later set up a photography business on his own. He was a handsome man, in the manner of the then contemporary matinee idol Wallace Reid, and he figures in his son's poetry only by his absence. Yet on the evidence of Randall's letters to his mother after the marital breakup—when he was living for a time with his paternal grandparents in California—he seems to have enjoyed a warm relationship with his father. This warmth extended to other members of Owen's family, especially his parents, who were known to Randall as "Mama" and "Pop," and who, along with "Dandeen"—the boy's great-grandmother—are featured in the three-part poem of recollection, "The Lost World," which Jarrell composed near the end of his life. Other relatives included Owen's uncle Billy Pearson and a married brother, Prescott. With this supportive family in fairly close proximity, Owen and Anna settled on a ranch outside Los Angeles where—as the mother recorded in her baby book—after a few months Randall had "obtained the healthy color common to westerners and began running around in the yard and talking." By November of 1915, when he was a year and a half old, Anna describes him as "an efficient little ranchman, attending his little chickens and rabbits and scampering all over the forty-five-acre ranch." Both the chickens and the rabbits—or rather, a single, symbolic representation of each kind—would play a significant part in his poetry.

Anna Jarrell was not only young but pretty and petite, with dark eyes, curly hair, and a skin so sensitive she needed to wear silk next to it and used only non-allergenic soaps and creams. An immaculate housekeeper and a dedicated mother, she loved to take care of her babies and did not stint herself: furniture and rugs, draperies and dishes were constantly replaced, and no leftovers were allowed to accumulate in the icebox. When she made her angel cake, said to have been delicious, she flushed a dozen egg yolks down the commode. But Owen's salary as a photographer's assistant was unequal to such extravagances; and when, after the birth of Charles, Owen moved the family away from Los Angeles and the relatives in order to open a studio of his own in Long Beach, relations between him and Anna became increasingly strained. With money tight and no family of her own or Owen's to turn to, her health suffered and she became, in the ladylike phrase, "delicate." (Eventually she underwent a hysterectomy.) There is a sequence in Jarrell's late poem "Hope" in which what the narrator refers to as "a recurrent / Scene from my childhood" is depicted in a rather arch tone:

> *A scene called Mother Has Fainted.*
> *Mother's body*
> *Was larger, now it no longer moved;*
> *Breathed, somehow, as if it no longer breathed.*

At such moments, certain procedures were followed by the family:

> *We did as we were told:*
> *Put a pillow under her head (or else her feet)*
> *To make the blood flood to her head (or else away from it).*
> *Now she was set.*

At the risk of confusing the poem's narrator with the autobiographical Jarrell, the rather flat and unadorned nature of this writing suggests that it has its roots in childhood memory; at least it fits well with what appears to have been his mother's "sensitive" and histrionic nature.

Finally the point came when in desperation she wrote to her brother Howell, a prosperous candy manufacturer in Nashville, who paid for his sister and his nephews to move back East. The parents divorced, and Jarrell would recall the separation from his

13

father as a determinative condition of his childhood. To a former sweetheart, Amy Breyer deBlasio, whom he envied for having grown up in a large, rooted Nashville family, he later wrote: "I've lived all over, and always been separated from at least half of a very small family, and been as alone as children ever are." With separation and divorce so common today, we are unlikely to credit that Jarrell's loneliness was wholly caused by his father's absence. And it may well have been that his sense of separation, of separateness, was inherent, and that it sharpened after the birth of his brother. As Suzanne Ferguson has pointed out, the brother who lived, Charles, is never a presence in Jarrell's poetry (in life their relations were less than satisfactory), while the sister who died is a recurrent motif—perhaps because there was no actual sister in competition with him for his mother's attention.

Jarrell's relations with his mother recall Robert Frost's, the poet about whom he was to write so brilliantly. Frost's parents were estranged early in their marriage, and when his father died, the mother moved East with Frost and his younger sister. That sister was at least as much a problem for Frost as Charles Jarrell was for Randall, and the "problem" may have begun with the younger child's birth. Nothing Jarrell said throughout his life gives any indication that he had any interest in having children himself. And yet, paradoxically, there is an extraordinary feeling for children expressed in both his poems and the children's stories he wrote late in life. Having "been as alone as children ever are" may have served as a reason—or at least a rationalization—for his disinclination to father a child of his own (his second wife brought two daughters with her into the marriage).

When Anna and her sons returned to Nashville, she took a job teaching English at a secretarial school. Her brother Howell's business success (his candy company produced Goo-Goo bars and Bell-Camp chocolates) did not inspire his nephew to similar exploits, although Randall was encouraged to deliver newspapers and sell Christmas wrappings door-to-door. In later life he wrote a fine poem about a paper boy ("Nestus Gurley"), but being one himself was no fun—indeed was something like hellish: "They had real gifts for finding me the most *awful* jobs. I wouldn't have minded delivering papers so much [. . .] if I could have hired someone to do the collecting. The people were so *bad*. They wouldn't pay, and they told lies. And I had to keep going back"—so Mary Jarrell recalls him saying decades after the event. Selling Christmas wrappings was at least as unpleasant ("*Imagine*, pestering people like that in their houses. Wasn't that a wicked thing to make a child do?"). Of course these are less statements of fact—the child's outcries against oppression—than they are statements of mind, the tonally extravagant complaints of a sophisticated adult.

As always, he performed well in school, though later, in his poem "The Elementary Scene," he would devote two stanzas to characterizing elementary school as sad and seedy. The best parts of many days arrived after school was out, when he would read in the Carnegie Library and dote on the librarian of its Juvenile Division ("She was young, and slender, had dusky red hair, and looked—still looks, in my mind's eye—just beautiful"). Some lines from "The Carnegie Library, Juvenile Division" suggest the depth of his romantic attachment to books, to reading:

> *Here under the waves' roof, where the seals are men;*
> *In the rhymes' twilight, where the old cup ticks*
> *Its gnawing lesson; where the beasts loom in the green*
> *Firred darkness of the märchen: country the child thought life*
> *And wished for and crept to out of his own life.*

A companion poem ("Children Selecting Books in a Library") puts it as a heartfelt directive:

> *Read meanwhile . . . hunt among the shelves, as dogs do, grasses,*
> *And find one cure for Everychild's diseases*
> *Beginning:* Once upon a time there was.

In an unpublished talk he once gave about libraries (the same in which the redheaded librarian occurs), he said of books: "The pages opened into life or something better than life, into a possibility without limits—if I had let go of the books wouldn't they have floated up into the sky?" As a reader he was insatiable: "I went to school, played, did what the grown-ups made me do; but no matter how little time I had left, there were never books enough to fill it—I lived on the ragged edge of having nothing to read."

The importance of reading, of "art," was established early in his life, so there was symbolic appropriateness when two sculptors engaged in making Olympian statues for the concrete replica of the Parthenon that adorns Nashville's Centennial Park invited him to pose for Ganymede, cupbearer of the gods. The boy's familiarity with myths and legends had charmed the sculptors (Belle Kinney and Leopold Scholz) to the extent that they not only immortalized him on the Parthenon (Nashville was proud to be known as the "Athens of the South") but even expressed interest in adopting him. Anna Jarrell refrained at the time from telling her son of their interest; when Jarrell later found out he said, "She was right. I'd have gone with them like *that*."

He did go off for a while, when in the summer of 1926 he traveled back to California to live with his grandparents and great-grandmother in Hollywood and to visit his father in Long Beach, where Owen and his partner ran a business called Jarrell-Kramer: Portrait Pictorialists. (Their motto was "Portraits for those blessed with the faculty of critical appreciation; who recognize the subtle distinction between merit and mediocrity.") Early in July Randall wrote—indeed typed, on his father's Remington portable—a longish letter home, which deserves attention for the way it brings the boy before us and also prefigures Jarrell's later epistolary self: "Dear Mother: I wish I could see you. I feel fine and am having a dandy time." He promises to tell her about the trip West by writing about it "in installments like a serial in a magazine," and assures her that he will "always stop in the most exciting parts so you will want to hear some more." He tells her that his grandfather, "Pop," has given him an unclaimed bicycle left in the front yard; it lacks a pedal, but his father will provide that and he himself will paint it. His father has just bought him a new pair of crêpe-soled oxfords and a new two-piece bathing suit in blue and white. He is going swimming that afternoon, and a big picnic with surf fishing is planned with "the folks" over the Fourth of July holiday.

As for the "exciting parts" of his trip, he passes along to her one episode that falls under the category of what he promises will be "hot stuff":

> We sure did see lots of buzzards on our trip. On one detour we saw four great big ones right in the road eating a dead chicken. They just stalked to the side of the road when we passed and then stalked back again. They sure are mean, ugly-looking birds. They just sail around in the sky, looking for some carrion to eat. They seem to say, "We'll get *you* someday, get you get you. We'll getyouyet, getyouyet, getyouyet. Just like choruses of songs that seem to run together.

The letter as a whole sounds equally natural, untroubled, happily alert to this or that circumstance and expressive possibility, very much in touch with things of this world like bicycles and bathing suits and buzzards. I emphasize the point, because the assumption that Jarrell endured a lonely, unhappy childhood (an assumption he sometimes encouraged) is too sweepingly neat to account for the lively particularities of a letter of this sort. Granted that he was markedly happier in California, the scene of his earlier childhood, than he had been in the brief Nashville interim or would be in Nashville afterward. Still, it is unlikely that life with his mother was devoid of pleasures. The postscript to this particular letter home—"Say, Mum, this is just about the same as a written four-page letter"—does not sound to me like the utterance of a boy full of bitterness at or disappointment in the mother from whom he had moved away.

When in 1962 his mother gave back to him the letters he had written home during the months he spent in California, Jarrell was animated by them and began to compose the remarkable poems —"The Lost World" and "Thinking of the Lost World"—which crown his work as a poet. They will be considered at the end of this book, but it is proper to mention here the shocking moment from "A Street off Sunset"—the third poem in the "Lost World" sequence—in which the child discovers death. That discovery is prompted by "Mama," the grandmother who one day enters the back-yard chicken coop, selects a hen, and wrings its neck. The child's eye registers the horror of that event:

> *The body hurls*
> *Itself out—lunging, reeling, it begins to run*
> *Away from Something, to fly away from Something*
> *In great flopping circles. Mama stands like a nun*
> *In the center of each awful, anguished ring.*
> *The thudding and scrambling go on, go on—then they fade,*
> *I open my eyes, it's over . . . Could such a thing*
> *Happen to anything? It could to a rabbit, I'm afraid;*
> *It could to—*

The unstated word is the stronger for its absence, and the sight of the flopping chicken combines in the child's mind with a story he has been reading about a wicked scientist who plans to destroy the world.

So it is with particular relish that the child looks forward to the arrival home from work of his grandfather, whom he greets as if he were the "All-Father." The poem ends with these lines:

> *He tells me about the work he's done downtown,*
> *We sit there on the steps. My universe*
> *Mended almost, I tell him about the scientist. I say,*
> *"He couldn't really, could he, Pop?" My comforter's*
> *Eyes light up, and he laughs. "No, that's just play,*
> *Just make-believe," he says. The sky is gray,*
> *We sit there, at the end of our good day.*

It is worth noting that the boy is not deluded: it *is* a "good day" in that moment of being together with "Pop," just as it was a very different kind of day when the flopping chicken or the evil scientist took stage center. Seeing the day as a good day involves a kind of play, both childish and theatrical ("play, / Just make-believe"), that is absolutely central to the poet's vocation as Jarrell was to conceive it. And to make something meaningful out of the chicken's violent demise demands as much artistic play as do more soothing forms of make-believe.

As a child writing letters, and as a man writing poems about his childhood, Jarrell strove to pay tribute to the mixed nature of life, good and evil growing together in its branches and issuances. He may not always have succeeded; the childhood he depicts usually features separateness and disaffection. Yet out of that solitude he became the wonderfully responsive, delicate reader who would produce throughout his life so many trenchant reports on his experiences of books. And out of whatever neglect or disappointment he felt in his mother's inadequacy, he became a man imaginatively fascinated by a number of women, and a poet who made women the center of many of his best poems.

The length of his stay in California was, apparently, indeterminate, since in August he wrote his mother hoping that she would not make him come back to her in October. Putting the best of reasons on his side, he assured Anna that "the schools are just wonderful here" and that he wanted to attend them (he did, with the usual high grades). The letters home were filled with sights and pleasures, some of which are later recalled in "The Lost World": family dinners with "chicken and squash and potatoes and biscuit and cornbread and peach homemade ice cream and cake and lots more things"; a trip to the new Los Angeles library with his grandmother to get a library card (he already had one at the Long Beach library); an afternoon playing with Tawny, the lion cub at a friend of the family's small lion farm; visits to museums. He watches the filming of a "picture show" being made with "dogs and Eskimos and igloos and icebergs and snow in it" ("They threw Christmas tree stuff in front of an airplane propeller and it looked like a blizzard"); and he is taken to *Ben-Hur*, "the best picture I've ever seen," by his grandmother. From reading these letters we sense that, in words from "The Lost World," the "blue wonderland

/ Of Hollywood" was a magnificent exaggeration of life, wholly engaging to his imagination.

There is no written record of his feelings about having to leave it all behind when school ended in June of 1927 and he returned to his mother in Nashville. That he was devastated by having to return, and took it out on his grandparents by never writing to them, is a sad fact which Mary Jarrell describes this way: " 'How I cried!' [Jarrell told her]. And he'd begged them so hard to keep him that when they wouldn't—or couldn't—he blamed them for being cruel and resolved never to think about them again or write them a word." Withholding the words he could display so lavishly and imaginatively was of course the cruelest thing the adolescent had in his power to do. Some lines from "The Lost World" address the matter as, in a dream, he plays dominoes with his great-grandmother and she tells him a story about how, when she was a little girl during the War Between the States, one of the Union soldiers put her on his horse:

> *She cries . . . As I run by the chicken coops*
> *With lettuce for my rabbit, real remorse*
> *Hurts me, here, now: the little girl is crying*
> *Because I didn't write. Because—*
>
>   *of course,*
> *I was a child, I missed them so. But justifying*
> *Hurts too: if only I could play you one more game,*
> *See you all one more time! I think of you dying*
> *Forgiving me—or not, it is all the same*
> *To the forgiven . . .*

One imagines how, as the original resolution *not* to write turned into a lengthening period of silence, he found it more and more difficult to break the rule and express his feelings of love and loss to his grandparents. It was not until the very end of his life that, in the poem, he finally made amends.

Back in Nashville he threw himself into becoming a tennis player, practiced hard at hitting balls against a backboard, hung around the city courts, and occasionally got to play with the better players. He was, and remained throughout his life, a fierce competitor. Robert Fitzgerald, a later partner, wrote of Jarrell's relishing "the craft and lore of the game, as of everything he took up. When he dropped the ball for his first forehand shot in practice, you saw a small ritual performed with attention and gravity." He was evidently not a player of great power or stamina, but had good strokes and excellent form. Fitzgerald also shrewdly noted his impression that Jarrell's interest in tennis "represented an attachment to common life." In addition, he shared with Frost and Ezra Pound (both of whom liked tennis) the sense that poet and athlete are akin in being performers. The "feats of association" that Frost said poetry consists of were like an athlete's craft and display.

At Hume-Fogg High School Jarrell participated in both journalism and dramatics. One of the leading members of the school's dramatic club when it put on Shaw's *Arms and the Man*, he played the lead, Bluntschli, with "a proper nonchalance" but (so the newspaper review tells us) was upstaged by a "buxom, shrill-voiced female impersonator" named Raymond Johnson, who hammed it up as Catherine Petkoff, the heroine's Bulgarian mother. In a then popular comedy, *The Nervous Wreck*, Hume-Fogg's "most important production of the year" (it served as the basis of Eddie Cantor's musical *Whoopee*), he played the title role of a "coughing and bespectacled figure." His sophomore-year contributions to the school magazine, the *Hume-Fogg Echo*, included a rather labored fantasy in which he sets out to interview Mark Twain, on the assumption that Twain's remark—"The reports of my death are greatly exaggerated"—has something in it. Twain's skeleton is encountered in a cemetery and an unsatisfactory conversation ensues as the skeleton keeps trying to tell bad jokes to an exasperated Randall Jarrell. (Although in later years he would recommend *Huckleberry Finn* and *Life on the Mississippi* as good books to read, Twain, like other nineteenth-century American writers, seems to have played a rather minor part in his literary constellation.)

More significant was the piece he contributed to the *Echo* the following year, an extended comparison of Shakespeare with Ibsen in terms of productions of *Hamlet* and *The Wild Duck* he had seen recently at the Nashville Little Theatre. He judged the production of *Hamlet* to be execrable and was especially disgusted that the players had used the debased First Quarto for their text. Not shy of letting his audience know what he knew, Jarrell wrote: "I happen to know the soliloquies and a number of the scenes in *Hamlet* by heart. So I am totally unable to control my indignation and dismay at hearing the 'To be or not to be' soliloquy [. . .] rendered thus" (he goes on to quote the First Quarto lines, substantially different from and inferior to the familiar ones). His remarks about the actors were aptly sarcastic and a preview of the poetry reviewer he would become. He confessed to breaking into laughter (much to the horror of the audience surrounding him) when the ghost tells Hamlet to "Swear-r-r-r." Of Laertes, he remarked that, since the son lost his mind at news of his father's death, he "cannot be held accountable for his actions. It is fortunate for him." Horatio, he said, "gave the impression of a retired business man." By contrast, he was rapturous about *The Wild Duck*, calling it "one of the in-tellectual experiences of one's life" and "the greatest play of the greatest dramatist since Shakespeare." On a note that is perfectly revealing of the precocious high-school student who has read a lot, he observed: "It is necessary for every person who considers himself cultured to have read it." It is also extraordinary to speak with the confidence Jarrell speaks with here, when he assures his readers (to whom he had earlier, in a parenthesis, introduced the play's author) that "there is nothing like it in all literature."

That someone with such enthusiasm and assurance about lit-erature should not have immediately headed for a literary career, or at least gone to college planning to major in English, may seem surprising. But Uncle Howell Campbell (like Hart Crane's father in a comparable situation) had hopes for Jarrell in his candy com-pany, and sent him to a commercial school in Nashville to study accounting and various secretarial skills. This was a disastrous experience, which Jarrell responded to by becoming seriously ill with pleurisy and borderline pneumonia; after weeks of convalescing, reading Marx and writing poetry, he closed out his short career as a commercial student and managed instead to convince his uncle to send him to Vanderbilt University. The arrangement was that he would live off campus with his mother and her new husband, Eugene Regan. The marriage did not please Jarrell, since it interfered with the mother-son relationship, especially the pleasant Saturday evenings at restaurants or at the movies—"She was so pretty people thought she was my sister, or my date," he said later. In the fall of 1932, he entered Vanderbilt as a student for the Bachelor of Arts degree.

At the beginning of Jarrell's first year at Vanderbilt, he was assigned to John Crowe Ransom's course in Advanced Composition, and, in the winter trimester, to Robert Penn Warren's section in the general survey of literature—one of the Beowulf-to-Hardy sort. Warren, then in his late twenties and himself a graduate of Vanderbilt, quickly recognized his student's brilliance (he had surely heard about him from Ransom), but he was also disturbed by Jarrell's incredulous and pained attitude toward his classmates' attempts to ask or answer questions. Little by little, Warren recalled, the other students huddled together, leaving Jarrell lordly and condescending. When Warren decided to have a talk with him, suggesting that perhaps he could help the other students rather than "terrorize" them, Jarrell was astonished and allowed that he had no idea how intimidating his classroom presence was. He resolved to turn over a new leaf, and Warren thereafter observed him gamely suppressing grimaces of pain when a well-meaning classmate spoke, even nodding his head stiffly as if attempting to approve of a good try. (The effect, Warren said, was even worse, but Jarrell's effort had to be commended.)

Ransom's testimony agrees with Warren's. Nobody could ignore Jarrell; an "insistent and almost overbearing talker," an "*enfant terrible*," were Ransom's words for him. And not just in English courses. In his sophomore year he took introductory psychology with Professor Lyle Lanier, who had heard about him from Ransom and Warren. Lanier recalls him sitting prominently in the front row, more or less alone in a classroom consisting mainly of pre-med students. When Lanier asked a question, Jarrell's hand would go up, and when called upon he would provide an answer of impressive lucidity and completeness. Lanier admired the young man—an admiration not shared by the other students, three of whom eventually showed up at the professor's office to tell him (politely) that they were tired of Mr. Jarrell's arrogant "lecturing." Lanier pointed out to them the distinguished character of Jarrell's scholarship, but agreed that his classroom participation might be toned down a bit.

In fact, Jarrell came to Lanier after the first class and requested a conference, at which he referred to what was—in Lanier's judgment—a prodigious number and variety of books about psychology and related fields. This led to a series of informal, irregularly held discussions between them, and eventually to Jarrell's changing his major, prior to his final year, from English to psychology, with a minor in philosophy. He completed the work for his degree in three years, taking summer courses at George Peabody, a teachers' college where Vanderbilt faculty often taught. His academic record at Vanderbilt consists of a string of A's, a few B's, two C's in French, and—most interestingly, considering his later fascination with the language—a single-term D in German. He made Phi Beta Kappa and received his B.A. in December of 1935 (graduating seventh in a class of 137), by which time he was doing graduate work in psychology.

He had shocked Lanier by coming to him before the 1935–36 fall term and saying that he wanted to take a master's degree in psychology. Lanier, who was virtually the whole psychology department, judged that Vanderbilt was not the place to pursue graduate study in that field; more importantly, he thought Jarrell's interest in becoming an experimental psychologist unrealistic, especially since he had been writing and publishing poems which his mentors praised. Lanier took him on, but insisted that, instead of taking more standard psychology courses, he do intensive background work in laboratory technology and in quantitative methods, so as to prepare himself for experimental investigation and for future teaching at an advanced level. This meant that Jarrell had to confront the fundamentals of electronics, as applied to physiological psychology (an area of interest to Lanier), and though he went at it with vigor, he gave up after a few weeks, telling Lanier he found it a deadly chore and had decided to go back to English. There was an incompatibility, Jarrell felt, between his main interests as a poet and critic and the pursuit of a career in "scientific" psychology (later he would write that trying to learn "radiophysics" pushed him back into literature). Lanier heartily agreed with him, and that was the end of Jarrell's official career as a student of psychology.

While an undergraduate he wrote a great deal for the college humor magazine, the *Vanderbilt Masquerader*. Whether, in fact, it was to be a humor magazine or a "serious" literary one was a question he took up as editor-in-chief in his senior year. Noting that several members of the faculty believed that it would be a bona fide literary operation, he opined, "We have never been able even to consider this suggestion seriously." Nobody would buy it, he said, nobody would advertise in it (thereby killing it), but most important, there simply wouldn't be enough good material to fill it: "College literary magazines are always greeted with satisfaction by their writers and with apathy by everybody else; curiously enough, we sympathize with the stolid majority." If this seems an unusual position for a young man with literary aspirations to take, it probably had to do with the fact that the young man had, the previous year, published five of his own poems in a New York magazine, *The American Review*. It is not likely that he would have welcomed his classmates' submissions of poetry and fiction with any more enthusiasm than he had shown their remarks in Warren's survey course.

His main—and indeed, to her recollection, only—abettor on

the *Masquerader* was a fellow student named Elizabeth Petway (she later married W. R. Moses, a poet who appeared with Jarrell in the *Five Young American Poets* anthology of 1940). Together Jarrell and Petway ran the magazine, the rest of whose editorial staff, she recalls, simply vanished, although their names continued to be listed on the masthead. As editor-in-chief of the humor magazine, Jarrell held a job prized by the fraternity set, to which 90 percent of the male undergraduates at Vanderbilt belonged. He by contrast belonged to no fraternity and inevitably was not popular with the conservative and conventional students whose eyes were set on business careers. Elizabeth Petway remembers him as careless of his appearance and sometimes oblivious of his environment; nor —to judge from the tone of *Masquerader* editorials—was he any more pious about hallowed college traditions than about the idea of a serious literary magazine. (He would later write a comic novel about academics.) In one editorial he mocked the notion that Vanderbilt was a "collegiate" college like Tennessee or Alabama, or like the "rah-rah" schools of so many 1930s Hollywood college musicals. On the contrary, he wrote, Vanderbilt had a tradition of "an almost complete lack of school spirit." As a football college it was equally pathetic: the Vanderbilt cheerleaders were "lousy," the band looked like the Salvation Army; the cheering section was "a lot worse than Hume-Fogg's." So, he concluded, the business of "school spirit" was overrated; there was no sense in being "rhapsodic and misty-eyed about 'dear old Vanderbilt.' "

In what was called the "Exam Number" of the magazine (December 1934), Jarrell inquired rhetorically into what had happened to his staff and concluded that they were all too busy worrying about exams to bother with the *Masquerader*. Therefore, as a challenge to his absent colleagues and the rest of the student body, he made up an examination of his own titled "Take This Exam." It consisted of a list of one hundred famous men to be identified by the exam taker. The first ten were easy ones like Shakespeare, Beethoven, Plato—figures so familiar that anybody in or out of Vanderbilt would more or less get them. But things soon became tougher: numbers forty to fifty featured Gibbon and Sainte-Beuve, Houdon and Poussin; by the sixties one had to contend with Pareto and Middleton, Frazer and Longinus; and at the end of the line appeared Boole and Strabo, Varèse and Vaihinger. Readers who did poorly on the exam were told they could console themselves by muttering, "After all, that's got nothing to do with how smart a guy is." But it would be safe to assume that in making up the exam Jarrell thought *he* was rather a smart guy, and, in fact, the gradations of difficulty by which the famous and not-so-famous names presented themselves were subtly arranged. Like his challenges to school spirit and to the "serious" literary magazine, the "exam" was an exercise in intellectual playfulness which aggressively separated him from his peers.

His life outside the classroom was stimulated and enriched by three families, the Milton Starrs, the Alfred Starrs, and the Bernard Breyers. Breyer was a prosperous manufacturer whose household—a wife and seven children—proved hospitable both to Jarrell (who was a classmate at Hume-Fogg of Breyer's daughter Lucie) and to Warren, who spoke of them as a family of great cultivation, whose "jolly Jewish dinners" offered lively talk and lots of lively children. Jarrell was especially fond of the son Bernard (a student of literature and professor-to-be), and even more so of his sister Amy, who was a few years older than Jarrell and a student of medicine at Vanderbilt. Amy, who was also doing graduate work in French, was not in awe of him ("She couldn't be awed by anybody," said Warren) and she had a feeling for poetry. She and Jarrell sometimes visited Warren in his house outside Nashville (a ramshackle place that lingered in Jarrell's memory), and to Warren they seemed to be in love, with Amy the older of the two not only in years but in emotional maturity.

Years later, after Jarrell entered the armed forces and published his first book of poems, he sent a copy of the book to Amy, who had returned to Nashville after an internship in New York, marriage, and a nervous collapse. In response to her letter of thanks, he wrote a long, intricate, and quite moving account (some of which

27

was quoted earlier) of how he now understood their relationship and why—at her wish—it had eventually dissolved. He told her that, when he thought of her and how "wonderful" she was, he didn't think, "How could I have suffered so much for this stranger?" but rather, "Yes, I was right to, it was worth it all." And he continued:

> It's all true about the growing up—you'd lived at home, in one place, in the middle of the Biggest Family in the World, and never been alone at all. I've lived all over, and always been separated from at least half of a very small family, and been as alone as children ever are. As long as I can remember I'd been so different from everybody else that even trying to be like them couldn't occur to me. I never realized at all that you felt I'd eventually "see through you" and leave you: how could I, when you were the only thing I had in the world, the only thing I cared about at all? Everything I did—I mean *everything*, really believe me—was just a way of wasting time while I was waiting to see you.

The letter doesn't ask for Amy's pity, but instead tries to convince Jarrell himself that she is secure, at the center of the Biggest Family, while he is separated, single, vulnerable, precarious—the lonely child, the poet, the one who is different. It is a testament and confession of how he wanted—or was fated—to see himself as above all else a romantic figure, indeed a romantic poet. Ten years later, he wrote a poem and sent it to another woman, Elisabeth Eisler, with whom he was then in love and from whom he was separated by an ocean and by the fact that he was married. Rooted in feelings about himself and Amy, it ends with a stanza expressive of much in Jarrell's character:

> *How poor and miserable we were,*
> *How seldom together!*
> *And yet after so long one thinks:*
> *In those days everything was better.*

The Breyer family was friendly with the Starr brothers, whose families—especially Milton Starr's—became significant to Jarrell. To some extent, the fact that they were Jewish families may have recommended them to him, insofar as he thought of himself as an outsider, not a part of the Vanderbilt mainstream. Milton and Alfred Starr were the two youngest siblings in a Nashville family of nine children. Milton attended Vanderbilt for a semester, then went into business, launching a chain of movie theaters for blacks which showed the usual B pictures of the period—westerns, horror films, etc. His younger brother, Alfred, graduated from Vanderbilt, where he became attached to the Fugitive group of poets. Through Ransom, he heard about Jarrell, whom he later would characterize as the brightest, most intelligent person who ever graduated from Vanderbilt. He welcomed Jarrell into his household, employing him (in the words of his daughter Cecile, a student at Louisiana State University at the time) as an "educated babysitter."

Those who were children at the time, in either Starr family, remember him as a marvelous storyteller. During summer vacations, he accompanied them to the coasts of Georgia and South Carolina. Cecile Starr, six years younger than Jarrell, was enchanted when, soon after they had met, he said to her, "I'll bet that I'm the first person you ever met who knows all the Beethoven symphonies." Nobody, she said, had talked to her like that before. Rather than being careless in his appearance, she remembers him as "smooth and clean and shining and radiant and happy with himself, full of energy to the point where he bounced when he walked." When she asked him what books she should read—always the question he liked best to be asked—Jarrell recommended *Out of Africa* (which had just been published) and *War and Peace*. Cecile Starr was struck by the way he saw literature—saw all the arts— as "life experience" rather than something to be studied. With *War and Peace*, he said, it was essential to get through the first 100 pages any way you could, by hook or by crook, and then—if you had to—you could skip the battle chapters, but you should try not to. She followed up on his recommendations, listened to Beethoven, read Dinesen and Tolstoy, and remembers with gratitude not just particular bits of advice but the manner in which they were given—without condescension, straightforwardly and passionately.

Milton Starr and his wife, Zaro, became long-term friends of Jarrell's. It is easy to understand the young man's desire to belong to a cultivated family interested in the arts, in good food and conversation. It is also easy to see why Milton Starr, whose education at Vanderbilt had been so brief, felt eager to associate with literary people and in time became a patron of the arts. In 1937, Jarrell spent part of the summer with the Milton Starrs at their summer place on Sullivans Island off the coast of Charleston, South Carolina. The idea was that he and Bernard "Junie" Breyer would serve as babysitters and provide lively company for the parents. Jarrell's prime object of affection among the Starr children was Sara, and she continued to be important in his life; the oldest child (age seven at the time), she was, in Zaro Starr's words, his "Alice in Wonderland." Jarrell's talent for babysitting was mainly displayed through his ability to tell hair-raising bedtime stories, which—Zaro Starr noted—kept her but not the children awake. That summer off the Carolina coast was the first of a number of vacations he spent with or near the Starrs, at Daytona Beach and later at Cape Cod.

Behind the superior student who intimidated his classmates, the humorist who sent up sacred cows like school spirit and "serious" literary magazines, and the fierce tennis competitor with his clean whites, cries of "Peachy" after a good shot, and general air of being pleased with himself—behind all these, or coexisting with them as yet another self, was Jarrell the poet. As a poet he was, to say the least, precocious; typically, his first recorded publication would be not one but five poems, and in *The American Review* rather than in a local magazine. *The American Review*, edited by Seward Collins, acknowledged Irving Babbitt as its main inspiration and thought of itself as a "minority organ" critical of various aspects of modern society. It published radical-conservatives such as G. K. Chesterton

and Wyndham Lewis, New Humanists like Norman Foerster and
Herbert Agar, and especially the Southern Agrarian-Fugitive writ-
ers, one of whom, Allen Tate, was invited to put together a Poetry
Supplement for the May 1934 issue. Tate assembled an impressive
group, including Warren, Ransom ("Prelude to an Evening"), Janet
Lewis, John Peale Bishop, Mark Van Doren, and Louis MacNeice
("An Epilogue for Christmas"). But the astonishing thing about
Tate's supplement was that it began with five poems by an un-
dergraduate named Jarrell.

Let us place this debut, rather roughly, by noting some books
by American and English poets contemporaneous with it. It was
the year after Yeats had published *The Winding Stair*. Eliot's *Ash-
Wednesday* had appeared in 1930 and he was on the verge of publishing *Burnt Norton* (1936). Hardy had died in 1928, the year his
last volume, *Winter Words*, came out; Housman's posthumous *More
Poems* would appear after his death in 1936. Robert Frost had
brought out his *Collected Poems* in 1930, the year Hart Crane's *The
Bridge* was launched (Crane leaped to his death in 1932). Auden
had made his notable appearance with *Poems* (1930) and *The Orators*
(1932). And very close to home, Ransom, Tate, and Warren were
producing work which the junior at Vanderbilt, who was reading
everything, of course knew well. In these earliest poems, Jarrell
sounds unintimidated, as if he had been writing this way for years:

> *In their thin eyes the sheeting of your name,*
> *The blood's rippling change casts in the form*
> *Of empty wakings and the vacant streets*
> *The lamentable torn possessions of their hell,—*
>
> *The running peoples on that bloody way*
> *Articulate your rank, the jeering names;*
> *It is you repeated in the shaking lights*
> *The child hangs sprawling in his vacant sky.*
>
> *You are uttered in the simple and forgetful words*
> *The homing seaman, the soldier falling to his stage,*

Pronounce in commentary on their state.
The child rocking in her empty room,

Patient, sleepless, haunted by your dreaming shape—
Helpless and suffering in a tale
That girl told in indifference and courtesy
She serves a symbol for that world.

This is the first half of the first of his five poems, "Fear," and it is pitched throughout in the same toneless, high-prophetic manner. With a couple of exceptions, each line ends with a monosyllable, often in the form of repeated words like "world" and "snow," "name" or "names," "form" or "forms." The elevated diction (sustained in the second half by words like "ermined," "argent," "mortal," and "inhuman") adorns declarative sentences jammed into the blocks of quatrains. Unlike Hart Crane's quatrains in "To Brooklyn Bridge" (which "Fear" at times recalls), Jarrell's are completely rhymeless, producing a sprawling and sometimes ungainly effect—as in the third stanza's "You are uttered in the simple and forgetful words," in which thirteen syllables limp into prose. (A similar effect is felt in other lines, like "That girl told in indifference and courtesy"—omitted from the revised version of "Fear" he published in *Blood for a Stranger* eight years later.) Audenesque abstractions (Auden's use of which Jarrell would later satirize)—the blood, the child, the soldier, and the seaman, "That girl"—haunt the atmosphere, serving as illustrative workings of "Fear" in its various shapes.

But the essential and perhaps the only thing that needs to be noted about "Fear" and the other *American Review* poems is their unvaried solemnity. Never descending from the grandiose, Jarrell remains precariously mounted on his high poetical horse. The humorous wiseguy who teased his classmates in *Masquerader* editorials; the man who, as Elizabeth Petway Moses recalled, couldn't stop laughing over the misfortune of a histrionic Vanderbilt law professor who dropped dead of a heart attack and rolled down the stairs of the administration building—this person now writes lines such as "The lamentable torn possessions of their hell,—" or "The passion of our ending world," proffering them to us with unblinking gravity. This makes for dullness, and four stanzas or so into "Fear" the reader suspects the poem isn't going anywhere; nothing that follows changes his mind. Jarrell's early poems lack the ironic wit found so abundantly in his prose criticism; instead, he gives us the irony-of-fate theme, of which young poets are often fond:

> *A child's words, swollen with weakness and pain,*
> *Could paint our sawn and mortal world,*
> *And scorn that sawdust-gushing wound*
> *Tended with pity and unmending love;*
>
> *But it's unfed and in the end betrayed,*
> *Sucked hollow by those gazing sheep-like forms,*
> *That dreaming and inhuman world,*
> *The forest of a winter night.*

These final lines from "Fear" may seem to invite thought, but in fact there is no profitable line of thought to take; one abstraction supplants another without adding up to an interesting argument or a gratifying sequence.

Yet these earliest poems contain moments of eloquence in which the language stirs with expressive possibilities, as here in the opening stanza of the untitled second poem:

> *O weary mariners, here shaded, fed,*
> *Dull as the wave, old hostages to sleep,*
> *Well-bearded, eloquent, the world's hands,*
> *Take what the kind sea brings to your feet—*
> *Shells, rays, tributes of the unsparing deep.*

With its echoes of Tennyson's "The Lotos-Eaters" and—more pointedly—Crane's "Voyages," this shapely sentence has an authoritative ring; yet the comma after "hands" in the third line seems to place "the world's hands" in apposition with the preceding adjectives describing the mariners, so that the fourth line ("Take what the kind sea brings . . .") must be read as a directive to the mariners, rather than a predicate of "hands." Such syntactical disruption or confusion (how deliberate it was on Jarrell's part is hard to say) is a gesture toward modernist "difficulty" and common to the poems he would write over the next few years. The lack of pattern extends as well to the rhyming, or the absence of it; "sleep" with "deep" gives the stanza a sense of completion, but also raises expectations not to be fulfilled in the following stanza or by the rest of the poem:

> *Here, perhaps, the shaved pinnacles of sand,*
> *Containing so much worth, will be abashed—*
> *Clouds torn by the storm and night of heaven*
> *Come home to you, rest dripping by your shores—*
> *And bend, magnificent, docile, proud.*

One begins to suspect that "Here" is really nowhere, that the poem offers only the merest excuse for any sort of realized situation. Its language feels showy and unrooted, its manner vacantly grand and portentous—as in Dr. Johnson's comment on Gray's odes: "He has a kind of strutting dignity, and is tall by walking on tiptoe."

Such criticisms are appropriate only in light of what Jarrell later accomplished. Given his age, one can see why no less a poet than Tate thought these poems worth pride of place in his supplement. Yet none of them was reprinted in the *Selected Poems* assembled two decades later, and it would be a long time before he could write lines like the following from "The Lost World," in which the child listens to someone playing the piano:

> *A prelude*
> *By Chopin, hammered note by note, like alphabet*
> *Blocks, comes from next door. It's played with real feeling,*
> *The feeling of being indoors practicing.*

Such writing creates a moment of time instinct with humor, the witty turn from "real feeling" to a sort of real feeling we hadn't

34

foreseen. Such a surprise, such a "turn," was completely foreign to Jarrell's early poetic practice; indeed, the *American Review* poems, rather than manifesting real feeling, display the feeling of being indoors practicing.

It is also possible that his development beyond the solemn, modernist, constricted, and "difficult" poems in *The American Review* may have been inhibited by his pronounced early success. He was admired and solicited by friends and mentors, the New Critics who at that time were assuming places of editorial influence. A year after Tate published his five poems, Warren and Cleanth Brooks began to edit *The Southern Review* out of Louisiana State University; three years later, Ransom founded *The Kenyon Review*. Jarrell was quickly assured of hospitable places for his work to appear regularly, and he had full confidence in his ability to produce. As a Vanderbilt senior he sent Warren a number of poems, and while he admitted that he was harried from writing up his psychology experiments, putting out the final issue of the *Masquerader*, and playing a tennis match every other day ("I've won all the matches I've had in games with other schools"), such activity did not deter him from his central task of writing poetry. If, he adds, Warren can print his poems in *The Southern Review*'s third issue, "by that time I'll have all the ones I'm writing finished, and some new ones written. I'll be able to give you thirteen or fourteen, I imagine, some of them fairly long."

He is not only winning all the tennis matches but writing all the poems. This confidence is worth remarking only because most young poets have to endure—as do most writers of any sort—a period during which the best they can hope for is a polite rejection slip, sometimes inviting them to try again with another submission. Instead of such slips, Jarrell from the first received the approbation of his poet-teachers, who promoted his work by publishing it in magazines. The facility and confidence he exhibited in his poems seems to have carried with it a relative inability or unwillingness to be very critical of them; certainly he had no hesitancy about their being published as soon as he wrote them. One thinks, by

35

extreme contrast, of the example of Frost, who wrote many poems in his twenties and thirties, a few of which were published, a few more rejected, the bulk of them not even submitted for publication until—on the verge of forty—he put together his first volume. Unlike Jarrell, Frost did not need, later on, to relegate his early poems to second-rate status by leaving them out of a selected edition.

On occasion, to be sure, one of his editors questioned a stanza, line, or phrase. When the first issue of *The Southern Review* was about to appear, Warren wrote Jarrell that he was dissatisfied with "the last two stanzas of the Asphaltine poem" ("Fat, aging, the child clinging to her hand," it begins), specifically with phrases he thought sounded "arbitrary and a trifle hysterical." Jarrell changed the offending phrases. On another occasion, he defended to Warren his use of the word "gibbous" in a poem, but agreed to alter another phrase in it, "the sick wind." But these were mild disagreements about the details of poems whose overall rightness neither Warren nor Jarrell seemed to have any doubts about. Sometimes this approval can be puzzling to someone on the outside, as when Warren refers to "the Asphaltine poem" as "so good otherwise that you shouldn't print it until the end is perfect." We may feel hard-pressed to understand what is so "good" about an obscure, apocalyptic meditation about History in which—as with Jarrell's other early poems—it is extremely difficult to figure out who is addressing us through the haze of rhetorical excitement ("The flame whirls up; time, and the scaffoldings / Swim like black phantoms through a darker waste— / The gutted balconies, bent under the moat, / Wake to some diver's peering and distorted face . . .").

The first issue of *The Southern Review* was impressive for its variety and the strength of its individual contributions: Ford Madox Ford writing about "technique"; stories by Katherine Anne Porter and John Peale Bishop; the first of three articles on modern poetry by Cleanth Brooks; Aldous Huxley on literature; poetry and fiction chronicles by Kenneth Burke and Howard Baker. The poetry se-

lection was led off by Wallace Stevens and included poems by
R. P. Blackmur, Warren, and—among a few others—two by Jarrell.
Like the *American Review* poems, they were untitled, an indication
—along with their vague focus and anonymous tone—of their
amorphous character. (Or perhaps Jarrell was simply imitating Auden's practice of not titling his poems.) The first of them ("And
did she dwell in innocence and joy") is about a carefree "child"
who is betrayed by experience into a violent corruption. Its final
two stanzas suggest the vagueness of the whole conception and
show the prosodic slackness Jarrell was prey to:

> *And, if she died corrupted, in the world's end,*
> *And that other, in misery and fantasy,*
> *Satisfied her shaved and corrupt heart*
> *With greed and longing, the empty clusters of delight,—*
>
> *The world's evil? Stand there waxen in the snow,*
> *Kind-hearted, ignorant, obstinate, secure; the*
> *Child of the world. Can one show*
> *The way of blessedness to the unsaved?*

Warren may have had his doubts about the poem, since he wrote
Jarrell that "Brooks and I want to look further at the 'Child'
poem"—but evidently the doubts were overcome. Yet it remains
of doubtful value, especially in its metrics. Jarrell may have been
attempting to imitate Ransom's sometimes Hardyesque ungainli-
ness; but the lines quoted above are grating to the ear and seem
uncertain about what sort of blank verse they are trying to be, or
whether and when they want to rhyme (the *snow/show* pairing in
the final stanza feels arbitrary, unprepared for). He never reprinted
the poem.

The second poem, however, was eventually rewritten and published under the title "The Elementary Scene." It appears to have
originated in a memory of schooldays in Nashville, though of course
the phrase "elementary scene" has more than local implications.
The poem's opening lines survive unchanged in the revised version,

37

and for the first time in his work a subject is focused on with some clarity and intensity:

> *Looking back in my mind I can see*
> *The white sun like a tin plate*
> *Over the wooden turning of the weeds;*
> *The street jerking—a wet swing—*
> *To end by the wall the children sang.*
>
> *The thin grass by the girls' door,*
> *Trodden on, straggling, yellow and rotten,*
> *And the gaunt field with its one tied cow—*

The remainder of the poem, in either its original or its revised form, has nothing so good as these lines. In them Jarrell forsook obscurity and vague gestures of profundity, perhaps because he was fully occupied in calling up images from the past—his own past—rather than in attempting to write grandly about History or Fear or Love.

Nothing is more noticeable, and in a way curious, than the contrast between the apocalyptic agonies of history and memory that Jarrell's early poems attempt to register—not very successfully—and the delightful, sanely humorous sense of himself and other people in his letters from the same period. When the letters were published in 1985, some reviewers said they provided only a superficial expression of the man, the real truth about whom could be found only in his poems. That truth, presumably, was a darkly gloomy one, in contrast to the cheeriness of his assumed epistolary style. Yet this is to privilege poetry; one could argue, contrarily, that the "assumed" style, the artificial one, was the one he was trying out in the poems—whereas in the letters spoke a natural, graceful, productive, and relatively happy person. There were of course two styles, two Jarrells; but one should not dismiss the non-poet as superficial or negligible. Consider the following sentences, written to Warren (who was teaching at Louisiana State) when Jarrell was in his second year as a graduate student at Vanderbilt. By then he had changed from psychology to English and was taking traditional courses like the English Lyric, Chaucer, Spenser and His Age, and a seminar in American literature:

> I am grading some of Mr. Ransom's papers, and writing a paper on Chaucerian shoes for Curry, and playing football every day. I have written about twenty poems since school started [. . .] I was sorry not to be able to send you a picture (for print in the Review)—and hadn't one, and the ones I got taken were too bad to send because by mistake all my hair was cut off. Amy is through with surgery and is starting obstetrics. Mr. Ransom is trying to write some poems. I am seeded one in the ping-pong tournament.

He was earning money by grading papers for two of Ransom's classes, and supplemented his income by writing and publishing poems at what sounds like an alarming rate (the letter was written in November, and he told Warren that since term began he had written "about twenty"). The "Chaucerian shoes" paper for Professor Walter Clyde Curry is a shade mysterious; but amusing when juxtaposed with news of Amy Breyer's medical studies, Ransom's struggles at poetic composition, and his own high seed in the ping-pong tournament. He proceeds to inform Warren that

> Tate made a speech here and he and Mr. Ransom made compliments to each other—but Tate wiggled while being complimented. Mr. Ransom was perfectly impassive; so I guess he won.

It is the mock-passivity of tone that makes the comedy satisfying, particularly in its deadpan postscript: "One girl wrote a paper for Ransom and quoted one of the Ten Commandments; she put a [1] by it and put a footnote 1: *Bible*, Exodus 20:14." In another letter to Warren at about the same time, Jarrell invited him and his wife to stay at Anna Regan's house in Nashville, since she and his stepfather would be in Florida. As an added attraction he noted:

39

"We even have some goldfish and a canary bird to play with. Mr. Ransom thought it was a wonderful idea—for you to play with the goldfish, I mean." Whatever "Mr. Ransom" did or didn't think about the potential spectacle of Robert Penn Warren playing with the goldfish (but perhaps ignoring the canary bird?), the fun here, as elsewhere in Jarrell's humor, lies in its cool juxtaposition of incompatibles: the poet of Original Sin, Time, Evil amusing himself with the fishes; the benign leader of the Fugitives smiling down his approval at the scene.

The summer before Jarrell entered graduate school at Vanderbilt, Cleanth Brooks had invited him to write what was known in the trade as a fiction chronicle for *The Southern Review*. In it a number of titles from the past three months' batch of fiction would be reviewed and connected one to another only by the reviewer's skill. Discounting the reviews he had done for the *Hume-Fogg Echo* and the *Vanderbilt Masquerader*, it was his first piece of published criticism, 6,500 words or so divided among ten novels. Brooks told him he was anxious to keep up standards for these long reviews (Kenneth Burke and Howard Baker had done them in the previous issue), and that "to some extent it will be well to keep them 'in the family' "—thus Jarrell was admitted to what he surely must have felt was good company. Pleased with the invitation, he proceeded to deal with Ellen Glasgow, Willa Cather, Stark Young, Erskine Caldwell, and a number of now pretty much forgotten names.

Ever the most ephemeral of forms, the omnibus chronicle of recent fiction is an attractive medium for the budding critic, since it allows him to test himself against reputations, established and not so established, to see whether he can come up with a few paragraphs for each which are both fair to his experience of the book and entertaining to the general reader. It is also a perilous form, insofar as it invites showing off and tempts the reviewer to indulge in spectacular one-liners (usually of a disparaging character) about the book in question. Although the one-liners in Jarrell's chronicle were not as deadly as those he later produced so effortlessly in his reviews of poets, the following examples show him with teeth already sharpened. About *Time Out of Mind*, by Rachel Field, he notes: "The author has the habit of quoting from the Old Testament, and her prose suffers from the comparison." Raymond Holden's *Chance Has a Whip* is dismissed with this crushing plot summary: "His hero has a very happy love affair; on the other hand, he almost dies of a burst appendix, his daughter commits suicide, he accidentally kills one of his wife's former lovers, and is accidentally killed by gangsters escaping from prison." Best of all is a sentence quoted from one of Stark Young's stories in which Young has tried to pass off as his own prose a large chunk of Wordsworth's writing about the Winander Boy in Book Five of *The Prelude*. Jarrell admits (with tongue in cheek) that it's a fine sentence, but "queerly enough, the best part of it reads almost like a paraphrase of Wordsworth." Since, he notes, Young in an essay has shown contempt for the English "nature poets" as compared with the Italian, "it is a pity he does not copy them instead of Wordsworth."

More complicatedly, the criticisms of Ellen Glasgow and Erskine Caldwell effectively mix praise and blame. Glasgow's *Vein of Iron* feels as though it was intended to be a great book, "yet the texture and details are too often commonplace, the words of the characters too often have the value of something overheard in the street or over the telephone—no more. Miss Glasgow has seen to the spirit, and let the letter take care of itself." Comparing Caldwell to Sophocles (a bold enough comparison), Jarrell says that "the blinding of Oedipus means something, it has an obvious relevance." By contrast:

> Mr. Caldwell would have told you of the act for its own sake, and besides have told you so vividly, and in so much detail, that you would virtually feel your own fingernail against your own eyes. The writer had better remember that even the most gruesome and tragic art must give the reader pleasure.

Finally, he identifies something important about Willa Cather's style, saying that, if the best style is one the reader doesn't notice,

41

hers almost satisfies the demand—"or at least, one notices the faults of her style more than its virtues [. . .] I mean that it is only by careful rereading that one sees all the virtues of Miss Cather's style." This may be considered an insight into Cather's work generally, not just the *Lucy Gayheart* he is reviewing here.

We may agree that a fiction chronicle is the sort of operation which, five or ten years out of college, a clever English instructor should be able to perform more or less successfully. In Jarrell's case he was performing the operation while still awaiting his undergraduate degree from Vanderbilt. His principles and standards of taste seem fully formed—certain, though not dogmatic, in their application. And there is always the ease and bite of wit. It is a performance that thoroughly anticipated the great reviewing to come, and repays examination for the way it demonstrates convincingly how Jarrell did not grow gradually into confidence as a literary critic but seemed to have had it built in from the beginning.

The Southern Review continued to provide him a useful forum. Over the next two years, they published fifteen more of his poems, none of which he later thought good enough for his 1955 *Selected Poems*. They were written—or finished—during his two years as a graduate student at Vanderbilt and at a time when his interest in Auden's poetry was at its height. He had written to Warren in 1935 proposing an article on Auden, which he offered to have ready for an early issue of the review, saying that he "really [knew] Auden's poetry pretty well" and adding, correctly, that, except for Warren's appreciation of *The Orators* in the aforementioned *American Review*, almost nothing had been written in America about Auden. Jarrell's essay was not to appear until 1941 and by that time he was at least as adversely critical of the poet and the direction his work had taken as he was appreciative. But his indebtedness to Auden earlier was immense. He planned to write his master's thesis on him, until the English department decided the subject was too recent, at which point he switched to Housman (who had conveniently died in 1936). And, although Audenesque touches crop up in many different poems, perhaps the most full-scale employment of them—though with important differences—can be seen in a *Southern Review* poem published in the autumn of 1937, after he had departed for Kenyon College:

> *Love, in its separate being,*
> *Gropes for the stranger, the handling swarm,*
> *Sits like a child by every road*
> *With begging hands, string-dwindled arms;*
>
> *Must be chafed, clothed, nourished, questioned,*
> *Its button glances, dunce's ways*
> *Wrenched and rasped till through them shines*
> *Love's logical obsessive face;*
>
> *Till of the simpleton's country scorners*
> *From grey-sored urchin to blinking miner*
> *Not one sticks hostile, holds out still*
> *Against love's ten-foot gentle stature.*

One thinks of the very early Auden poem beginning "Love by ambition / Of definition / Suffers partition / And cannot go / From yes to no," or the one which begins "Oh Love, the interest itself in thoughtless Heaven." As can be seen from the way Jarrell's verse proceeds, it has some of Auden's playful, off-rhyme shuttling, and some of his compressed, jammed way of presenting abstract characters who go off on mysterious, purposeful missions—though Jarrell's touch is not nearly so light or skillful, nor is his tone so deftly menacing, as Auden's. Instead, "Love, in its separate being" seems concerned to wind itself up into a violent denouement, a torrent of words that issues in cloudiness and obscurity:

> *From the tamer, the crammer, the trainer,*
> *The torturers' shredding hours,*
> *Who would have dreamed for a minute*
> *That love and love's perfection flower?*
>
> *Where love moved, a home-sick stranger,*
> *By bare shires and foreign shores,*

> *Earth crackles with love's repeated look:*
> *The subject's glance, the heart each shares*
>
> *To be ignorant, to be innocent,*
> *Welcome the warship sent for the exile,*
> *Divine in his words the perfected world*
> *Of—grown giant, gracious—the exposed child;*
>
> *Yield the great keys, the graves, and the charter—*
> *In the bared head, over the soldiers' song,*
> *See sparkling, rising and murderous in their grace,*
> *The emblems of that butchered king;*
>
> *And up the choked mouth and closing way*
> *The doomed men cry: He is one of us.*
> *But, necessary, triumphant, beautiful,*
> *Love laughs and is not magnanimous.*

As the conclusion is neared, words begin to get in each other's way. With "To be ignorant, to be innocent," the rhythm suddenly falls to pieces, and the syntax yields no satisfactory disposition of the poem's various figures—"love," "the subject," "the heart," "the exile," "the exposed child," the "butchered king," "the doomed men," and so forth.

In his discussion of Auden and Jarrell, Bruce Bawer has argued that, in its striving for impersonality, in its insistence on the "universal perspective" as opposed to the personal, Jarrell's early poetry (like other early work from what Bawer calls "the Middle Generation" poets—Lowell, Berryman, Schwartz) was written under the dictates of T. S. Eliot. Yet (as Bawer admits) the style is Auden's, only manipulated less skillfully. Jarrell was later to say, when questioned directly about his early work's debt to Auden, that in fact the Auden he most cared for—*Poems* (1930) and *For the Time Being*—had *not* influenced him; presumably, we may guess, because it was so special and inimitable. But there was a more available Auden, the poet who in the middle 1930s and beyond wrote about Love, History, Guilt, Fear, Disease—the poet of civilized ironic pity and terror about whom Jarrell, by 1941, when he published his essay on him, had very mixed feelings. "Love, in its separate being" was an attempt, only partly successful, to write in the mode of one whose shoes were too large for him to fill comfortably. In poems written after 1937, and especially after he had broken off with Amy Breyer in 1938, he attempted to express a more personal view of some of these issues, by bringing the abstractions down from their heights and at least trying to suggest a particular situation and an individual human voice speaking out of it. In becoming less disillusioned and world-weary, his poetry became more vulnerable, and eventually shed the all-too-knowing manner in which he had encrusted himself.

T W O

Academical

I N February of 1937, the winter of his second year as a graduate
student, Jarrell decided that his prospects for receiving a fellowship from Vanderbilt for a third year were not as rosy as
he had assumed. He wrote Warren that, despite Walter Clyde
Curry's assurance that he had a "very good chance" of getting
one, he probably would not, and he expressed irritation at Vanderbilt for not rewarding him in the way he deserved. Considering
his varied activities as student, published poet and reviewer, and
reader-assistant to Ransom, he certainly looked deserving; at any
rate, he asked Warren about fellowship possibilities at L.S.U.,
suggesting that he could also read proof for *The Southern Review*.
Warren replied that reading proof would pay only twenty-five
dollars a month, but that he might nonetheless apply to L.S.U.
if Vanderbilt fell through. This less than happy alternative was
dropped when a more attractive one presented itself in the spring
of 1937. Kenyon College made an offer to Ransom at a salary
which topped his Vanderbilt one, and which included a rent-free
house and the establishment of a new literary review with Ransom
as editor. An intensive and complicated effort was then mounted,
led by Allen Tate, to persuade Vanderbilt to match Kenyon's offer
and keep her distinguished professor; Jarrell and some three

hundred other students signed a petition urging the chancellor of the university to direct his strongest efforts at keeping Ransom in Nashville. Although the university eventually did offer him a higher salary, it was still less than Kenyon's, and Ransom seems to have been attracted by the idea of making a fresh start in an environment where he could devote more time to his own writing.

Jarrell's relationship with Ransom was more complicated than that of admiring student and approving mentor. Although Ransom recognized Jarrell's brilliance, he tended to think of it—at least in the memoir he wrote, and also in letters to Tate while Jarrell was alive—as that of the irrepressible child, the "*enfant terrible*" who had shown up as a freshman in his writing class at Vanderbilt. With reference to some lines from "The Lost World," Ransom says that the figure who appears in the poem is "a prodigy of a child, but no more of one than was in the young man in his teens who later presented himself at Vanderbilt." Repeatedly Ransom thought about his student in childlike terms, as when he writes of another of Jarrell's late poems ("Thinking of the Lost World") that "Randall was announcing the beginning of his 'second childhood.' " (This view of Jarrell was apparently common: Lowell, in one of his sonnets, calls him "Child Randall.") And at Kenyon Ransom expressed mixed feelings about the childlike habits and behavior of his student and assistant. As for Jarrell's attitude toward Ransom—who was always "Mr. Ransom"—there seems to have been a mixture of reverence, gratitude, amusement, and more than a touch of skeptical irreverence. As a graduate student at Vanderbilt, he wrote to Warren:

I've seen Mr. Ransom a good deal—he is engrossed in aesthetics. We rather argue [. . .] I reread Croce and said the original part in Croce (the intuition as expression) was purely psychological, or to use a word he loves, behaviouristic; he gave me a thoughtful look, with doubt, concern, and regret mixed in, and said he had never seen it looked at from that

47

point of view before. I have more fun talking with him than
I used to; I like to talk shop, and aesthetics more or less is,
politics and freeing the slaves not much.

It might be gathered that the last two subjects were "Agrarian"
ones in which Jarrell had no interest; for someone born in Tennessee he writes as if the War Between the States never took place.
Or, rather, he is aware that the war is over and has no ambivalence
about "the slaves" having been freed; in saying that he would rather
argue with Ransom about non-political matters like aesthetics, he
recognizes that his loose, quasi-Marxist-Freudian inclinations were
hardly a useful foil to Ransom's courtly conservatism, radical or
reactionary in its tone.

In another letter to Warren from Kenyon, Jarrell writes that he
is seeing a lot of "Mr. Ransom, who is well and wise but not writing
poetry; I guess from posterity's point of view it would be better to
have him sick and silly, but writing." By 1937, when Ransom left
for Kenyon, he had written nearly all the poems for which he is
remembered, but his career as a literary critic and theorist was just
coming into fruition. He had determined to leave behind subjects
like regionalism and Agrarianism, and to concentrate on what he
called "pure literary work." In part, this may have been an attempt
to rationalize his leaving Vanderbilt and accepting the Kenyon
offer; but in retrospect it spoke truth. In 1938 he published a
collection of literary essays, *The World's Body*, then began to edit
The Kenyon Review, while devoting the remainder of his life to
literature and criticism—to "aesthetics." From Jarrell's point of
view, Ransom's invitation to accompany him to Kenyon as (in
Jarrell's phrase) "a sort of part-time instructor" was a godsend,
since he could finish his M.A. thesis and teach the general survey
of English literature. Beyond that he would be "Director of
Tennis," which meant coaching the impressive Kenyon team,
whose number-one player had recently played a hard-fought match
with the world's second-ranked player, Baron Gottfried von
Cramm.

Robert Lowell, who at Merrill Moore's suggestion had gone to Vanderbilt to study with Ransom, also followed him to Kenyon. Lowell and Jarrell shared a room in Ransom's attic, and early on in the fall of 1937, Ransom wrote Tate that both young men were "pretty good company; both good fellows in extremely different ways. Randall has gone physical and collegiate with a rush; tennis is the occasion; good for him. Cal is sawing wood and getting out to all his college engagements in businesslike if surly manner." By the following April, however, Ransom had become slightly disturbed by what he felt was Jarrell's insufficiently serious attitude toward teaching and his own future: "So advanced in his thought that he wants just to pitch into some college department and work with the big professors; which is not too likely a prospect with his rather untactful manners and unimpressive public speech." Ransom insisted that he thought highly of Jarrell and that the young instructor was highly thought of at Kenyon, indeed had more than justified his position there. But a month later, again writing to Tate, he returned to the subject of this "very strange boy" whose career prospects looked dubious. Jarrell's poetry, said Ransom, was almost ruined by attempting to put William Empson's doctrine of ambiguity into practice, while "as a teacher he's extremely animated when he is interested, and spares no pains, and gets pretty good results; but the other day he asked me if I ever got bored, and intimated that this was rather his stock condition teaching Freshmen. A man of his age and ill prospects has no business getting bored by his job." In Ransom's eyes the prospects were ill because Jarrell showed insufficient seriousness about pursuing an academic literary career through the usual channel of a doctoral dissertation. Ransom's severity here is understandable, especially if we allow that there was a slight hint of mischief in his pupil's asking him whether he ever found teaching boring. After all, he was the *enfant terrible* who made unsettling remarks, as Warren attests with an incident he probably heard about from Ransom. Robert Frost, at a party in his honor at President Chalmers's house, made a rather lengthy point about metrics, then looked round at the other guests for corroboration and approval. In the silence, Jarrell was heard to say, "I don't believe that." Frost, who had good selective hearing, managed not to register the comment.

One of Lowell's sonnets about Jarrell, written in the 1960s, recalls the Ohio scene of the late 1930s:

> *Thirty years ago,*
> *as students waiting for Europe and spring term to end—*
> *we saw below us, golden, small, stockstill,*
> *the college polo field, cornfields, the feudal airdrome,*
> *the McKinley Trust; behind, above us, the tower,*
> *the dorms, the fieldhouse, the Bishop's palace and chapel.*

In the fall of 1938, he and Jarrell were joined by Peter Taylor—who had transferred from Vanderbilt to Kenyon and who would eventually become Jarrell's best friend—as well as by Robie Macauley and John Thompson, entering students just beginning what would be distinguished literary careers; Macauley as novelist and editor, Thompson as poet and critic. The five shared a house, and Taylor has described their tenancy in his autobiographical story "1939":

> We were all independents in Douglass House. There was no spirit of camaraderie among us. We were not the kind of students who cared about such things as camaraderie. Besides, we felt that there was more than enough of that spirit abroad at Kenyon, among the students who lived in the regular dormitories and whose fraternity lodges were scattered about the wooded hillside beyond the village.

But if camaraderie was the wrong name for the inhabitants of Douglass House, there was plenty of walking and talking going on among them:

> We walked the country roads for miles in every direction, talking every step of the way about ourselves or about our writing, or if we exhausted those two dearer subjects, we talked

about whatever we were reading at the time. We read W. H. Auden and Yvor Winters and Wyndham Lewis and Joyce and Christopher Dawson. We read *The Wings of the Dove* (aloud!) and *The Cosmological Eye* and *The Last Puritan* and *In Dreams Begin Responsibilities*.

Taylor points out that these books were outside the range of the "formal courses" they were taking.

He and Lowell have provided memorable portraits of Jarrell during his Kenyon years; Lowell remembers Jarrell, who thought Shakespeare's sonnets were richly and satisfyingly ambiguous, arguing with Ransom, who had written an essay detailing their faults: "I can see and hear Ransom and Jarrell now, seated on one sofa, as though on one love seat, the sacred texts open on their laps, one fifty, the other just out of college, and each expounding to the other's deaf ears his own inspired and irreconcilable interpretation." Both Lowell and Taylor were especially struck by Jarrell's ability to entice members of the opposite sex to knit mufflers and suchlike apparel for him; indeed, Taylor notes that he even persuaded Ransom's wife to remodel an old fur coat of his mother's for him. Taylor also remembers seeing Jarrell out one night with one of the high school teachers he was dating at the time: "The two of them were looking in a shop window, and Randall was pointing out a sweater he admired. Already you could practically see the knitting needles flying in the girl's hands." Carried away with his fantasy that all the female population of Gambier, Ohio, and environs were ministering to Jarrell's sartorial needs, Taylor mentions a mother and daughter who ran a restaurant in town and "were somehow persuaded to darn Randall's socks. They may even have done his laundry." And with respect to the latter half of Jarrell's double title on the Kenyon faculty—"Instructor in English, Director of Tennis"—Taylor writes that by the end of the director's second year, members of the crack Kenyon tennis team could be seen "sitting about the soda shop reading Auden and Chekhov and Proust." If these stories are too good to be true, they testify to their subject's power as an inspirer of campus myth, certainly as someone about whom it was fun to tell stories.

Kenyon was a small college, with an enrollment of three hundred or so students, and its English department consisted of five or six varieties of professor, with Jarrell the only "Mr." Along with Ransom and the others, he taught elementary writing to freshmen— the course in which, as he confessed to Ransom, he sometimes got bored—and a course of his own in American literature. Taylor enrolled in this course, which met at 8:00 a.m., and Jarrell, who sometimes arrived late for the class, could be seen, according to Taylor, "sprinting down the Middle Path, often eating his breakfast as he ran." More than once he failed to arrive by the second bell, after which many of the less-concerned students bolted the classroom, leaving the happy few who remained to talk about literature with their instructor. In addition to his tennis duties, he was a member of a committee titled "Freshman Writing and Use of Library," an appropriate appointment since, as Ransom later wrote about him, he had "read more books from the library than any student we had, and of wider range than any professor would have chosen." Besides teaching and writing (and having socks mended or sweaters knitted for him by admirers), there was little to do but read in this tiny academic community in southern Ohio. As he wrote Warren the fall of his first year there: "Gambier is rather like Siberia with nothing to do but otherwise rewarding." Later that same year he noted, again to Warren, that he had been skiing a lot and that Gambier was better "for sheep and for sports than for writing poetry." The skiing activity on one occasion drew from him the ecstatic cry "I feel just like an angel," rumored to have disturbed Kenyon's President Chalmers in its lack of moderation.

Meanwhile, he continued producing poems and criticism at an impressive rate. In the winter of his second year at Kenyon, Tate wrote him from the Woman's College of the University of North Carolina in Greensboro (Jarrell's eventual place of employment) that Scribner's might possibly be interested in publishing a book of his (Jarrell's) poems. Naturally the idea appealed to Jarrell, who was also, through Warren, looking into Louisiana State University Press. Along with the poems, he was writing prose criticism, and in a letter of thanks to Tate, he admitted to being hard at work on a review of Yvor Winters's book about American literature, *Maule's Curse*. By the end of April 1939, he had sent his corrected and expanded master's thesis to Donald Davidson at Vanderbilt. Some of the "corrections" had to do with manner of presentation, since he wrote Davidson that he hoped "the tone is formal enough now," and that he had substituted an analysis of a Shelley lyric for what was originally an analysis of one of Jarrell's own poems. (When we recall that he had wanted to do his thesis on Auden but desisted when told the subject was too recent, then these deferrings to authority were consistent with his earlier practice.) It was, of course, unthinkable for the writer of a learned essay for an advanced degree to propose to discuss one of his own poems! Jarrell's disinclination to advance further on the academic ladder—to undertake a doctoral dissertation—was of a piece with his preference for a witty, informal critical style, and his feelings about being centrally a poet rather than a scholar. Out of these feelings, or along with them, came the irreverence about teaching that annoyed Ransom, who was surely never late to his classes.

Jarrell's thesis was titled "Implicit Generalization in Housman," and while finishing it he was also preparing an article on Housman, lifted from the thesis, to appear in Ransom's new magazine. In fact, he appeared in the first three issues of *The Kenyon Review*, the earliest of which contained perhaps his most grandiose poem, "The Winter's Tale," an exercise in the apocalyptic mode that ends with a line announcing "The fall of the western hegemonies." A more impressive contribution was his review of Yvor Winters in the next issue, his first mature review of a single book and writer. "The Morality of Mr. Winters" is a mixed and totally clear-headed response to the challenge and provocation of an original critic. Winters's *Maule's Curse* dealt mainly with nineteenth-century

53

American writers (Hawthorne, Cooper, Melville, Jones Very, Emerson, Dickinson, and Henry James) and how their New England heritage emasculated and impoverished them. It also contained the first of Winters's many attacks on Emersonian romanticism from the standpoint of his own unromantic notion of morality.

That notion Jarrell refers to, summarily but fairly, as "an absolute moral dogmatism, an aesthetic that reduces art to morals, and a metaphysic conscious of hardly any problems except those of determinism." In a fine sentence, he noted that Winters "writes as if the last three hundred years had occurred, but not to him," a formulation that aptly characterizes the tone of aggrieved certainty informing Winters's writing. This moral dogmatism went along with an aesthetic one, and Jarrell became the first critic of Winters to call attention to some of his notorious judgments and preferences which "a tactful admirer might characterize as trembling on the brink of absurdity":

> Mr. Winters calls Jones Very "one of the finest of poets"; thinks Elizabeth Daryush great, the "finest British poet since T. Sturge Moore"; ranks Bridges (whom he considers a thoroughly major poet) above Hopkins, Moore above Yeats [. . .]; thinks Lady Winchilsea's "The Tree" and "The Change" "flawlessly beautiful poems" which typify almost uniquely the traditional norm of English poetry; puts Gray and Collins below Churchill, a great poet who "all but equals Pope's brilliance and range."

And so forth, these perversities having been taken not from *Maule's Curse* but from Winters's earlier *Primitivism and Decadence*.

Having said as much in disparagement, with a generous and invigorating turn of mind Jarrell offers an enormous "But":

> But these are the lapses of a critic whose thoroughness, clarity, and real penetration are almost unequaled today; *Maule's Curse* is the best book on American literature I ever read, and I

make so great a point of its author's vices only because his virtues are apparent and indeed overwhelming. He puts into exact and lucid shape judgments informed by an unusual sensitivity, a rigorous intelligence, and a dismayingly thorough knowledge. He reads each writer as if he had never been read before; he is a critical instrument completely uninfluenced by any fear of ridicule or consideration of expediency.

"He reads each writer as if he had never been read before": it is a tribute any critic would be pleased to have been paid, though Winters was good at resisting compliments. But it is also an apt characterization of Jarrell's own critical procedure, seen here in an early instance.

The review also presents two of the distinguishing traits that marked him as a critic: first, the aggressive informality he took pains to remove from his master's thesis and which typically expresses itself through humorous one-liners (as when, speaking of Winters's chapter on Poe, Jarrell parenthetically confides to us that it "leaves him [Poe] looking like a china shop after a visit of the Marx brothers"); second, a habit—or so it soon came to be—of praising the object in front of him by insisting that it is too good for any words he can summon up ("If I said just how good the essays on Melville and James are, I should seem extravagant"). We cannot question the critic's judgment, since the object of his praise (which praise, he assures us, is inadequate) is superior to any vocabulary through which that judgment could be expressed. This rhetorical gambit can sound at times like an evasion of the issue, but it had its roots in passionate enthusiasm, which in the review of Yvor Winters was as fresh as the voice that gave it utterance. An original style of criticism was emerging, as sharp and informal as any to be found in America.

The essay on A. E. Housman, which appeared in the third issue of *Kenyon*, is titled, modestly, "Texts from Housman," and is an extremely compressed demonstration—it examines only two poems—of Jarrell's concern with what, in his thesis, he called

55

"implicit generalization" in Housman's poems. In the review of *Maule's Curse* he had noted that, for Winters, good poetry was "entirely unambiguous." By contrast, Jarrell admired Empson's work (to the extent where, as noted above, Ransom deplored the latter's influence on his poetry), and it may be that, having been refused permission to write his thesis on Auden, Jarrell chose Housman as a writer whose "simple" but highly concentrated style contained ambiguous statements from which the implicit generalization had painstakingly to be inferred. In any case, his discussion of Housman's "Crossing alone the nighted ferry" and "It nods and curtseys and recovers" treats them as poems which (like Shelley's brief "To the Moon," also discussed in the thesis) contain generalizations so complicated as perhaps to escape altogether the reader's notice.

His procedure with each poem is to begin, as the good teacher does, by quoting it in its entirety (a substitute for reading it aloud) and then subjecting its "statements" to a rigorous stretching and bending in order to see what combinations of meanings they may accommodate. A single example of this exercise will serve to illustrate his tone and method, as they focus on the concluding utterance of a Housman stanza:

> *Crossing alone the nighted ferry*
> *With the one coin for fee,*
> *Whom, on the wharf of Lethe waiting,*
> *Count you to find? Not me.*

One might find the tone of those last two words unremarkable, but Jarrell found it rich with meanings:

Its casualness, finality, and matter-of-fact bluntness give it almost the effect of slang. It is the crudest of denials. There is in it a laconic brutality, an imperturbable and almost complacent vigor; it has certainly a sort of contempt. Contempt for what? Contempt at himself for his faithlessness? contempt at himself for his obsessing weakness—for not being faithless

now instead of then? Or contempt at her, for being bad enough
to keep things as they are, for being stupid enough to imagine
that they will be so always? The tone is both threatening and
disgusted. It shivers between all these qualities like a just-
thrown knife.

He concludes with a generalization of his own that was implicit in
his analysis: "Variations of this formula of alternative possibilities
make up one of the most valuable resources of the poet." (This is
of course the central assumption of Empson's *Seven Types of Ambiguity*.) Thus in "Texts from Housman" Jarrell is very much the
New Critic, wholly concerned with the words on the page in their
dramatic and tonal relationships. The essay mainly reveals his
capacity—the one he admired in Winters—to read each writer and
each poem as if they had never been read before. Certainly Housman had never been read this way, with such a fullness of attention,
a set of antennae working to tune in on the poem's range of sounds
and implications.

In the letter to Tate criticizing Jarrell's fecklessness as a teacher,
Ransom also said that his pupil was returning to Kenyon for one
more year. Thus by the winter of 1939, while completing his thesis
and writing for *Kenyon*, it was time for Jarrell to look for a job.
Although Tate had mentioned as a possibility the Woman's College
in Greensboro, where he was currently teaching, Jarrell's real hope
was the University of Texas. With written recommendations from
Tate, Ransom, and Warren, and an M.A. soon to be awarded (he
received it in the fall of 1939), his prospects were strong. Of his
three advocates, Tate was now moving to the fore as a mentor,
what with Ransom's only qualified approval of him and Warren's
kindly but somewhat detached interest. Fifteen years older than
Jarrell and with strong opinions about everything, including, centrally, the state of poetry, Tate was a good instrument to stir up
the younger poet-critic's mind. Unlike Warren, Tate took a great
interest in actively shaping the careers of younger writers whose
work he respected—Lowell was a case in point. And although—

as is the case with most people who wrote letters to Jarrell—Tate's letters have not survived, we can see from the four which Jarrell wrote to him in the spring of 1939 that Tate had struck a responsive chord.

Jarrell's fullest response is contained in one of the best letters he ever wrote, a longish one in which—in reply to remarks Tate had made about the relation between science and poetry (one of Tate's favorite subjects)—he took the opportunity to engage in a bit of self-analysis. Referring back to his Vanderbilt studies in psychology, he says that it was Gestalt psychology that interested him because it was "non-positivistic" and was mixed up with philosophy. He scoffs at psychologists who, like some English professors, pretend to use "scientific method" (complete with tables and formulas) to make up for the fact that their subject is not quantifiable. He is dubious (perhaps with I. A. Richards in mind) about whether psychology can be of any use to the criticism of poetry, but adds that at any rate no such putatively useful psychology had begun to emerge. Then the following excursion into self:

> I feel very frivolous and unconcerned about it anyway; I think all in all I've got a poetic and semifeminine mind, I don't put any real faith in abstractions or systems; I never had any certainties, religious or metaphysical, to lose, so I don't feel their lack [. . .] I think my mind is *really* unsystematic; along with that or perhaps because of it, I can't help thinking the world [. . .] is too.

In a manner reminiscent of Samuel Johnson refuting Bishop Berkeley by kicking the stone, Jarrell says he feels "that when I'm good I *am* good. And when poetry's good it *is* good—that the values are really values, and thoroughly important." So he claims not to be bothered by contradictions and inconsistencies, and says that when he hears people arguing solemnly about "ideas" he can't help thinking to himself, " 'How ridiculous for these two grown-up men to take all this so seriously and finally'—and so forth [. . .] When

I know something I *know* it: I mean, as if I were the thing (or at least I hope so) and not as if I were—O, Mattheiessen (or however you spell his absurd name—this is a Freudian block, I'll bet a dollar) or a sociologist."

Years later, when he was living in New York and serving as temporary literary editor of *The Nation*, Jarrell insisted to Philip Rahv on one occasion that (in William Barrett's words) "the whole of Existentialism was philosophically meaningless." Rahv, Barrett says, was aghast and insisted that surely it was not meaningless to talk about the meaning of death; yet Jarrell remained unwavering in his insistence on the nullity of all such philosophical talk. Barrett admits to being puzzled that a poet should have been so cavalier about such a central human subject, but neglects to say that Jarrell in his poetry paid a good deal of speculative attention to death. Aside from any possibly mischievous teasing of Rahv that may have been going on (the *enfant terrible* from Nashville knocking down New York–*Partisan Review* icons), the exaggerated, unqualified insistence on Jarrell's part tallies with his earlier assertion to Tate about the impossibility of taking seriously two grown men arguing about ideas. His strategy, and it was a repeated one, was to isolate himself from—by elevating himself above—certain kinds of in-tellectual, certainly ideological, controversy; to cultivate his "*really* unsystematic" mind; to put the stress on feeling "frivolous and unconcerned" while everyone around him (so the fantasy ran) was acting deadly solemn about such matters as the science of criticism or the meaning of Existentialism. One word for Jarrell's sort of behavior is of course arrogance; yet the letter to Tate is filled with an attractive, youthful conviction of powers ("When I know some-thing I *know* it: I mean, as if I were the thing") that seems more self-perceptive than self-inflated. It feels as if these powers were speaking through the twenty-five-year-old and that all he needed to do was heed their promptings, whatever the world of ideas and systems and men arguing might say. The "poetic and semifeminine mind" was what really mattered.

That mind was on display again in six poems Brooks and Warren

59

published in the Winter 1939 issue of *The Southern Review*. They showed little development beyond earlier ones he had printed there, and although he would write Amy Breyer deBlasio, after *Blood for a Stranger* was published, that many of the poems in it were her private poems, the Audenesque manner Jarrell adopted protects him from personal exposure. One of those poems, "On the Railway Platform," was the first of the six in *The Southern Review* and also would open *Blood for a Stranger*. He wrote Amy: "What you say about 'On the Railway Platform' and about what it meant about us and Kenyon, is all so." Speaking of another poem, he told her: "I guess nobody else but you would know." Nobody, certainly nobody but the poet and Amy, would know that the opening lines of the railway platform poem had a personal edge, since they might very well have been written by Auden:

> *The rewarded porters opening their smiles,*
> *Grapes with a card, and the climate changing*
> *From the sun of bathers to the ice of skis*
> *Cannot hide it—journeys are journeys.*

> *And, arrived or leaving, "Where am I going?"*
> *All the travellers have wept; "is it once again only*
> *The country I laughed at and nobody else?*
> *The passage of a cell between two cells?"*

> *No, the ends are hardly indifferent, the shadow*
> *Falls from our beaches to the shivering floes,*
> *The faces fail while we watch, and darkness*
> *Sucks from the traveller his crazy kiss.*

The landscape, the diction, the compressed mode of speech, the "frontier" situation, the journey, the abstracted "travellers" and "traveller," the stage props of grapes and bathers, beaches and floes, the knowing superiority of tone are all Auden's, who two years previously in *Letters from Iceland* had written:

> *And the traveller hopes: 'Let me be far from any*
> *Physician'; And the ports have names for the sea;*
>   *The citiless, the corroding, the sorrow;*
>   *And North means to all: 'Reject!'*

In Auden's final stanza "Tears fall in all the rivers," while Jarrell's railway platform poem proceeds to tell us "And the tears fall. What we leave we leave forever: / Time has no travellers."

Often Jarrell's early poems begin promisingly, sometimes with an elegant lyricism, as in "When you and I were all," another of the *Southern Review* poems of 1939 in the Auden style:

> *When you and I were all,*
> *Time held his trembling hand,*
> *Fall's leaves lay long, the snows*
> *Were grave on wire and wand;*
> *Along the echoing ways*
> *Our steps were lucky on the stone;*
> *And, involved in our embrace,*
> *Man's intent and mercy lay*
> *Dazed through love's exacting day.*

It is the manner of Auden lyrics like "Fish in the unruffled lakes," or "Dear, though the night is gone," or the famous "Lay your sleeping head, my love," and Jarrell even employs one of Auden's favorite words, "lucky" ("Warm are the still and lucky miles," begins an Auden lyric), while moving around abstract counters such as Man, Love, and Time. But what in the first stanza looks to be a rhyme pattern loosens and becomes unpredictable as the poem continues, uncertainly, through six stanzas, to end in disillusionment:

> *The towel and the ewer scraped*
> *The blood from our consent; our kiss*
> *Was acquiescence, but we knew*
> *The dooms would fall no less if its*
> *Wet sanction were untendered. We*

> *Might stammer to the magistrates, "You too*
> *Are housed and nourished with that crime;*
> *And who is there that hears but is*
> *Its and the world's accessory?"*

After receiving the poem, Warren wrote to Jarrell asking him to consider "the general rhythmical structure of the last stanza," with an eye—the hint is—toward improving it. Jarrell in response defended the stanza by claiming that its rhythm was "purposely broken and stammering in some parts," but he also said that it was probably "wrong" and he would try to fix it. On the evidence of the published poem, there is no sign that he fixed anything, since the tongue-twisting of its final lines, the rough, wrenched enjambing of one line with the next, and the unpleasant, grating sound effects all remain. In 1939 he lacked—as most poets lack—Auden's matchless ear.

Yet to an extent, at least, he was becoming aware of his tendency to assume an apocalyptic, vaguely prophetic manner about the world—life, love, history, and so forth—at the expense of those particularities of situation, character, and speaking voice he so admired in Hardy and Auden. When at the end of 1940 Tate wrote him about *Five Young American Poets*, evidently objecting to the limpness of some of his lines, Jarrell admitted the charge and replied, unconvincingly, that when people got used to reading accentual verse they would find his lines stronger (he had just begun that fall, he said elsewhere, to write accentual verse). But, more important, he defended his current practice to Tate as "an occupational risk, a defect of a quality. In other words, I'd rather seem limp and prosaic than false or rhetorical, I want to be rather like speech." These contradictory impulses toward "rhetoric" (as displayed above in the final stanza from "When you and I were all") and "speech" (as something aspired to, not yet present in the poems) would not be resolved by a simple choice of one over the other. The matter needs to be considered in light of Jarrell's notions about the situation of modern poetry as he would describe it, first in his short preface for *Five Young American Poets*, then in a longer article for *The Nation* in 1942, "The End of the Line." Those prose pieces coincided with the publication of new poems—"90 North" and "Children Selecting Books in a Library"—which are far better than anything he had previously written, and in which speech and rhetoric co-exist within a plausibly imagined situation. But these literary events took place after he had been hired by the University of Texas, had parted from Ransom and Kenyon, as well as his friends Lowell and Taylor, and had taken up residence in Austin for three years of teaching and writing that would be ended by the Second World War and his enlistment in the armed services.

THREE

Making a Reputation

DURING the three years Jarrell taught at the University of Texas, his main correspondent was Allen Tate, and soon after he began teaching there in September 1939 (and after visiting Tate that summer) he summed up his happy sense of the new place:

> Texas is lovely: the students meek, the professors amiable or indifferent; I am taking piano lessons, and have written about 150 lines since I've been here. I've got an office on the twenty-third floor, a really enormous one: the book shelves would hold several hundred books, and look comic with my six or eight. So far I've met nobody who knows anything about poetry, but I should worry. Nobody knows anything about me, either—except I've become famous, since I'm the best badminton player, at the university, and am getting a permanent modest look (*very* unbecoming) from responding to compliments. My classes are nice and not too much work: all in all, it's a lot nicer for me than Kenyon.

He would never again speak so genially of it. The meek students turned out not to know much of anything, as illustrated by a humorous anecdote he later passed on to Tate about a class of forty-five sophomores in which only *one* of them had heard that faith and works were religious terms. All the rest went to church, 5 or 6 were Catholics, too. I said, "What do your preachers talk to you about?" One girl said (I thought), "About election."

I thought of you, the Ode, I mean [Tate's "Ode to the Confederate Dead" contains the line "Of heaven to their election in the vast breath"], and was going to answer, "Well, that's a good thing to talk about," when I realized that she had used the plural.

He wonders how "exceptional" Tate finds the students at Princeton, where he was teaching, and says that he, Jarrell, has one who, "at eighteen, has read Rilke, Kafka, Proust, Spengler, everybody, but she's European and doesn't count. The rest make up for her." In fact, he seemed much more pleased by the football team ("I confess that if Texas played Vanderbilt I'd be yelling myself hoarse for Texas") than by his students. He says he has met some of the players, even played touch football with them, and he is delighted by the presence in his class of an all-state freshman back who runs the hundred-yard dash in 9.7 and is also "cold as a corpse—possibly owing to the fact that he's an undertaker's assistant in the summers."

As for his colleagues in the English department—and with the exception of two of them his own age, Herschel Baker and Guy Steffan, with whom he became friendly—their amiable indifference and inattention to poetry, including Jarrell's poetry, was soon to be spoken of with more asperity. In his third year at Texas, when Tate was arranging for him to give a lecture at Princeton, Jarrell looked forward to it, he said, since—along with the fact that *The Atlantic Monthly* had paid him a dollar a line for one of his poems—"it would really have more effect on the department than having a couple of books published. The people here are the usual lunatics: I've been told that several disapprove of my having things in 'that radical magazine, *The Nation*'; others said that they disapproved of my having so much published, since it must mean that I was neglecting my classes." He allows scornfully that, if he had

had equal amounts of his work published in *PMLA*, he would be a full professor. In fact, for part of his stay at Texas he was allowed to teach only three-fourths of a full load. Being invited to lecture at Princeton, he said, would probably mean an additional course to teach, thus an increased salary.

Tate was a valuable patron on various fronts. He suggested to James Laughlin, publisher of New Directions books, that Jarrell deserved a place in the first volume of Laughlin's projected anthology series, *Five Young American Poets* ("young" meaning in their twenties—Jarrell and John Berryman were each twenty-six when the book appeared in 1940). And he sent the manuscript of *Blood for a Stranger* to Scribner's, his own publisher, offering as well to advise Jarrell on which poems should go into the New Directions venture, and which additional ones, and in what order, should be included in *Blood for a Stranger*. When things did not work out at Scribner's, Tate put in a word to his friend Lambert Davis at Harcourt, Brace, which eventually published the book. Not surprisingly, Jarrell's letters to Tate during this period are filled with many graceful thank-you's for this and that favor.

Eventually, Tate came to feel that Jarrell was insufficiently grateful for such efforts on his behalf. An early and relatively minor instance of the student not appreciating his mentor as the mentor thought appropriate occurred in 1940, when Tate suggested to Edmund Wilson at *The New Republic* (to whose attention Tate had brought Jarrell) that the best poem Jarrell had yet written, "90 North," could be improved if its fifth stanza were excised. Jarrell courteously but firmly explained to both Tate and Wilson that such an excision was a very bad idea. A more serious breach, at least in Tate's mind, occurred when his protégé failed to follow his advice about the organization of *Blood for a Stranger*: "Select well, O Allen, or—but I can't think of any threat horrid enough," Jarrell had humorously ordered, but then proceeded, quite properly, to exercise his own final judgment on the poems and their sequence. Years later, in a memorial volume for Jarrell, Tate's contribution was a short one and revealed a long-standing hurt still festering:

"For an inscrutable reason—I never understood Randall—he liked me very much for some years around 1940, but not much later on. He dedicated to me his first book, *Blood for a Stranger*; he had previously asked me to go over the manuscript and arrange the order of the poems; this I did; but he then gave them his own order, writing me a letter in which I appeared to be a little obtuse." (The letter has not surfaced; in the same year as the memorial volume appeared, Tate expressed himself rather less guardedly when he wrote to Arthur Mizener that, in his opinion, Jarrell was a "gifted, self-adulating little twerp.") At any rate, before Jarrell left Texas for the army, he had removed himself from under Tate's wing and taken full charge of his career as poet and critic.

At the end of his first academic year at Texas, he married Mackie Langham, a colleague in the English department whom he referred to in one of his letters to Tate as "somebody with judgment" (she had, among other things, liked a poem of Tate's shown her by Jarrell). Mackie Langham, who had a master's degree from Texas, was—on the evidence of photographs—small, dark, and pretty. She looked older than Jarrell and (according to one observer) was protective of him, though certainly not to an extent which excluded teasing and irony from their mutual dealings. Some months after their marriage in June of 1940, Jarrell wrote Tate that "Mackie's latest game is calling me all the names she can get from letters on reviews complaining of me. I rarely get called anything but *arrogant and pretentious creature* or such. I just answer scornfully, Brilliant! brilliant! Wittier than *anybody*!" Of course he believed it too, and at least in the early years of their marriage there is no indication his wife disagreed. They had moved into a rural retreat which he made sound attractively down-at-heels—"a big river thirty yards from the door, cows to the left, horses to the right—like Red's old place except rattier. Kitten loves it: he was born in the nearest house." "Red's old place" was the house outside Nashville where Jarrell and Amy had visited Warren; it recurs more than once in the letters as the archetypal Good Place to live. The fact that "Kitten" loved it too was at least as significant, for Kitten was the black Persian cat, born the fall after the Jarrells' marriage, who was made much of over the years to come by both of them, but especially by Randall. The following from a letter to Louise Bogan (the letter apropos of a controversy in *The New Republic*) may be cited as a humorously idyllic rendering of the Jarrells' life at one point during the first year of their marriage:

> I was interrupted in writing this letter by the extraordinary arrival of a poor wonderfully scrubby half-starved four-months-old dark brown Persian; the extraordinary comes from the fact that very obviously—from his looks and some more data—he's the half-brother of our own Kitten, who at the age of seven and a half months weighs twelve pounds. We fed him; he was wonderfully good, and our cat was too; they're both fast asleep on the floor, looking like the lion and the lamb (I don't think the new one weighs two pounds). My wife's also asleep on the floor, everything's perfectly dark and quiet except for a cow that moos occasionally outside; I feel as if I'd wandered into the Sleeping Beauty's castle.

There was no place where he would rather have found himself, it may be presumed.

The colleague in the English department whom Jarrell was closest to was Herschel Baker, later to become a distinguished Renaissance scholar and professor at Harvard. Jarrell and Mackie became lifelong friends of Baker and his wife, Barbara, who remember Jarrell organizing games of touch football in which they were all supposed to play (though Barbara Baker was at one point allowed to decline, being pregnant), or eating out together and deciding between the thirty-five- and seventy-five-cent Mexican dinner at a local restaurant. To the Bakers, Mackie seemed warm and intelligent, an intellectual, but not "superior." At one point, they all decided to enroll in a night-school class in carpentry, and Baker recalls that Jarrell "couldn't tell a screwdriver from a claw-hammer." Yet he noted also that, when Jarrell decided to learn to do something, he usually did it well, carpentry being the evident exception that proved the rule. If his efforts at carpentry were abortive, his enthusiasm for handwriting analysis, which he had begun to practice, took strong hold. After he had analyzed a sample from each of the Bakers, he remarked to Barbara, somewhat regretfully, "Yours isn't nearly so intellectual as Herschel's." Jarrell admired Baker's facility with languages and his musical ability. Years later, after visiting him and Barbara at Harvard, he summarized Baker's talents by saying, "He is very intelligent and wonderfully educated: knows Greek, Latin, French, German, Anglo-Saxon, plays the piano and organ, etc. [. . .] He's extremely well-read and has better taste than any scholar I've ever met—and better than any but a few critics." Since on his own part Jarrell lacked both a command of languages and the ability to play a musical instrument, his list of Baker's virtues has in it a slight note of regret.

In November of 1940, the autumn of his second year at Texas, *Five Young American Poets* was published. After originally declining James Laughlin's invitation to be one of the five, Jarrell deferred to Tate's advice (and to further explanations from Laughlin about the book) and signed on. But he was reluctant to contribute the short prose preface Laughlin asked each poet to write. "I think I'll wait until I can have a few hundred pages before I tell the world what I think about poetry," he told Laughlin, who was, however, not to be put off. The interesting result was that Jarrell ended up writing not merely "A Note on Poetry" (the standard title for each of the five poets' prefaces) but setting forth a striking new perspective on modern poetry and its relation to what preceded it. "The End of the Line" would later extend and complement the preface, and taken together, these two pieces of writing can be considered Jarrell's theoretical underpinning—something he always insisted he had no need of or taste for providing—not only to his contribution to the anthology, but to *Blood for a Stranger*, and to the ten or so poetry reviews he wrote during this prewar period. These, along with his longer essays on Auden and Yeats, constitute his early criticism and should be placed in the context of the

polemics he was developing a taste for—or at least developing—
in the pages of *The New Republic*. There is of course no reason to
expect the poems and criticism of a writer to square with the theory
propounded in a particular essay or two; but—like Wordsworth's
and T. S. Eliot's—Jarrell's theories and practices become more
interesting when placed next to one another.

The other poets in Laughlin's volume were Berryman, W. R.
Moses, George Marion O'Donnell (an old Vanderbilt rival), and
—after an extended discussion about what (somewhat token) female should be chosen—Mary Barnard. Of the group, only Jarrell
proceeded in his preface to talk historically about what modern
poetry was. After some introductory grumbling about having to
sound off in this medium, which might perhaps cause readers to
confuse his life and opinions with his poems ("I look like a bear
and live in a cave; but you should worry"), he stated his thesis:
that "modern" poetry was an extension of romanticism—"it is what
romantic poetry wishes or finds it necessary to become." Because,
he argued, the best modern criticism of poetry was anti-romantic
in its tendency (he cites Eliot, and might have cited his own mentors, Ransom and Tate), one may mistakenly assume that modern
poetry is "classical." But consider a list of the qualities manifested
by "typical modernistic poetry":

> Very interesting language, a great emphasis on connotation,
> "texture"; extreme intensity, forced emotion—violence; a
> good deal of obscurity; emphasis on sensation, perceptual
> nuances; emphasis on details, on the part rather than on the
> whole; experimental or novel qualities of some sort; a tendency
> toward external formlessness and internal disorganization
> [. . .]; an extremely personal style—*refine your singularities*; lack
> of restraint—all tendencies are forced to their limits; there is
> a good deal of emphasis on the unconscious, dream structure,
> the thoroughly subjective; the poet's attitudes are usually anti-
> scientific, anti-common-sense, anti-public—he is, essentially,
> removed; poetry is primarily lyric, intensive—the few long

poems are aggregations of lyric details; poems usually have, not a logical, but the more or less associational structure of dramatic monologue.

He concludes: "This complex of qualities is essentially romantic; and the poetry that exhibits it represents the culminating point of romanticism."

No critic of modern or "modernistic" poetry (he uses the words "modern," "modernist," "modernistic" interchangeably) had produced as forcefully comprehensive a list of its qualities. Like all such lists, it fitted some poems better than others; still, it was a telling attempt to fix a movement in a sentence, coming from the pen of a modern poet whose shortest poem in the anthology was titled "The Machine-Gun":

> *The broken blood, the hunting flame,*
> *The pierced mask and the flowering shell*
> *Are not placated—nor the face*
> *That smouldered where the searchlights fell;*
>
> *Our times lie in the welded hands,*
> *Our fortune in the rubber face—*
> *On the gunner's tripod, black with oil,*
> *Spits and gapes the pythoness.*

Connotation, "texture," intensity, violence, some obscurity (though less than in most of Jarrell's early poems), emphasis on sensation, details, the unconscious (as in a dream), the "removed" poet, associational rather than logical structure—these qualities pretty well fit "The Machine-Gun." (In fact, this little poem has more organization and more "restraint"—is, in Jarrell's sense, less "modernistic"—than a number of its neighbors in the anthology.)

As a contribution to literary criticism or history, the insistence on continuity rather than discontinuity between romantic and modern poetry is a salutary one which only years later was taken up and developed by critics like Frank Kermode and John Bayley.

71

Jarrell was concerned to avoid the two basic ways of simplifying literary history he had encountered in university theorizing: the first was an old-fashioned, rather Arnoldian one that loved Shakespeare, Spenser and the Elizabethans, Milton, then—after an eighteenth-century lapse into neoclassicism—the glorious romantics and Victorians. (Modernism was a reaction to romanticism that should be regarded with suspicion.) The second simplification found in modernism a return to true principles, as observed in the metaphysical poets or French Symbolists but not in most of the romantics or Victorians. This more or less Eliotic line had been recently laid down assertively by Cleanth Brooks in his *Modern Poetry and the Tradition* (1939).

By contrast, Jarrell's attempt was catholic in its thrust, insofar as it singled out no period or style in preference to another and castigated no period or style as a deviation from true poetry. He was honest enough to admit that of course there were differences between romantic and modernist poems, matters of tone and posture that would be evident to anyone who looked. But by overstating the case, by insisting on the similarity and continuity between the two kinds of verse, he hoped to counter the enormous effort that had gone into stressing their differences. Further, and in the title of the longer essay on the same subject, we were witnessing "The End of the Line": "How can poems be written that are more violent, more disorganized, more obscure, more—supply your own adjective—than those that have already been written?" he asks. An alternative was that poets could go back and repeat the ride, as it were, or could resort—these "last romanticists"—to odd varieties of neoclassicism. He points out that a similar development has occurred in modern music (although he mentions no names, he may be thinking of Stravinsky or Prokofiev, of *Pulcinella* or the *Classical Symphony*), and he alludes to Yvor Winters as a contemporary poet who has simply repudiated the whole system of modernism.

"The End of the Line" was published in February 1942, after America had entered the war, and there may be something appropriately last-ditch to Jarrell's tone, as if after him the deluge. The contemporary poet, he wrote, has a variety of styles he can choose from, but no guarantee that one is any more or less legitimate or fertile than any other. In a sense it is an embarrassment of riches; in another sense, an anarchy. As in "A Note on Poetry," he defers to "economics" as determining literature, even as he insists that poets can't avoid making the choice to write in this or that style: "Young poets can choose—do choose—to write anything from surrealism to imitations of Robert Bridges; the only thing they have no choice about is making a choice. The Muse, forsaking her sterner laws, says to everyone: 'Do what you will.' " Jarrell is not concerned to use this situation as an opportunity for exercising superior irony, any more than he is concerned to indict romanticism or modernism: "I hope I am not such a fool as to condemn a century and a half of a world. (Besides, I liked it—a lot of it, anyway.)" And there is the possibility that, even at the end of the line, wonders may follow. In his eyes, Auden is—or rather was until recently—one of those wonders: he was what Jarrell referred to in "A Note on Poetry" as "a departure from modernist romanticism," and what he now called, in "The End of the Line," "the most successful and novel reaction against modernist romanticism."

Where does this leave Jarrell himself, a young poet at the end of the romantic-modernist line? In concluding his preface, he anticipated a reader's asking such a question by suggesting that we may have been thinking, "Does he really suppose he writes the sort of poetry that replaces modernism?" He is sorry he must decline that soft impeachment. In some sentences he added to "The End of the Line" when he revised it in 1951, he was less personal and less coy, saying only:

Originality can no longer be recognized by, and condemned or applauded for, its obvious experimentalism; the age offers to the poet a fairly heartless eclecticism or a fairly solitary individuality. He can avoid being swept along by the current

73

—there is no current; he can congratulate himself on this, and see behind him, glittering in the distance of time, all those bright streams sweeping people on to the wildest of excesses, the unlikeliest of triumphs.

Here surely we have a bravura instance of what Harold Bloom has termed "belatedness." For Pound's Hugh Selwyn Mauberley, at least "the age demanded" something that the poet could set himself in resistance to, refusing to provide "an image / Of its accelerated grimace." Jarrell's post-modern era demands nothing from the poet, since it scarcely knows the poet is there; it offers, rather, a "fairly heartless eclecticism" or a "fairly solitary individuality."

As for his own position in relation to this matter, we probably should not hold him hard to terms thrown out in a moment of eloquence in a critical essay; but whether "heartless" or not, the word for his poems in the anthology of five poets and in *Blood for a Stranger* is eclecticism. In her invaluable and detailed study of the poetry, Suzanne Ferguson does not use the word about Jarrell's early work but suggests something like it by speaking of the poems' "surprising anonymity in style and content," their indebtedness to a number of poets, primarily Auden, and their "sociological" tone toward things: "situations and characters are generalized in imagery that is concrete without being specific, and in extended personifications that dramatize abstract conditions of love and suffering." What they do not dramatize is the presence of a personal voice. Jarrell's early poems never seem to have much of anything at stake that might relate to a particular case or person; it is an anonymous speaker, rather, who seemingly has foresuffered everything and thus knows all.

Blood for a Stranger adds twenty-seven poems to the nineteen from the anthology, but shows no new style or attitude toward experience (indeed many of its poems were published before the anthology ones). Jarrell joked about the title, which he had decided on years previously, writing to Tate that it was "a happily or unhappily characteristic title, I'm afraid." It derived from the volume's final poem, "Che Farò Senza Euridice" in which "your blood sprang / To the hands of the strangers, the fishers of the river / Of death." This portentous rhetoric is, unhappily, characteristic of more than one poem in the book. Nor was the business of flowing blood merely metaphorical; in May of 1941 he wrote Tate: "I've been writing stuff that flows glibly off, without emotion but wittily, I hope, anyway—why it comes out I've no notion," and quoted from his poem "Esthetic Theories: Art as Expression": "Poems, like lives, are doing what we can / And very different from what we know. / They start surprisingly, like blood in bones. / The unlucky wake up bleeding at the nose." In August 1942, again writing to Tate, he noted: "My nose has been bleeding every day for the last week, why I don't know; and I've noticed that the blood is the freshest gayest most innocent red imaginable, without a thought in its pretty head." Since *Blood for a Stranger* was to be published in a month, Jarrell may have been giving the book a little publicity, or have had unlucky forebodings. For in the language from "The End of the Line," a "fairly heartless eclecticism" produced too many poems in that volume which were "stuff that flows glibly off." On the other hand, and in the words of his other possibility for the post-modern poet at the end of the line, the book has moments in which a "fairly solitary individuality" shines out —suggestions, amidst the facility and predictability of most of *Blood for a Stranger*, of the kind of poetry he would come to write.

Evidence for such a claim is found especially in three poems he published in *The New Republic* in 1941. One of them, "The Christmas Roses," would (like most of the others in *Blood for a Stranger*) be excluded from his *Selected Poems*; a second one, "Children Selecting Books in a Library," was almost completely rewritten for that volume; the third, "90 North," survived virtually intact. In these poems Jarrell was able to express and explore what, in the letter written Tate from Kenyon, he called his "poetic and semi-feminine mind," by focusing on what might be considered unmanly situations: a patient lamenting in her hospital bed; a child seeking to escape the pain of life through reading books; an adult reflecting on how the child wakes from the dream of a meaningful life into a real world of meaninglessness, darkness, and pain. All three poems avoid the heavy-handed rhetoric about history and the individual he often indulged in. Their generalizing ambitions, though strong, are at least partially anchored in particularities of dramatic situation, and in a speaking voice with some recognizably personal character. In other words, we hear for the first time the distinctive note of a human voice in Jarrell's poetry.

This is not to say that the poems—at least the first two—were satisfactory as wholes, as he himself later acknowledged by suppressing the first and rewriting the second. "The Christmas Roses" eventually chokes on its own repetitions and banalities ("And now I'm dying and you have your wish. / Dying, dying; and I have the only wish / That I had strength or hope enough to keep, / To die"). But it opens on a compelling note:

> *The nurse is at the tree, and if I'm thirsty no one minds.*
> *Why don't they finish? . . . If it's metastasizing*
> *I wish that it would hurry. Yesterday it snowed.*
> *The man they took before me died today.*
> *When I woke up I thought I saw you on the bed,*
> *You smiled at me and said, "It's all all right,"*
> *And I believed you and went back to sleep.*
> *But I was lucky: the mortality's so high*
> *They put it in a foot-note or don't mention it.*
>
> *Why don't you write to me? . . . The day nurse sits and holds*
> *The glass for me, but yesterday I cried*
> *I looked so white. I looked like paper.*
> *Whiter. I dreamt about the pole, and bears,*
> *And I see snow and sheets and my two nurses and the chart*
> *I make all by myself with my thermometer*
> *In red that's like the roses that are like the blood*
> *That's gone, that's gone for good—and what's left's spoiled,*
> *The silly culture I keep warming for my death.*

Writing to Tate, Jarrell remarked about the poem that it was supposed to be "*said* (like a speech from a play) with expression, emotion, and long pauses" and that it needed a "girl" to do it: "I'd like to hear it done really nicely by somebody like Bette Davis," he added, possibly without irony. (He also said he could say it aloud when he was alone, but got embarrassed in front of other people.)

In her edition of the letters, Mary Jarrell invites us to see the poem as having sprung from her husband's "painful feeling of abandonment" concerning Amy Breyer. Looked at from this angle, "The Christmas Roses," which in subsequent stanzas goes on to stress the patient's feelings of having been abandoned by her lover, is Jarrell's attempt, only partly successful, to try out or try on feelings of sickness, pain, loss by projecting them through the voice of a woman (although "she" is never specifically identified as a woman). It is the first in the long line of dramatic monologues he was to write with a woman at the center of things; but its situation is rather melodramatically conceived, inasmuch as the hospital setting introduces potentially extreme, even desperate elements. As in many of the poems in *Blood for a Stranger*, "blood" appears in "The Christmas Roses," and like Jarrell's nosebleed and much of the poetry he was writing, it flows off too glibly—the speaking voice is unchecked in its wanderings. Yet some of the juxtapositions and transitions in the above stanzas are artfully and wittily managed ("but yesterday I cried / I looked so white. I looked like paper. / Whiter. I dreamt about the pole, and bears, / And I see snow and sheets"), and move in the direction of the "speech" he was trying to get into his poems.

"Children Selecting Books in a Library" was the first of three poems he would write about that institution he so much loved. In his previously mentioned talk about libraries, he made a fine and final argument for the essentialness of open stacks to a good library: "We become cultivated, educated, by all the books we look at and don't get; the ones we read a little in, standing up, and then put down; the ones that we read a little in, and read more in, and sit down and read, and then take home and read—books we discover for ourselves by looking at, walking around among, living for a while in the midst of, books [. . .] A good library has to have its stacks full of readers." In the poem's third stanza—the only one which survived intact in the revised version fifteen years later—the narrator tells us why children ("They hunt among the shelves, as dogs do, grasses") should select the books they select—why, in short, they should, must read:

> *Their tales are full of sorcerers and ogres*
> *Because their lives are: the capricious infinite*
> *That, like parents, no one has yet escaped*
> *Except by luck or magic; and since strength*
> *And wit are useless, be kind or stupid, wait*
> *Some power's gratitude, the tide of things.*

There is an awkward moment here—the confusion of "be kind or stupid" hanging in midair—but compared to much of his early poetry, the lines have a serene and grave authority, that of an experienced voice which knows the way things inevitably are and speaks out of that knowledge with sympathy and grace—as in the lovely touch of "like parents," those "ogres" whom indeed no one escapes except perhaps by the luck and magic of reading (and even then only *while* reading). That Jarrell is speaking out of a firm conviction about his own lot is, I think, undeniable. As he would put it in another poem, "The soul learns fortitude in libraries."

The attempt to be "rather like speech" instead of "false or rhetorical" (in the words of a December 1940 letter to Tate); the impulse, concurrently, to speak in a gravely authoritative way about human experience; and the sense that somehow the child is importantly connected to that way of speaking come together in the third poem, "90 North," one of the poems that Edmund Wilson had accepted. "90 North" is about the difference between "there" and "here," between discovering the North Pole, as a child dreams of doing, and—as an adult—discovering that the discovery is meaningless. The poem's first two stanzas are about the child's voyage and its end; the remaining six stanzas give us the adult "here" and speculate on the difference between childish illusion and adult disenchantment. It is the first of Jarrell's poems that one wants and needs to quote in its entirety:

At home, in my flannel gown, like a bear to its floe,
I clambered to bed; up the globe's impossible sides
I sailed all night—till at last, with my black beard,
My furs and my dogs, I stood at the northern pole.

There in the childish night my companions lay frozen,
The stiff furs knocked at my starveling throat,
And I gave my great sigh: the flakes came huddling,
Were they really my end? In the darkness I turned to my rest.

—Here, the flag snaps in the glare and silence
Of the unbroken ice. I stand here,
The dogs bark, my beard is black, and I stare
At the North Pole . . .
                              And now what? Why, go back.

Turn as I please, my step is to the south.
The world—my world spins on this final point
Of cold and wretchedness: all lines, all winds
End in this whirlpool I at last discover.

And it is meaningless. In the child's bed
After the night's voyage, in that warm world
Where people work and suffer for the end
That crowns the pain—in that Cloud-Cuckoo-Land

I reached my North and it had meaning.
Here at the actual pole of my existence,

79

Where all that I have done is meaningless,
Where I die or live by accident alone—

Where, living or dying, I am still alone;
Here where North, the night, the berg of death
Crowd me out of the ignorant darkness,
I see at last that all the knowledge

I wrung from the darkness—that the darkness flung me—
Is worthless as ignorance: nothing comes from nothing,
The darkness from the darkness. Pain comes from the darkness
And we call it wisdom. It is pain.

This is a child who, selecting books in the library, found and read one about polar exploration and has now submitted himself to a dream narrative in which, heroically, he meets his meaningful end—"In the darkness I turned to my rest." But that was "There in the childish night"; "Here at the actual pole of my existence," he has nowhere to go but down, back south with the fruits of knowledge that are indistinguishable from ignorance, the "wisdom" that is really pain. The poem is attractive for the richness with which the child's voyage is filled out—clambering like a bear up the "impossible sides" of the globe; standing there amid the "huddling" flakes, black beard, furs, dogs, and all. And rich, too, in the repetitions which, in its later stanzas, create pace and continuity in sound and syntax: "here," "where," "world," "alone," "darkness," "pain" are some of the recurring words which make for echoes that drive the poem along by engaging the ear. In many of Jarrell's early poems, their pessimism about life and the world feels unearned; the Waste Land syndrome, the "life is sterile" line, as adopted effortlessly by so many modernist poets, all too easily takes over the poem. By contrast, "90 North" enacts its discovery of the world as pain *within* the poem, instead of laying it on from outside. It does so in a declarative mode made stronger by the short phrases, and now and then short sentences, of which it is composed; yet the poem's discovery is effected with wit and charm—with the sorts of things that a bookish child, grown into adulthood, may also find are a part of him. Writing to Wilson and insisting that the poem needed its fifth stanza (the one Tate had suggested dropping), Jarrell said that "anyone who writes such a pessimistic poem ought just to nod with gloomy satisfaction at seeing it spoiled." But he laid claim to no such heroic consistency, insisting correctly that the stanza was essential to the whole poem. At any rate, "90 North" is exactly the poem to illustrate the "fairly solitary individuality" he predicted for the poet of the early 1940s, at the end of the line, just where the man in the poem finds himself. It was the strongest early intimation of Jarrell's distinctiveness as a poet.

Ever since Tate had published five of his early poems in *The American Review*, and Brooks and Warren, then Ransom, accepted others for *The Southern Review* and *Kenyon*, Jarrell had been appearing regularly in little magazines. (By 1939 *Partisan Review* and *Poetry* were also taking his verse.) But it was Edmund Wilson who introduced him to a somewhat larger audience than that of the quarterlies, and who also encouraged his work as a reviewer and critic. Since Wilson kept up with *Partisan*, he would have seen and been pleased by the first "omnibus" poetry chronicle Jarrell published there in the March–April issue of 1940. (Philip Rahv, one of *Partisan*'s editors, was another early admirer of his poetry and criticism.) In that review Jarrell pulled out all the stops and exuberantly played his role as the clever young man ready at the drop of a hat to say the most outrageously witty things about anybody. The lineup of poets included a few forgotten ones, but also Archibald MacLeish, Kenneth Patchen, Robert Graves, Muriel Rukeyser, Dylan Thomas, and Auden. Of the ten, only Auden—and to an extent Thomas—emerged unscathed over the course of 1,500 words, while Graves received an inadequate treatment that Jarrell would atone for years later with a full-length essay.

What must have struck the reader in 1940—and what surely strikes us now, largely uninterested as we are in whether the reviewer was "right" or "wrong" about the individual volumes—is Jarrell's capacity for the devastatingly dismissive sentence. His talent for one-line invective had already been on display in his fiction chronicle for *The Southern Review*, but it came to full flower in "Poetry in a Dry Season." Given pride of place as the first book under consideration was one titled, memorably, *Chorus of Bird Voices, Sonnets, Battle-Dore, Unconventional Verse, etc.*, by William Bacon Evans. "While ailing in Syria," Jarrell announced, "he wrote a song for every species of North American bird (I am no ornithologist, but there *can't* be any more of the damn things)":

> This is poetry which instructs its writer and entertains its reader (the functions of poetry, I have read); a missionary could hardly be more harmlessly employed. Mr. Evans is an amiable, unpretentious, and tolerant person—he apparently dislikes nothing but cigarettes—and won my heart immediately: more than I can say for most of the poets I am reviewing. But then, Mr. Evans is no poet.

Fully warmed up, he proceeds to skewer Florence Becker: "If I were a dust jacket, I should call *Farewell to Walden* 'sonnets of love and social protest'; being what I am, I can say only that they are all Italian, all regular, and all bad."

With MacLeish, his strategy was to pretend that the book, *America Was Promises*, knowingly parodied MacLeish's public-speaking manner, since its argument "might have been devised by a YMCA secretary at a home for the mentally deficient." After all, who would believe, he says, that any serious poet could end a serious poem with "Believe / America is promises to / Take! / America is promises to / Us / To take them / Brutally / With love but / Take them. / [Big gap] O believe this!" With Patchen, it was another kind of sentimentality: "His poetry has a big violet streak of Original Swinburne-with-a-dead-baby; and his detailed version of 'Sex is *wonderful*' gets much worse than Swinburne's 'It's *wicked*.'" Patchen has "a real, but disorganized, self-indulgent, and rather commonplace talent"; although, he adds, this is not Patchen's opinion of himself, nor was it the opinion of William Carlos Williams, who had called him "a hawk on the grave of John Donne." "I should have called him a parrot on the stones of half a cemetery," says Jarrell.

It is hard to stop quoting, but this sampling may suggest the sort of critical operation he went about performing. To call it acerb and deadly, as everyone has, is but part of the story. One needs also to emphasize the sheer creativity, the comic brilliance of association and juxtaposition, that is the mark of its style. It is one thing to abuse Kenneth Patchen's poetry; it is a rather different thing to speak of it as "Original Swinburne-with-a-dead-baby." One almost imagines that, if he had read those words, Patchen might have been slightly amused, even though they were uttered at the expense of his verse. At least one poet who received a crushing review from Jarrell later testified that, oddly enough, he was not crushed: "I felt as if I had been run over but not hurt," said Karl Shapiro, speaking of a 1948 review of his *Trial of a Poet* that Jarrell had called "a sort of bobby-soxer's *Mauberley*." And even those poets who had quite clearly been hurt by his dispraise often had to admit, as Conrad Aiken did in 1941, after Jarrell had attacked him, to having "a lot of respect for Jarrell." Despite his annoyance, Aiken found him "damned intelligent," and that intelligence was inseparable from the distinctive idiom in which it was phrased.

It was this style and intelligence to which Edmund Wilson proposed to introduce *New Republic* readers. In the last quarter of 1940, Wilson returned to the magazine for a three-month stint as literary editor. (He was to leave it for good in 1941 as America prepared to enter the war.) Under Wilson's editing, Jarrell published three poetry reviews, each of which considered two to four poets. Lively as always, they contain little of permanent value other than acute remarks about Pound's *Cantos* LII–LXXI, the "Chinese" and "John Adams" cantos, two of the least admired sections. Jarrell called them simply "the dullest and prosiest poetry

83

that [Pound] has ever written," and said: "These cantos are so bad that they would not seem his at all, if they were not so exactly like the very worst portions of the old ones." He went on to speculate why this had happened to such a highly admired modernist poet. There was some fallout from the Pound review, but his onslaughts on lesser figures, particularly on Frederic Prokosch and Conrad Aiken, especially hit home. Prokosch, rightly characterized by Jarrell as a "decerebrate Auden, an Auden popularized for mass consumption" ("the poems pour out like sausages, automatic, voluptuous, and essentially indistinguishable"), said in a letter to *The New Republic* that, "clever and entertaining" as the reviewer was, he, Prokosch, had resolved to publish no more poetry in America, since it had met mainly with "vituperation." Others wrote in, some in support of Jarrell's reviewing style, some deploring it; a few went on to extend their adverse criticism to the whole business of poets reviewing other poets. Indeed, Malcolm Cowley, who had by now replaced Wilson as boss of the magazine's literary pages, felt called upon to publish a piece titled "Poets as Reviewers," in which he claimed that it was unfortunate when—as in the case of Jarrell on Aiken—a reviewer's clever style assumed more importance than the subject he was reviewing. By being negative about such a distinguished friend to and practitioner of poetry as Conrad Aiken, Jarrell (Cowley said) was making it that much harder for deserving poets to find an audience.

In due course, Jarrell replied to Cowley's charge with a coolly amused statement that even in its first paragraph pretty much won the contest hands down, since its own style was so much more engaging than the question of what to do about serious poets getting bad reviews. Cowley had paid the usual homage to Jarrell's talents as a poet and wit as a reviewer, to which the reviewer replied:

I am so flattered at Mr. Cowley's overestimation of my wit that I hardly like to object to his underestimation of my judgment. Besides, there is something agreeably odd about reviewing a book for a magazine and having the review reviewed, as a typical crime, by one of the magazine's editors; I feel as if my decision had been overruled by the Supreme Court.

He went on to make probably the only case an honest reviewer can make for his trade, by saying that "a good many of the books I get to review do seem bad to me, and I say so—a string of sober *no's* would bore any reader, so I try to phrase my *no's* as well as I can. But so far as I know I've never been dishonest enough to say unfavorable things for a chance to be witty." Writing to Wilson after the event, he said that he had to "laugh unbelievingly when I think of three little unfavorable reviews by a quite unknown reviewer making such a mess—it's completely absurd."

Absurd or not, he came out of the scuffle not quite so unknown as when he went in. He was not only invited by *The New Republic* to write an article on contemporary poetry criticism, but Margaret Marshall, literary editor of *The Nation*, began to solicit reviews for her book pages. In addition, the poems of his own which appeared in *The New Republic* that year (three in Wilson's "supplement" in April, another three near the year's end) stood to gain more attention from readers who, having observed his fierceness with other poets, wondered what his own poems sounded like. Further, he seems to have discovered himself as a writer of prose, and to have been rather pleased with what he found, thanking Wilson for suggesting the *New Republic* reviews. (Wilson had also pushed Jarrell's poetry at both *The New Yorker* and *The Atlantic Monthly*, both of whom published him in 1941.) He deferred to Wilson's expertise, and at one point, when the older man took him to task slightly for committing some rather emptily "positive" phrases, leavening a mainly negative review of Marya Zaturenska and Horace Gregory, Jarrell admitted that, when he tried to talk about the virtues of a poet, his style collapsed and his wit disappeared. What he was encountering here, of course, is exactly the sort of thing encountered by anyone who reviews frequently and often "negatively": the fact that—as with a novelist creating "evil" rather than "good" characters—it is easier to blame than to praise, to scoff at rather than exalt. Or at least it is easier to do so in lively sentences. That Jarrell took Wilson's criticism to heart, insofar as he later went on to become—in his essays on modern poets—an encomiastic critic of great power rather than of emptily positive phrases, is one of the heartening turns in his literary career.

Jarrell's immediate notoriety as an "executioner," who sentenced poets to death and carried out the sentences with his own pen, was a matter of hyperbole encouraged by a magazine like *The New Republic*, which thrived on controversy. So when Jarrell replied, humorously and modestly, to Cowley's charges, the latter couldn't resist adding in a further note that he had reread some of the reviews in question, in which Jarrell had "skillfully dispatched the fifteen remaining poets, covering their bodies with quicklime and strewing salt over their graves." Cowley went on to compare him to the hanging judge Jeffreys, whose behavior toward revolution-aries at the Bloody Assizes in 1685 had immortalized him, and who was—like Jarrell—"also a witty man." Such heady publicity was probably responsible for Jarrell's defining himself more strongly as a critic; on the one hand, standing out against the soft reviewers who tried to have a good word for everybody and to look on the positive side of things; on the other hand, against the schol-arly academics (his University of Texas departmental colleagues) who were simply living in a different time and world. After the *New Republic* piece in which he criticized Pound, he wrote Wilson about the review: "It was neither a success nor a failure here, nobody read it. Out of 11,000 students and 750 professors, not one even mentioned it." These people presumably didn't read Pound; why, then, should they read an adverse review of Pound? When he came to write at length about contemporary criticism of poetry, he pointed out that at present the only "commercially prac-ticable" sort of criticism had to be bad, since it had to sell the books under consideration: "Good criticism, which points out bad-ness or mediocrity, and actually scares away buyers from most books, is something the publishers necessarily cannot tolerate." Nor, he added, does the commercial public care much for that sort of thing. At the same time, real criticism is no more to be found at the universities than in most reviews: "Our universities should produce good criticism; they do not—or, at best, they do so only as federal prisons produce counterfeit money: a few hardened prisoners are more or less surreptitiously continuing their real vocations."

So this hardened prisoner, unread by his colleagues and rebuked by some readers of his reviews, was finding out that he had a real vocation as a critic. There were various responses available to his relative isolation in Texas, such as the construction of a comic routine out of the ignored Pound review; he wrote Wilson that "to make up for that, I read it several times, and laughed and applauded." More seriously, he could identify himself with the species poet-critic; with a number of men who had produced—as he says in "Contemporary Poetry Criticism"—"the best modern criticism" in an age which is unique for its production of "so much extraordinarily good criticism of poetry." This criticism was the work of writers like Empson, Eliot, Blackmur, Tate, Winters, Brooks, Ransom, Warren, and Delmore Schwartz. Like himself, they were poets to a man who wrote "*hard* criticism, of unusual depth and complication," that made great demands on readers, and—unlike more "general" critics like Wilson or Kenneth Burke—writers whose politics were usually conservative, even reactionary. Jarrell, who thought of himself as Marxist in social orientation and who admired Freud, was politically apart from these poet-critics, but at one with them in their devotion to writing, reading, and criticizing poetry in intensive ways. And that he was able to get along—more or less without serious argument or dispute—with two such politically different figures as Tate and Wilson shows not merely that the younger Jarrell was diplomatic in his approach to each but that his detachment from "ideas," whether Marxist or Southern Agrarian, could be formidable.

There is, of course, a difference between writing cleverly incisive reviews in which the poet under scrutiny receives a page or a paragraph of characterizing comment and attempting the extended, "hard" criticism which Jarrell held up for admiration in Empson, Blackmur, and other contemporaries. He had done such criticism in his master's thesis on Housman; further examples were the essays on Auden and Yeats he published in the Autumn and Winter issues of *The Southern Review* in 1941–42. The Yeats essay— written for a special issue devoted to the recently dead poet—is the shorter of the two. It makes a just (though by now familiar) point about Yeats's poetic development by noting the drastic difference in vocabulary between his early poems and his later ones. Jarrell provides, by way of illustrating this distinction, two lists of words, the first containing "dream," "rose," "heart," "lonely," "wandering" (the first five of forty-six such "dream" words he lists), the second made up of the likes of "passionate," "ignorant," "malicious," "crazy," and many more. Oddly enough, he spends so much time on a biographical sketch of Yeats's early life, in hopes of making the stylistic change understandable, that (as he admits at one point) Yeats's poetry is neglected—there are no analyses of individual poems. This was quite unlike standard New Critical procedure, and is also untypical of his own later habit. The essay on Yeats has survived, however, because of the vividness with which the two lists of words are juxtaposed; it was a starting point for further argument and qualification about the continuities and discontinuities of the poet's achievement.

More significant as literary criticism—although it, too, shies away from detailed examination—is the much longer essay titled "Changes of Attitude and Rhetoric in Auden's Poetry," a piece of writing which began as an idea for his M.A. thesis, then was worked on over a period of years. It is important not only as the first searching consideration of Auden's lyric poetry from the 1930s (it remains today as fresh and lively in its perceptions as it must have seemed almost fifty years ago) but as a surprising, if necessary, act for Jarrell the poet: a simultaneous celebration and killing off of Auden as his most significant poetic father. By saying this I am not invoking Harold Bloom's theory that all poets are burdened by the anxiety of influence and must enact a significant "swerve," of one kind or another, away from their precursor. I mean only to point out how getting Auden off his back was a way of freeing himself for the poetry he would go on to write, most immediately during the war years to come. It was a task that could be accomplished and rationalized only by a rigorous, intelligent account—laced with all the wit Jarrell possessed—of how Auden obtained his "effects" and what had happened to those effects between the publication of *Poems* (1930) and his most recent book, *Another Time* (1940).

He separates Auden into "early" and "late," and the essay's first section traces how those early poems divided the world between "We" and "They," the "We" a myth made from such sources as Marx and Freud, notions of "the folk, the blood [. . .] mysticism, fairy tales, parables"; the sciences, especially biology; "boyish" sources of value like flying and polar exploration; and homosexuality. On the other hand, "They" represent everything from Business and Industrialism all the way down to people who say "I *mean*" or have a room called "the Den." "We" is the future, struggling against the dead past of a "They." In the second half of the essay, Jarrell proceeds to analyze the "peculiar language" of Auden's early poetry and insists (this is a sticky point, granted) that it is "language" rather than "rhetoric" which counts in those poems. By contrast, in the later poems—and particularly in *Another Time*—it is the rhetorical machinery Auden depends on, as he becomes increasingly abstract and public. Jarrell's notion of "language" as opposed to "rhetoric" may be illustrated by the following lines from XXV of *Poems* (1930), his favorite poem from the early Auden:

> *Metals run*
> *Burnished or rusty in the sun*
> *From town to town,*
> *And signals all along are down;*
> *Yet nothing passes*
> *But envelopes between these places,*

> *Snatched at the gate and panting read indoors,*
> *And first spring flowers arriving smashed,*
> *Disaster stammered over wires,*
> *And pity flashed.*

The lack of tone in this voice, the difficulty of assigning its words to some imaginable speaker in a recognizably personal or social situation, forces attention on the words themselves—on what Jarrell calls their "tough magical effects." But he doesn't use the word "magical" in order to excuse himself from analyzing those effects taken in the mass; rather, in the essay's two most extraordinarily packed pages, he offers a list of twenty-six characteristics of early Auden. The list is grammatical and philological in its focus, consisting of items such as "frequent omission of articles and demonstrative adjectives," "constant inversion, consciously effective changes of the usual word order," and so forth. Any reader of the early Auden will recognize these items, which Jarrell goes on to illustrate by various phrases and formulations from individual poems.

In a phrase from Kenneth Burke's *Attitudes Toward History* (a book he singles out for special acknowledgment, and which must have suggested the essay's title), Jarrell claims that in his later poetry Auden has "bureaucratized" his imagination, has learned a method that can be applied to any material, "guaranteed to produce insights in any quantities." The wittiest example of such bureaucratized application—Jarrell discusses several of them—is Auden's use of the "capitalized personified abstraction," of which use he is extremely conscious, expecting the reader to recognize it as "different and exciting, a virtuoso performance" meant to make us say, " 'Why, he got away with it after all.' " I quote only a part of the long, hilarious paragraph of illustrations of how Auden in his later work has become "like someone who keeps showing how well he can hold his liquor until he becomes a drunkard":

At first he made all sorts of ingenious variations: he made capitalized personified abstractions out of verbs, adverbs, pro-

nouns, or whole phrases. But at last even his ingenuity disappears; he is like a man who will drink canned heat, rubbing
alcohol, anything. There is a thirteen-line menagerie where
I Will, I Know, I Am, I Have Not, and I Am Loved peer
idiotically from behind their bars; nearby, gobbling peanuts,
throng the Brothered-One, the Not-Alone, the Just, the
Happy-Go-Lucky, the Filthy, hundreds of We's and They's
and Their's and Our's and Me's, the Terrible Demon, the
Lost People, the Great, the Old Masters, and the Unexpected.

This list continues through another twenty-five or so items, at
which point Jarrell concludes: "Reading *Another Time* is like attending an Elks' Convention of the Capital Letters [. . .] All this
is a squeamish business, a pilgrimage through some interminable
Vegetarians' Cafeteria."

One reason for dwelling on this passage from the Auden essay
is that it so concentratedly shows the serious uses to which, in a
"scholarly" critical essay, Jarrell could put his smart-aleck, seemingly offhand, informal reviewer's style. The canned heat, the rubbing alcohol, the fantasy of not just a convention of capital letters
but an *Elks'* convention of them, the Vegetarians' Cafeteria that
feels interminable—these and other inventions combine to make
a telling point about Auden's style, its excesses and its limitations,
but make it in such a way that (unlike more sober assessments) it
stays in the mind. Another reason is that, as already suggested, it
was important for him to say hard things about his once revered
master's recent excesses as a way of clearing the decks for his own
first book of poems—some of which, at least, he must have been
uncertain about.

He was to say later that the Auden he liked best—early
Auden—he was not influenced by. But the later Auden (whom,
as this essay shows, he did not like nearly so well) had influenced
a good deal the poems he wrote in the late 1930s. At the close of
"Changes of Attitude and Rhetoric . . ." he speculates that, while
Auden has managed to make his poetry more accessible, and has
responded more to "political or humanitarian interests," this was

a high price to pay—that his solution was "too conscious, too thin, too merely rational." At this moment Freud entered the picture, reminding Jarrell that poetry "represents the unconscious [. . .] as well as the conscious, our lives as well as our thoughts; and [. . .] has its true source in the first and not the second." The price of too "rigorous supervision" of the sources of poetry may mean that those sources are drained of their power.

I would not claim that the poems about to appear in *Blood for a Stranger* were, like Auden's recent ones, products of a "far too conscious and controlled" method—they were often too inexpert for such an identification to be plausible. But they were certainly poems filled with "rhetoric," and, as Jarrell himself acknowledged, full of the influence of later Auden; thus it is not fanciful to suggest that he was attempting in some measure to distance himself from his own poetry. What is the "solution" to Auden's problem, he asks, and answers that he does not know, except that it will be found "in the work of the next first-rate poet." Jarrell wanted to be *that* sort of poet, but was conscious he had not as yet become it. In what would grow into a typical way of ending one of his critical essays, he says in a note of mild self-deprecatory apology that his treatment of Auden may seem an "ungrateful return for all the good poetry Auden has written," and that he is embarrassed at having done "so much Analysis and so little Appreciation." But—he concludes—analysis even of faults is a way of showing appreciation. This is no idle or lame excuse, since the essay shows as deep an appreciation of Auden as, in my judgment, he was ever to receive. And if, as Jarrell developed his own voice as a poet, Auden necessarily ceased to be a major presence in his work, Auden would continue to occupy him as a challenge to critical judgment.

What with writing poetry, reviews, and essays, and teaching his classes, plus the usual tennis and touch football, Jarrell's life was packed and did not include significant diversions. He and Mackie went places during the summer: to Cape Cod after they were married in June of 1940, to visit the Milton Starr family; to Mexico in the summers of 1941 and 1942; and back to Nashville and Baton Rouge (where he saw Cleanth Brooks and Robert Lowell). As vacations these trips seem to have been pretty nominal, as may be gathered from the tone of the following letter to Tate in the fall of 1941, revealing that life in Mexico was not essentially different from life in Austin: "In Mexico, after the first week, I wrote like a mechanical horse—reviews and an absolutely endless article on Auden ($125 worth—just enough to pay doctors' bills, without counting hospitals and such)." The medical bills had to do with the pneumonia his wife contracted on the day they were to leave for Mexico. In August he wrote Edmund Wilson from Mexico City: "The most amusing thing I've done in Mexico is to help coach a boys' football team—I don't know any Spanish, so the operation of coaching is pretty funny." Otherwise he remarked on the presence everywhere of colorfully dressed policemen and soldiers, also what seemed to him the extraordinarily large number of "big contented dogs" lying about the pavements and aisles of the markets. He confided to Wilson: "If a Mexican dog barks at anyone he is taken to a psychoanalyst." Although the Jarrells revisited Mexico in 1942 (this time, with America at war, he had to get permission from his draft board), they tired of it and came back early: "We got so sick of Mexico—which is like a pageant or *Everyman*, full of highly visible Evil." A couple of undistinguished poems came out of the Mexican enterprise.

In the fall of 1941, as he began his last year of teaching at Texas, he wrote Tate that, although he had written a lot of poetry the previous spring, "I have the impression that I'm at a sort of dead end; though not when I'm writing, then it comes easily enough, too easily I guess." By Christmas he had arranged with Lambert Davis at Harcourt, Brace that they would publish *Blood for a Stranger*, and with those poems headed for book form he was uncertain where to go next. What the "dead end" feeling has to do with is lack of a subject: one of the Mexican poems ("An Indian Market in Mexico") was not published until years later and barely justifies itself over its fourteen lines; a number of other poems he published in the spring of 1942 never found their way into any volumes during his lifetime. With hindsight we can say that what he needed for a subject was World War II: the pilots, planes, barracks, landing fields he would experience and which it was appropriate—even necessary—to write about without the rhetorical obscurity that disfigured many of his early poems.

For the first time, and more or less coincident with the feeling of being at a poetic dead end, his letters complain about being ill. After mentioning his wife's pneumonia the previous June, he says, writing to Wilson, he's been "pretty sick" himself, disease unspecified. Some of the discomfort was the result of combat on the gridiron, as when, in the fall of 1941, he wrote to Brooks at *The Southern Review* that he was having trouble writing his essay on Yeats since he had a broken rib and two teeth shoved out of place—"and I can't even turn over in bed or sneeze without my side's knotting up." In the winter of 1942 he wrote Tate that he had been "very sick for about seven weeks" and hadn't done anything, was still in bed: "some kind of blood poisoning with abscesses—the lymph glands in my left arm and chest were infected, and I was enormously swollen, feverish, and aching." Further descriptions follow of lancings and drainings, and (so he says) rubber bands stuck in the infections—altogether "the most miserable disease I've ever had." When the Jarrells returned to Mexico the following June, he fell sick again ("sick or dopey half the time," as he described it to Tate), which doubtless contributed to their abbreviated vacation.

He was well enough in April of 1942 to travel to Princeton ("on the choo-choo," as he wrote his publisher) to deliver, under Tate's auspices, a *Mesures* lecture titled "Levels and Opposites" (other *Mesures* lectures were given by Burke and Blackmur). In a letter to Wilson describing the talk, he said that it was about how the "logical" structure of poetry "is, very often, roughly dialectical, this with many examples." Though the lecture has not survived, it appears to be a continuation of his concern—as in the thesis on Housman—to show that good poems don't look in a single direction but rather combine "alternative possibilities." He wrote Wilson that he had found an apt quotation from Blake to serve as an introduction to the talk: "In poetry Unity and Morality are secondary considerations" (he added, "I'm kidding—halfway"). He made good use of his few days in the East, with a trip to New York City, where he stayed with Lowell and Jean Stafford, and a side trip to Cape Cod to see Wilson at Wellfleet. Vladimir Nabokov was also visiting Wilson, who was then married to Mary McCarthy, and she remembered giving a lunch at which Jarrell was appalled by the "Cape Codder bohemia" she had invited. (Her amusing way of putting it was that he followed her around "screeching in a whisper," wanting to know why she wasted her time with "these *people*.") In New York he failed to get to the Bronx Zoo, which he had hoped to see, but did consult with his publisher about the binding of *Blood for a Stranger*. He took the manuscript with him on the train back to Texas and there worked out a final arrangement for the poems, different from the one Tate had suggested. In a further show of autonomy, he wrote no thank-you letter (until August) to Tate for arranging the Princeton lecture; this silence helped cool their relationship.

Blood for a Stranger was published in September 1942 to—in the main—respectful reviews. The most intelligently critical of them was by his old editor (and corrector) Malcolm Cowley, in *The New Republic*, who devoted most of his review to listing Jarrell's borrowings from his modern predecessors—Auden, Crane, Eliot, Yeats. But Cowley found the poems lacking the "central core of belief" those predecessors demonstrated; Jarrell's poetry, he said, showed "fragments of several great mosaics" that didn't combine together into a pattern. The conclusion of his review distinguished a number of further Jarrell-selves besides the accomplished echoer of other poets, and among those selves could be found the Jeremiah prophesying destruction, or the "swaggering rhetorician" working overtime at coming up with stunning phrases. (This rhetorician, Cowley suggested, "ought to be kept on a lean diet.") Yet there was for him a final and more attractive self than any of these—"a young man wounded by life, intense and honest in his feelings, hesitant about revealing them, then at last coming forward to offer

95

his blood for a stranger." When these various poetic selves managed to come together (which they had not yet done), and—Cowley might have added—had corrected and modified their particular excesses, then "we should have not echoes but the Poem." If Jarrell smarted under any of these criticisms, he should have been pleased by the overall tenor of the review, and especially at its shrewdness in imagining the "intense and honest" young man who was the best thing about *Blood for a Stranger*. But by the time the book was published, he was about to enlist in the army and begin the life that would occupy him until his discharge in February 1946, three years and four months later.

FOUR

In Service

EXCEPT for the academic year he spent at Princeton in 1951–52, no other period of Jarrell's life is so well documented as his years in the armed services. This is especially true for the first year or so, when, living apart from Mackie (who eventually joined him at Davis-Monthan Field, Tucson, Arizona, in November 1943), he wrote her frequently and at length. These letters give a richly detailed, bitterly humorous picture of life in the "immense worm" of whose "digestive processes" he had become a part. In their combination of satire and sympathy they are unique; at least I know of nothing comparable written about the mundane life of a Stateside enlisted man during World War II. In letter after letter, Jarrell turned the routine, the boredom, the loneliness and wastefulness of army life far from the zones of combat into the figures of something like art—an epistolary art more complex and satisfying than any of his "real" art, the poems he had hitherto written. At the same time, the style and tone of his own poetry changed significantly; the "dead end" he had written to Tate about in late 1941 opened up into a new way of thinking and feeling about the world. For the first time, his poetry confirms that what he wrote to Amy Breyer deBlasio that month he enlisted was something more than a pious protestation: "For to write what you can about the world makes it almost bearable."

Any account of how bearable Jarrell found his army service must rely chiefly on his letters to Mackie and must take into consideration that in writing to his wife he would want to avoid alarming her. The letters home would show her that he was surviving, making out all right, and able to cope with things, even though a poet. Years later, after he and Mackie had separated and she had returned his correspondence, he wrote his wife-to-be, Mary von Schrader, that he had been reading and enjoying very much his army letters to Mackie and that he was struck "with how (relatively) cheerful and determined I managed to stay," even though the letters didn't say "how bad a lot of it was." Whatever his feelings about his situation, the letters to Mackie—and later to literary companions like Tate and Lowell—show him able to cope with things not in spite of but because of his being a poet, with a poet's genius for turning dreariness into witty, imaginative life. Consider this paragraph from a letter to Sara Starr, written after he had been in service for eight months, explaining how it was that he had been cut from the pre-flight program for which he had originally signed up:

> For about two months, back around Christmas [of 1942], I flew all the time, sometimes twice a day; then I got washed out because the chief pilot thought I did some maneuvers badly. (I guess he was right, too.) I didn't like flying much because it isn't very thrilling—instead of seeming to move fast you just seem to stand still, with the world moving around you very slowly, as if it were a motion picture. Besides, we always had to fly at *just* so many miles an hour, at *just* such an altitude, in *just* such a direction—it was too much like one long examination.

The young lady (she was thirteen at the time) is being entertained here through a fantasy that explains Jarrell's failure as mainly a deficiency in flying itself (even as, casually, he admits that the chief pilot was right to fail him). The trouble with flying, an activity usually connected with thrills and glamour, is that—of all things —it's not thrilling enough. One has instead to follow these rules and get those details exactly right, while the promise of free move-ment is merely an illusion: "you just seem to stand still, with the world moving around you very slowly, as if it were a motion pic-ture." So Sara Starr is advised that, really, flying is no more than an extended version of the examinations she took in school.

The tone adopted in this letter to Sara Starr is scarcely different from the one he took toward his wife. With hopes of becoming a ferry pilot or flight instructor in the Army Air Corps, he had enlisted in October 1942 and sat through hours of classes in ground school (which he said was easy) at the University of Texas—living in a dormitory and taking his meals in the school cafeteria, while ex-periencing a minimum of military discipline. After flunking the flight part of the program, he had hopes of becoming a ground instructor, but was sent instead to Sheppard Field, in Wichita Falls, Texas, a "replacement center" with some 50,000 soldiers of all sorts and conditions, which prompted him to make this observation to Mackie:

> Being in the army is like being involved in the digestive pro-cesses of an immense worm or slug or something—being involved in them along with tens of thousands around you and millions out of your sight; it doesn't seem terribly stupid or at all malicious, just too big to have any sense or meaning—a mess, rather.

Although there were times, especially during the course of the next six months, when the army indeed came to seem "terribly stupid" to his sense of things, Jarrell never wavered from his original con-viction that it was a "mess" but not a malicious one. Neither in his own experience nor in the poems that came out of it does the individual usually appear as the good, helpless victim of an essen-tially malign institution; although his familiar rhetoric from the early poems about the impersonal state grinding down the person still occurs, it ceases to sound an exclusive note. For the first time in his life, as part of the processes of that immense worm the army, Jarrell could observe at first hand and apply his witty intelligence to a phenomenon that—"too big to have any sense or meaning"

—was a challenge to the meaning-making poet. To meet it he had to move on from what he once referred to as his " 'political economy' style"—the knowing, abstractly analytic rhetoric that filled the poems in *Blood for a Stranger*—into his " 'army' style," in which, as he soon put it to Mackie, "some good, dreary poems" might be written.

This change of emphasis, observable in the poems he began to write in the spring of 1943, did not mean that he had changed his mind about how the individual was victimized by the state. In fact, he defended the rightness of his earlier poetry by insisting that it fitted the army perfectly: "just the bulk of the Army passively suffering, doing what it's told, not knowing why anything's happened, helplessly ignorant and determined." And whatever bits of childishness marked those early poems also fitted: "for most of the army seems under 21, and almost all of it juvenile in so many ways. It's so *dumb*: the poor soldiers are as dumb as the way they're treated, almost." Even so, the reason Jarrell's "army style" had a new kind of power was that it helped him resist his impulse—up to then plentifully indulged on all subjects—to be too knowing too quickly, too much in control of what he was observing. The dumbness, the ignorance, "the bulk of the Army passively suffering" needed to be treated in ways more complicated than as a satiric target for the superior poet to look down on with pity and contempt.

There is, however, plenty of satiric commentary in the letters written home during his tenure at Sheppard Field, enlivening commentary because it is tinged with more humor than bitterness. At Sheppard he took the general classification test (on which he thought he did poorly—too many questions about spatial relations) in the hope that it would place him in officer candidate school. For a time he still wore civilian clothes ("I believe I'm the only person in 50,000 without a uniform"); then, after receiving a uniform and waiting to be assigned a job, took further aptitude tests and ended up in the mail room. He hoped to get out of Sheppard and into a training program at some college or university where things were more congenial than he found the replacement center and its occupants to be. What most impressed or distressed him about those occupants was the way they talked: "The conversation is on a level that makes you disbelieve even in the existence of say, Proust [. . .] You know, I've never seen any conversation in a book (well, naturally) that reproduces the way people like these talk: the intelligence, variety, vocabulary, etc.—all *surprisingly* low." What sort of country did he think he was living in? Granted that the army experience is a great eye-opener, his eyes seem to have been very much shut, especially for one who fancied himself sensitive to economic and class differences. But Jarrell frequently surprises us by the enthusiastic naïveté of some of his notions. What saves his perception about his mates from being merely snobbish and narrow is the relish with which he records their strange ways with words: "When I got here one guy was just back from a march; he was telling how far it was: 'Fourteen miles, they said; but really it was 15, it was such a hazardous course.' When he said *hazardous* he moved his hand up and down to indicate the hills and valleys." So far, he said, that was the "only bright flower of rhetoric" he had encountered, though others came later on: "In a lecture today we were twice told that we must obey orders 'promptly and willfully'; isn't that charming?" And while being read the Articles of War (the "opium of the soldier," he called it), he and his companions were warned that they must not make "provoking or reproving *guestures* to a soldier [. . .] I spell it the way he said it."

That the clever professor-poet was amused by the antics of mere ordinary folk could be judged tiresome, indeed heartless; yet Jarrell truly sounds charmed by their mistakes. As part of the immense worm, he was part of them as well, although his educational credentials would open doors closed to them. But he also soon realized that "they" were something more than just plain "dumb." "In many ways they're unbelievably barbarous," he wrote Mackie, but they were also different from what he had expected:

They are very generous: I've never seen anybody getting things to eat without immediately going around offering them. When

everybody's cleaning barracks they are quite willing for someone who feels bad to do nothing; they'll even, half the time,
not say anything to somebody who just doesn't want to do it.

Later on, when he was assigned to interview soldiers with an eye
to placing them in one or another unit, he wrote that some of those
interviews actually brought tears to his eyes—"when the people
are so very young and homesick, or are soft, gentle, with wives and
babies. It's so disquieting to read under a soldier's year of birth
1925." As he approached his thirtieth birthday, he was disquieted
by the spectacle of these mere eighteen-year-olds; and while he
avoids any direct assertion of sympathetic identification, his description of sleeping in the barracks at Sheppard shows, I think,
that he was affected by his surroundings in more than a negative,
recoiling way:

> The barracks is queer at night; you're in the middle of a just-
> moving sea of sleeping people who cough, or make little snor-
> ing sounds, or give little moans—at any time you wake there
> is someone making some sound. At 4:30 you are wakened by
> a *very* queer sound: somebody running down the street as fast
> as he can blowing a whistle—the whistle gets louder and
> louder (accompanied by footsteps) and then vanishes away.

He could be moved also by the odd individual one would never
have expected to encounter, such as a "tall fat cadet from the east
who could recite almost all of A. A. Milne—he did for the whole
fifteen minutes we were in line. It felt so unlikely and pleasant."

Jarrell cultivated such unlikely and pleasant events as an antidote
to the repetitive stupidity of army life; indeed, he went so far as
to put himself forward—in the eyes of his fellow soldiers—as
someone who would do and say unlikely and pleasant things. Early
along he noted to Mackie that his mates spent great amounts of
time writing home, but also would ask how to spell half the words
they used: "About six people have learned to spell *bivouac* and
they're in *great* demand." We may presume he was one of the six,

and he proceeded not merely to help the men with their spelling but to instruct them on the condition in which they found themselves, asking them, for example, what profession army life might prepare them for. His answer, which one presumes nobody came up with, was "being a convict." Presumably his mates were amused, and at least in the eyes of some of them he figured as a rather special person who, among other things, did not speak as they did: "It would be ridiculous to try to seem even remotely as spotted as these creatures. So I sound calm, clear, and cultivated, and no one seems to mind or think it odd. I count just as a different variety, and one that they tend to be slightly respectful to."

Perhaps the most engaging of his anecdotes about the other men's sense of his specialness has to do with waiting in line for breakfast and receiving an unexpected gift: "One of the K.P.'s who liked me took a bottle of milk and poured all the cream on my cereal, instead of mixing it. Another K.P. reproved him, 'Hey, don't do that! Think of the poor guys that get the bottom.' He answered simply this: 'It's Jarrell.' I was so pleased with this that I smiled all morning." Things hadn't really changed all that much for him since he was the prize pupil in Warren's class at Vanderbilt, except that now, instead of terrifying his mates (as Warren said he did the other students), he endeared himself to them. From his own accounts, and unless he desperately misled himself and misjudged his audience, they liked to hear him talk, liked to hear him hold forth on such subjects as what was wrong with the army, or what the war was really about.

As for what he thought of that war and America's position in it, no clear attitude emerges from the letters to Mackie—and there is no reason to assume he would hold such thoughts back if he had them. The vaguely Marxist analysis of the state found in his early poems seemed not to touch the reality of daily army life. There is no patriotic talk about the necessity of defeating Nazism, nor is there any mention of Japan. At one point, good news from the Russian front is saluted in a brief sentence. After he had begun again to write poetry, he noted "how much I write about the army and how little the war." Certainly the most memorable set pieces from the letters home are about the army in its dailiness: dishwashing on K.P.; standing in line; men doing calisthenics in the "tremendous dust-pile" of Sheppard Field; or mail call:

> Mail call is a very pretty ceremony: everyone's wedged in at one end of the barracks, lying on beds, the tops of double decker beds, standing, sitting on the floor; there's always a big stack of letters for C.Q. (raised above the rest) to distribute. He reads the names out in a tough rapid rather charming voice: each answers *Here* or *Ho* or *Yoho* (one boy really said that) and gets the letter flung at him like a leaf out of Shelley: the letter dives under a bed or hits somebody on the head and is rapidly passed on to the owner.

His description of being "chief operator of an enormous dishwashing machine full of clanks and steam" is even more of a performance, too long to quote and on the face of it too trivial to bother with. Yet it is also a striking confirmation of how much his letters, like his poetry, were about the army rather than the war.

Often the imaginative effort in the letters was to see himself as a sort of Child Randall, miraculously and happily converting the stuff of routine into something rich and strange, as Emerson had defined the proper task of the American Scholar. At the end of his portrait of the artist as young dishwasher, Jarrell says that he forgot to mention "the stupendous uproar: the dishwasher, the bangs of thousands of pieces of metal, everybody's agitated cries —it was a very enlivening scene, and half the time I felt fine and sang aloud—though, like the tree in the forest, nobody heard me." There is a fairy-tale quality to the way in which the charmed hero —at least for half the time—is buoyed up rather than overwhelmed by circumstance. When, at the end of April 1943, his orders for Link trainer school came through and he was able, thankfully, to depart Sheppard Field, the train trip to Chanute Field in Illinois took on aspects of an enchanted journey. In transit, he wrote: "Here I am somewhere in Missouri, looking, like one of Wordsworth's little girls, at the trees, grass, and beautiful irregularities of the ground" (Sheppard Field was flat, dry, and dusty); and his eye fixed on Missouri's Wordsworthian equivalent of the special child: "Last night we stopped on the outskirts of a town, and a little girl, in her back yard, about four, kept waving at us and calling excitedly, 'Hello, soldiers.' She had a beautiful big snow-white puppy with her, who jumped up and down and wagged his tail."

Admittedly, the note he strikes, in efforts to recount or create these "charming," surprising interludes to standard army life, sometimes sounds fey, inviting parody from a just slightly unsympathetic reader (whose ears the letters weren't meant for anyway). At Sheppard Field, for example, after a scrambled-egg supper for soldiers at the YWCA, he played a little tennis and was told by the woman in charge that he could borrow rackets from the USO at any time: "Isn't that charming? It felt *wonderful* to hit a tennis ball; and the lovely feminine tea room atmosphere of the Y.W.C.A. supper almost made me weep with joy." As if to admit that he's on the edge of self-parody, he vows that in the next war he'll "get an executive job with the Campfire Girls." One of the letters to Mackie goes on at great and amusing length about how and what the men sing as they march or do calisthenics (there is an elaborate description of "I've Been Working on the Railroad" and its addenda). He admits that the singing is pretty bad, but that there are compensations:

> While making the long calisthenics marches people (a) trip each other (b) step on each other's heels (c) hit each other in the back (d) grab each other (e) push each other, and so on and so on and so on; all this comes under the head not of Song but of Humor.

He adds: "They do this almost entirely with close friends, though, or at least with people they know quite well—so I'm not bothered."

Taken both as a whole and as representative of many others, these examples suggest how Jarrell contrived to lead a "literary life" while he served his country—or, like a convict, served time.

More open to question is whether he was able similarly to transform into poetic terms the various jobs he performed. When he was made a sorter in the mail room at Sheppard Field, he wrote to his wife that his correspondence would probably suffer, since letters about letters were an unpromising genre. After being transferred from the mail room, he worked as a classification interviewer and seems to have taken serious interest and some pleasure in talking to the men and trying to situate them where their talents might be of use. Later, at Chanute Field, he says little about the Link trainer program except that it was "very pleasant to sit under the hood with the instruments, shut away from all the army." When, at the conclusion of the program, his class was told that the army didn't need them, Jarrell enrolled in a further course where he was trained as a celestial navigation tower (CNT) operator: "Some complicated mechanism (like a Link Trainer surrounded by a miniature plan-etarium)" was how he described the phenomenon in which the flyers were taught. The advantage of this program, he thought, was that it would mean less moving around, a better location, and better ratings: "The army is like a mighty maze," he said, alluding to Pope, "and all without a plan: that is, there are always several additional openings for you, none of them leading anywhere." An opening did, however, lead him in November 1943 to Davis-Mon-than Field in Tucson, Arizona. There he remained for the duration, as an instructor-trainer for navigators in their last three-month course of training before combat.

He felt pleased and lucky to be sent to Tucson, since it had the oldest and best CNT department and the best field in the Second Air Force. Mackie and Kitten joined him, and the three lived off post in a way that felt quite unlike the army he had been used to. Writing to Tate, with whom he resumed correspondence briefly in 1945, he described his job with some engagement:

> What I do is run a tower that lets people do celestial navigation on the ground. In a tower about forty feet high a fuselage like the front of a bomber is hung; it flies the way a Link Trainer

does. The navigator (sometimes pilots and bombardiers too) sits in it, and navigates by shooting with his sextant the stars that are in a star dome above his head—we move them pretty much as a planetarium operator does. Also we have radio transmitters he can get radio fixes from, and a sort of movie-projector arrangement that he can do pilotage with. He flies a regular four-hour mission; besides running and setting up the tower, we record his fixes and other stuff, correct them if he's made mistakes, and so forth. It's extremely useful: a navigator improves as much after five flights in our trainer as he would after ten or fifteen regular flights. One trainer in a year certainly saves five or six bombers and five or six crews: there'd be that many crashes in the same number of real flights.

So there was the sense, at last, that he was doing something useful, short of flying the planes himself. Probably only someone who operated a celestial navigation tower could really understand what Jarrell describes here, but in the terms he uses, it certainly has a quotient of the poetic, since not everyone in the army got to move the stars around.

The only misfortune in his settling down with Mackie at the Tucson airbase is that we are deprived of the minute, almost daily characterizing of army life in his letters to her. Overall, the impression given by that correspondence is one of resiliency and ebullience—however much at times he may have forced himself to assume such tones. The letters are exhilarating for the way they present us with outstanding moments in which something that has nothing to do with the army suddenly assumes possession of a man's spirit: like observing the trees on the University of Illinois campus at Urbana he visited while on a pass from Chanute Field (he titled a poem "The Soldier Walks under the Trees of the University"); or hearing "a wonderful performance of Schumann's piano concerto," which "sounded so beautiful—and nothing else —I was overwhelmed"; or, and as always, reading something wonderful. "Today, in the pay line and so on, I did what's one of the pleasantest things I do in the army: I read *Out of Africa*. It's so much everything the army isn't that here it beats, almost, any other book at all [. . .] Somebody wanted me to move ahead and called, 'Hey, Africa, see if you can get in front of that guy.' " To have that soldier's remark on top of the pleasure of reading Isak Dinesen was perhaps the kind of bonus only being in the army made possible.

About a month after he reported to Sheppard Field, Jarrell found himself in the hospital with what was called nasal pharyngitis—a bad cold, fever, and a sore throat. He found the place delightful, provided ecstatic descriptions of the food ("The biggest fresh lima beans I ever saw, and spice cake"), and hailed the chance to sleep from nine to six ("how nice it is to be waked up at 6. And isn't *that* a pathetic remark?"). Best of all was the time it gave him to read; from this short stay in the hospital we receive a useful idea of just how fiercely he devoured books, and although what he read there was less than fully demanding of his powers, still the report is daunting. He claims his reading speed has increased to the point where it "frightens" him:

> I read *Lost Horizon* in 45 minutes today. From about 12 one day till 12 the next I read two detective stories, novels, that is, *Penrod*, a book of reminiscences about World War Q Ships, the *Green Bay Tree*, *Collier's*, the *Saturday Evening Post*, and *And Tell of Time* (the most obliviously Confederate reactionary book I ever read, about). Except for the Q-ship one, I wouldn't recommend a one to a chimpanzee.

A couple of days later he has read novels by Somerset Maugham and Sholem Asch, a biography of William Pitt the Younger, "and *Tom Sawyer* and *Life on the Mississippi* and *Mysterious Stranger* and such, and more I don't remember. The library has a lot of good books, but I've read them all; I can reread goodish stuff or read poor."

A month or so later, while working in the mail room, he predicted that, given the time, he could write "some good, dreary poems about the army, and the war," and soon afterward spoke of working on two or three poems (and a play, which never saw the light), even as he sent his wife a copy of "The Carnegie Library, Juvenile Division," probably begun before he entered the army. By the end of June, when he was installed at Chanute Field, his letters to her are full of talk about particular poems, of which he claims to have written thirteen since his arrival at Chanute. In other words, within a matter of months after joining the army he had regained what he called "my beautiful old feeling that I can always write good poems—just give me the time and a subject, any subject; I'd lost it in my last year before I got in the army." He sounds like the confident student of Vanderbilt days who informed Warren of how many poems he had written over the past couple of months. One notes his faith in subjects as all that's really necessary (given enough time to work them up) to make "good" poems, and also the conviction—shared by other American writers like Norman Mailer and James Jones—that in the army and the war a great subject was to be found.

Over the next four years he would write and publish close to fifty poems dealing with war, the army and air force, prisoners, concentration camps, hospital wards, and barracks life. Unlike Karl Shapiro, whose *V-Letter and Other Poems* won the Pulitzer Prize in 1945 and who announced in the book's introduction (written from New Guinea in the South Pacific) that he had tried to be on guard against becoming "a war poet," Jarrell appeared to welcome the role, devoting his full attention to military situations and materials he had experienced or imagined. Although he saw no combat and remained in the States, he wrote so convincingly about the actions of pilots, navigators, and gunners that a contemporary of his, R. W. Flint (who had himself been a gunner on a carrier), was astonished to discover in the poems details that he had missed while in the center of the flak. Flint reminded himself that the great poets of the American Civil War were Whitman and

Melville—noncombatants; surely Jarrell's safe distance from battle helped make his poems happen.

His attitude toward both the war and the notion of being a "war poet" was expressed most fully and intelligently in a review of Marianne Moore's *Nevertheless* in 1945. This volume contained her often-quoted "In Distrust of Merits," and in that rather high-pitched poem, Moore rhapsodically salutes the fighting and dying soldiers (her brother was a career navy chaplain) by contrasting them with her own—and everyone's—necessary attempt to fight with and conquer the evil in the self. The poem swells to an affirmation—

> *If these great patient*
> *dyings—all these agonies*
> *and woundbearings and bloodshed—*
> *can teach us how to live, these*
> *dyings were not wasted.*

—and concludes that "Beauty is eternal / and dust is for a time." Jarrell, who had written appreciatively about an earlier book of hers, politely but firmly declined the invitation and detached himself from this sort of celebratory war poem:

> She does not understand that they are heroes in the sense that the chimney sweeps, the factory children in the blue books, were heroes: routine loss in the routine business of the world. She sees them (the recurring triplet is the major theme of the poem) *fighting fighting fighting*; she does not remember that most of the people in a war never fight for even a minute—though they bear for years and die forever. They do not fight, but only starve, only suffer, only die: the sum of all this passive misery is that great activity, War.

He goes on to criticize the "blindingly moral terms" in which her poem thinks about the war, and says that she should have distrusted the "peace" "of which our war is only the extrapolation." Still, Moore is more admirable, he concludes, than those American poets who are blind to the war and claim that "*they* are not going to be foolish enough to be 'war poets.' " "How could they be?" he asks bitterly. "The real war poets are always war poets, peace or any time." There is a notable grimness about the remark, suggesting that, when Jarrell told Amy that "to write what you can about the world makes it almost bearable," he wasn't just or even mainly talking about the world at war, 1941–45, but saying that cruelty, suffering, stupidity, and death must always be the subject of a real poet, "peace or any time."

Jarrell's ambition—and in his best poems he succeeded in realizing it—was to write about war, about being a soldier or a flyer, in a style that avoided Marianne Moore's eloquently painful, self-accusatory celebration of the "fighting," while on the other hand avoiding Karl Shapiro's certainty that the war was (in Shapiro's phrase) a "gigantic slapstick" to which the poet could feel superior. (In fairness to Shapiro, his war poems from *V-Letter* do not exhibit the poet as superior to the "slapstick" and even call into question the appropriateness of the term.) By contrast, Jarrell's war style cultivated anonymity of viewpoint and, at times, a flatness of tone, rather than the kind of "dramatic" speaking voice that, through its turnings and self-questionings, invites us to identify with it—as, say, we are invited to identify with Yeats's voice in "Easter 1916" or with Auden's in "September 1, 1939" ("war poems" insofar as they address themselves to relations between the poet and an imperiled civilization).

My aim here is not to define what "war poetry" really is or is not. As can be seen from Oscar Williams's nearly five-hundred-page anthology *The War Poets*, published in 1945, anything goes; anyone can be included so long as someone (the anthologist) detects a relevance, a connection between one thing and another. Sergeant Randall Jarrell was prominently represented in that anthology by seven poems (after he described Williams's own poems as giving "the impression of having been written on a typewriter by a typewriter" he was dropped from Williams's subsequent anthologies). But in response to a letter from Lowell praising some of its contents, he called it a "silly anthology," then offered some mainly deflationary comments on poems by Empson, Richard Eberhart, Tate,

Warren, and others Lowell had singled out. In the course of his remarks, he noted that "a good deal of Owen is the best anybody did with the first world war," so it is reasonable to assume that he thought about Wilfred Owen's example as he attempted to do something comparably good with the Second World War.

Owen's remark about poetry and war has often been quoted: "Above all I am not concerned with Poetry. My subject is War, and the pity of War. The Poetry is in the pity." It certainly has the ring of memorableness, but its meaning is not especially clear: just where is "the pity of War" located, and how is "the Poetry" *in* this pity? We may be said to sense "the pity" of war in Owen's evocation (in "Anthem for Doomed Youth") of "The shrill, demented choirs of wailing shells; / And bugles calling for them from sad shires"; or his portrait of the soldier in "Disabled," who notices "how the women's eyes / Passed from him to the strong men that were whole"; or in the bewildered, gassed company of soldiers in "Dulce et Decorum Est." Although Jarrell never talked about pity as the war poet's stock-in-trade, both speakers in James Dickey's 1955 dialogue-review of *Selected Poems* stress it as central to his treatment of the helpless individual, subjected to the state's relentless purposes. Dickey's speakers A and B disagree about how fine the war poems are, but agree that pity is an important element in them. Putting the anti-Jarrell case, B asks rather scornfully if one can imagine any war poet *not* pitying individual soldiers; yet B is disturbed because none of that pity is brought to bear on anyone in particular. He asks, "Did Jarrell never love any *person* in the service with him? Did he just pity himself and all the Others, in a kind of monstrous, abstract, complacent, and inhuman Compassion?" Since B finds only "types" in the poems (The Ball Turret Gunner, The Dead Wingman, etc.), he claims that we are prevented from caring about them as individuals.

Speaker A objects— I think rightly—that Jarrell wrote, after all, about the impersonal side of a war fought almost entirely by machines, with the men as almost an afterthought; thus it was right not to focus on individual personalities. (Jarrell pointed out to Lowell that he had never written a poem about himself in the army or the war: "Unless you're vain or silly you realize that you, except insofar as you're in exactly the same boat as the others, aren't the primary subject of any sensible writing about the war.") The question A does not go on to ask is whether Jarrell's best poems are so wholly in the service of Pity or Compassion (speaker B calls those attitudes "monstrous") as both of Dickey's speakers assume, or whether those poems achieve their effects in a more complicated manner. There is no question that in the more didactic of the war poems Jarrell approaches his helpless soldier in a pitying manner. "The Sick Nought" begins:

> *Do the wife and baby travelling to see*
> *Your grey pajamas and sick worried face*
> *Remind you of something, soldier? I remember*
> *You convalescing washing plates, or mopping*
> *The endless corridors your shoes had scuffed;*
> *And in the crowded room you rubbed your cheek*
> *Against your wife's thin elbow like a pony.*

One notes first how different this style is from that of *Blood for a Stranger*. Plates, mops, scuffed corridors, and a homely simile ("like a pony") replace the rhetoric and abstractness of earlier poems. Typically Jarrell doesn't attempt to individuate the "I" who speaks here and who is simply a vehicle for the gravely understanding and pitying voice which asks—since there are so many convalescents, so many soldiers—

> *How can I care about you much, or pick you out*
> *From all the others other people loved*
> *And sent away to die for them? You are a ticket*
> *Someone bought and lost on, a stray animal:*
> *You have lost even the right to be condemned.*

But pity is held in check by the angrily hopeless comparisons—a ticket, a stray animal—and moves at the end of the poem into a rhetorical question Jarrell has asked before: "What is demanded in the trade of states / But lives, your lives?—the one commodity." Taken together, the poem's combination of feelings includes pity, but also something close to contempt and ironic self-knowledge: "How can I care about you much, or pick you out." There is a hard edge to the compassion; it lacks the complacency James Dickey's speaker B found pervasive in the war poems.

Early in his stay at Chanute Field, Jarrell wrote Mackie that he was working on his "poem about sleeping soldiers." This turned into "Absent with Official Leave," the first of five poems printed in *Poetry*, August 1943, signaling the beginning of his wartime production. It may be that he never wrote a better army poem than this one, although he later remarked to Lowell (who had praised it) that it was "a quiet poem and people don't notice it much." Aside from its virtues as a poem, it is useful as an example of how a situation that looks perfect for the exercise of pity turns into one which summons other emotions. In "Absent with Official Leave," a soldier dreams himself away from the army, back into the old ordinary world of peace where he is welcomed, cared for, exalted, and from which eventually he wakes up, back in the barracks and the reality of service. The poem begins by opening out into the country of dream:

> *The lights are beginning to go out in the barracks.*
> *They persist or return, as the wakeful hollow,*
> *But only for a moment; then the windows blacken*
> *For all the hours of the soldier's life.*
>
> *It is life into which he composes his body.*
> *He covers his ears with his pillow, and begins to drift*
> *(Like the plumes the barracks trail into the sky)*
> *Past the laughs, the quarrels, and the breath of others*
>
> *To the ignorant countries where civilians die*
> *Inefficiently, in their spare time, for nothing . . .*

114

Like many of the poems Jarrell would write, this one promises to tell a story and begins to do so in an attractively unhectic way, with a calm, measured musical rhythm carrying us along from one stanza to the next ("Past the laughs, the quarrels, and the breath of others // To the ignorant countries"—the lines' enjambment over the stanza break is both powerful and natural). Its gravity does not exclude a quiet, rather rueful wit by which dying in the war is contrasted with "the ignorant countries where civilians die / Inefficiently, in their spare time, for nothing"—for nothing but, as it were, the ordinary things people die of or for, unofficially. The soldier absent from his army, with the "official leave" that a dream —or a poet—has given him, finds himself first dismayed, then increasingly enclosed by a surrealistic sequence in which he is ministered to as a child:

> *The curved roads hopping through the aimless green*
> *Dismay him, and the cottages where people cry*
>
> *For themselves and, sometimes, for the absent soldier—*
> *Who inches through hedges where the hunters sprawl*
> *For birds, for birds; who turns in ecstasy*
> *Before the slow small fires the women light*
>
> *His charmed limbs, all endearing from the tub.*
> *He dozes, and the washed locks trail like flax*
> *Down the dark face; the unaccusing eyes*
> *That even the dream's eyes are averted from*
>
> *See the wind puff down the chimney, warm the hands*
> *White with the blossoms it pretends are snow . . .*

The "unaccusing eyes"—distinguished from the "dream's eyes" which the soldier sees—are not clearly specified, but somehow lead into the "beings" or "causes" who, in the remainder of the poem, preside above the soldier-turned-child and finally precipitate him (if it is they who do it) back into wakefulness:

He moans like a bear in his enchanted sleep,
And the grave mysterious beings of his years—

The causes who mourn above his agony like trees—
Are moved for their child, and bend across his limbs
The one face opening for his life, the eyes
That look without shame even into his.

And the man awakes, and sees around his life
The night that is never silent, broken with the sighs
And patient breathing of the dark companions
With whom he labors, sleeps, and dies.

Whatever difficulties certain moments in this dream-narrative present, the poem gathers splendidly to its beautiful and inevitable-sounding close, as the man ("child" in the original version) awakes into adulthood once more. We are reminded of the child in "90 North," whose dream-journey to the North Pole was heroic and meaningful but who, when he waked into manhood at the "actual pole" of his existence, found, like all men, that he was alone and that the "Pain [which] comes from the darkness" was indeed pain, not wisdom. In "Absent with Official Leave," the soldier wakes to silence and his "dark companions" (Jarrell noted in a letter how close one slept to those companions in the barracks arrangements), and to the invariable round of work, sleep, death.

The poem enacts a dignified acceptance of the human lot as regimented into a collectivity by the fact of war, and does this without pitying the soldier or asking us to pity him. If it is a pity things should be as they are, it is also the way in this world they must be: the final stanza makes us feel that the awakening is both touching and final. The strong and unexpected rhyme in that stanza's second and fourth lines is crucial in creating this sense of finality; of equal weight is the way the stanza's single sentence continuously unravels right down to the closing sequence of verbs: "With whom he labors, sleeps, and dies." Jarrell often had trouble ending poems and tended to go on too long, explaining and diluting things: "Absent with Official Leave" knows exactly when it's time to stop, the mark of a superbly finished piece of writing.

When in 1955 he came to arrange his *Selected Poems*, he divided them into two parts, the second of which consisted of the war poems, subdivided into the following categories: "Bombers," "The Carriers," "Prisoners," "Camps and Fields," "The Trades," "Children and Civilians," "Soldiers." These categories overlap and need not be regarded with great seriousness; nor is there any progression in the war poems between the earlier ones that appeared in *Little Friend, Little Friend* (1945) and the slightly later ones that formed a good part of *Losses* (1948). The man who composed "Absent with Official Leave" early in his stay at Chanute Field was not about to "improve" but rather, as is suggested by the various categories, to turn his gaze on other scenes and experiences. Taken together, the war poems have perhaps been respected more than they have been enjoyed. They are typically so unflashy, so reluctant to grip the reader through striking dramatic postures or appealingly theatrical rhetoric, that they run the risk of being overlooked, or read only dutifully because of their "important" subject matter. In his fine short appreciation, R. W. Flint calls them one of the two "peaks" in Jarrell's poetic career (the other, presumably, is *The Lost World*) but notes that it takes time "to absorb [their] general monotony of effect, the mind they make, their static grandeur of sentience." This may seem to damn with faint praise, but is in fact an accurate comment on poems which take a great deal of getting used to, not because of individual complexities so much as the typical way in which they achieve their effects. Their flat assertiveness discourages the sort of analytical paraphrase and explicative commentary that (for example) Robert Lowell's poems from the same period so much invite.

Consider a poem which Flint quotes as exemplary but says almost nothing about, "A Front" (located under "Camps and Fields" along with "Absent with Official Leave," though it could as well belong in the "Bombers" section of *Selected Poems*). It is set in a fogged-in base at which one bomber manages to land, while the

others head south to a more accessible field—except for one plane
that loses radio contact and eventually crashes:

> *Fog over the base: the beams ranging*
> *From the five towers pull home from the night*
> *The crews cold in fur, the bombers banging*
> *Like lost trucks down the levels of the ice.*
> *A glow drifts in like mist (how many tons of it?),*
> *Bounces to a roll, turns suddenly to steel*
> *And tires and turrets, huge in the trembling light.*
> *The next is high, and pulls up with a wail,*
> *Comes round again—no use. And no use for the rest*
> *In drifting circles out along the range;*
> *Holding no longer, changed to a kinder course,*
> *The flights drone southward through the steady rain.*
> *The base is closed. . . . But one voice keeps on calling,*
> *The lowering pattern of the engines grows;*
> *The roar gropes downward in its shaky orbit*
> *For the lives the season quenches. Here below*
> *They beg, order, are not heard; and hear the darker*
> *Voice rising:* Can't you hear me? Over. Over—
> *All the air quivers, and the east sky glows.*

Flint usefully identifies the technical ingredients of Jarrell's war
poetry: "A ground tone of swaying iambics varied by spondees and
syncopation, paired and tripled adjectives in wistful or angry
clumps, a recurring litany of abstractions: the State, the States,
Death, Dream, fire, the years, the cities—the soldier-prisoner-
patient, his wife, mail, and cat." More than most, "A Front" is
free from this litany of abstractions and relies wholly, in a phrase
of Pound's, on the "dignity of sheer presentation." Flint doesn't
mention the repetitions—"no use," "voice," "hear" (with "here"),
"Over, Over"—which make the poem primarily an aural experience, for all its visual, informational load. And, as with the final
stanza in "Absent with Official Leave," a strong rhyme surprises
us and reverberates in the mind—I am thinking of how "The

lowering pattern of the engines grows" is unexpectedly confirmed and completed by the poem's last line, in its violence of conclusion: "All the air quivers, and the east sky glows." Flint is daringly right to speak of Jarrell as a "fastidiously inhibited poet"—remember his shock at how crudely his barracks mates spoke—who was nevertheless prepared to "swallow the war whole, to make it his" in something like "an epic of acceptance." This is how "A Front" comes to terms with the world, and its "poetry" is more difficult to locate than in something called, abstractly, "the pity."

The famous, or infamous, "The Death of the Ball Turret Gunner," favorite of the undergraduate neophyte poetry reader, is in fact quite untypical of the war poems generally—and not merely because it is far and away the shortest:

> *From my mother's sleep I fell into the State,*
> *And I hunched in its belly till my wet fur froze.*
> *Six miles from earth, loosed from its dream of life,*
> *I woke to black flak and the nightmare fighters.*
> *When I died they washed me out of the turret with a hose.*

Although it plays with the recurrent theme of waking from the dream of life into the harsh reality of "the State," its imagistic brevity sets it off from the other poems, and its final line is altogether more spectacular than the sort Jarrell usually produces in the war poems. Not all readers have approved of the ending; one of them, Donald Hall, spoke of it as "the portentous ending of a tiny poem," and (referring to the popular 1950s TV show) said that "like the oracular remarks of Sergeant Friday on *Dragnet* [. . .] it chokes with the softness of toughness." Thus, for Hall, the poem was sentimental, a charge he brought to other Jarrell poems.

In recorded performances of his poetry readings, Jarrell often provided extended commentary on the images and materials which went into his work, and with "The Death of the Ball Turret Gunner" he described the tiny size of that gunner's perch and the sort of steam hose which would be turned on the plane to clean it. There is no question of the poet's not knowing what he's writing about—quite the opposite, and the poem is the stronger for that knowledge. But Donald Hall is objecting to something else, to a "tough" tone of voice that is really sentimental and that titillates the sensationalistically minded reader with a shocking image. What nobody including Hall seems to have thought about is the oddity of having the dead gunner speak at all—who invited him to explain?—and the consequent difficulty of pronouncing on how "portentous" are his remarks. (Would it not have been more portentous to go on at some length about the State and the Individual?) Surely the little poem is a tour de force rather than—like most of Jarrell's other war poetry—a leisurely, detailed, expository presentation of some scene or action. "The Death of the Ball Turret Gunner" doesn't demand long acquaintance for its impact to be made; nor does it grow in the mind on rereadings. It is an immediately available poem whose popularity is easy to account for.

Jarrell felt that perhaps the best war poems he wrote were "Siegfried" and "Burning the Letters," the first about a gunner who has his leg amputated and is sent back to the States; the second in which the wife of a pilot killed in the Pacific tries to divest herself of his memory. Both poems are on the long side, are marked at times by rather tortuous writing, and are spoken in a wholly serious, even solemn, narrative voice. Each teeters on the edge of the lugubrious:

> *If it is different, if you are different,*
> *It is not from the lives or the cities;*
> *The world's war, just or unjust—the world's peace, war or peace;*
> *But from a separate war: the shell with your name*
> *In the bursting turret, the crystals of your blood*
> *On the splints' wrapped steel, the hours wearing*
> *The quiet body back to its base, its missions done.*

(from "Siegfried")

> *The lives are fed*
> *Into the darkness of their victory;*

The ships sink, forgotten; and the sea
Blazes to darkness: the unsearchable
Death of the lives lies dark upon the life
That, bought by death, the loved and tortured lives,
Stares westward, passive, to the blackening sea.
In the tables of the dead, in the unopened almanac,
The head, charred, featureless—the unknown mean—
Is thrust from the waters like a flame, is torn
From its last being with the bestial cry
Of its pure agony.

                     (from "Burning the Letters")

These are poems which in their reiterated insistence never let up, but purchase their intensity at the cost, perhaps, of wearing out the reader—for all the vividness of individual passages.

In fact, more often than not, it is to passages or stanzas that one responds, rather than to the poems in their entirety. On occasion, Jarrell wrote relatively short ones, such as "A Ward in the States" or "A Field Hospital," which are strongly bonded by stanzaic and rhyming patterns, and in which the poet makes a continuous argument, carried through to its conclusion—as in the third stanza of "A Field Hospital":

A cot creaks; and he hears the groan
He thinks his own—
And groans, and turns his stitched, blind, bandaged head
Up to the tent-flap, red
With dawn. A voice says, "Yes, this one";
His arm stings; then, alone,
He neither knows, remembers—but instead
Sleeps, comforted.

This is expert, but perhaps not as original as when Jarrell avoids constructing well-made patterns and instead risks the "general monotony of effect" Flint speaks of. Consider the following passage (the first half of "Second Air Force"), which takes its landscape from what, in a letter to Lowell, he said a "heavy bomber training-field was like" (the landscape resembles Davis-Monthan Field):

> *Far off, above the plain the summer dries,*
> *The great loops of the hangars sway like hills.*
> *Buses and weariness and loss, the nodding soldiers*
> *Are wire, the bare frame building, and a pass*
> *To what was hers; her head hides his square patch*
> *And she thinks heavily: My son is grown.*
> *She sees a world: sand roads, tar-paper barracks,*
> *The bubbling asphalt of the runways, sage,*
> *The dunes rising to the interminable ranges,*
> *The dim flights moving over clouds like clouds.*
> *The armorers in their patched faded green,*
> *Sweat-stiffened, banded with brass cartridges,*
> *Walk to the line; their Fortresses, all tail,*
> *Stand wrong and flimsy on their skinny legs,*
> *And the crews climb to them clumsily as bears.*
> *The head withdraws into its hatch (a boy's),*
> *The engines rise to their blind laboring roar,*
> *And the green, made beasts run home to air.*
> *Now in each aspect death is pure.*
> *(At twilight they wink over men like stars*
> *And hour by hour, through the night, some see*
> *The great lights floating in—from Mars, from Mars.)*
> *How emptily the watchers see them gone.*

There are nominal human beings here—a mother visiting her son at his base—but they are subordinate to the world created by these lines. In replying to Lowell—who in a letter had expressed reservations about the "rhetoric" which fills the poem's second half, saying that it "pretty well obliterated the mother and her situation" —Jarrell said that she was "merely a vehicle of presentation, her situation merely a formal connection of the out-of-this-world field with the world." And indeed, the best part of this passage—and poem—occurs when an out-of-this-world place is created, with the loops of hangars swaying like hills, the dunes rising as "dim flights" move over them ("over clouds like clouds") and the little mechanical men (the "armorers") equipped for their warlike task, looking homely and innocent in their sweat-stiffened, patched clothes. The planes, instruments of death, are really charmingly awkward—like funny animals in the zoo—while the men are no less awkward as they climb "clumsily as bears." There is the poignant touch of a parenthetical "(a boy's)" to identify the head disappearing into the plane's hatch, after which "the green, made beasts ["made" is a fine, surprising touch] run home to air." As with the sleeping men in "Absent with Official Leave," or the plane trying to land in "A Front," Jarrell succeeds in investing the scene with both dignity and oddity: the poet's eyes don't quite believe what they see, and there is surprise that unfolds as those eyes move from one observation to the next. The largeness and alien quality of the experience take it beyond any "moral" attitude of condemnation or rueful superiority, as in the three-line parenthesis about homecoming planes:

> *(At twilight they wink over men like stars*
> *And hour by hour, through the night, some see*
> *The great lights floating in—from Mars, from Mars.)*

The origin of the bombers has to be repeated to be believed.

As Jarrell's letters make abundantly clear, he managed to get along in the army at least in part because of his appreciation of the absurd, his delight in incongruities, his deadly ear for the speech he heard around him (orders must be obeyed "promptly and willfully"). Yet it is a fact that very little, almost none of this humorous sense of things gets into the war poems. In part, this had to do with avoiding a satirical perspective on Karl Shapiro's "gigantic slapstick of modern war," and out of a related decision not to feature himself (as Shapiro often did) as a character in the poems. More deeply, it had to do with his not trusting himself to be humorous in a poem. Robbed of the "I" who performs so entertainingly in the letters, the prospects for comic or ironic effects were small; the "good, dreary poems" he wanted to write about the war would be built out of something else. His aim in poetry was to do something like what he so admired and handsomely praised in his appreciation of Ernie Pyle, written shortly after Pyle's death in the Pacific theater. Jarrell felt that Ernie Pyle "wrote like none of the rest," and that the quality of his writing was uniquely able to express "the real war":

> What he saw and what he felt he said. He used for ordinary narration a plain, transparent, but oddly personal style—a style that could convince anybody of anything; but when his perceptions or emotions were complex, far-reaching, and profound, he did his utmost to express their quality fully—at his best with the most exact intensity, at his worst with a rather appealingly old-fashioned spaciousness of rhetoric.

Like the cartoonist Bill Mauldin, whose work Jarrell also greatly admired and was moved by, Pyle was "always conscious of the shocking disparity of actor and circumstance, of the little men and their big war, their big world." In a closing tribute, he says that Pyle's style of writing, like his life, was "a victory of the deepest moral feeling, of sympathy and understanding and affection, over circumstances as terrible as any men have created and endured." That this tribute to Ernie Pyle was Jarrell's first real piece of encomiastic writing is interesting, especially since it was directed at a "popular" writer about the war rather than a poet or a novelist. The latter types most often brought out his ironic and satirical side, his penchant for striking off a writer's faults with sentences that bit. Toward Pyle, by contrast, his tone is as measured, declarative, and affectionate as he thought the correspondent's own to be—and as, perhaps, he hoped were the poems he himself was writing about the army and the war.

Perhaps Jarrell's most engaging and successful attempt to express the "real" army came in a poem he wrote—or finished—after his discharge, and which was not published until 1949. By this time, he had begun to experiment with breaking up and generally relaxing his poetic line and had become aware of the attractiveness of poets like Frost who worked at getting conversational voices into their work. In "Transient Barracks," he devoted himself to nothing more than conveying the feel of ordinary barracks life, first through an all-seeing perspective, then more particularly through that of a gunner who has returned to the States, assigned now (Jarrell says in his note to the poem) to serve as a gunnery instructor. It begins distinctively:

> *Summer. Sunset. Someone is playing*
> *The ocarina in the latrine:*
> *You Are My Sunshine. A man shaving*
> *Sees—past the day-room, past the night K.P.'s*
> *Bent over a G.I. can of beets*
> *In the yard of the mess—the red and green*
> *Lights of a runway full of '24's.*
> *The first night flight goes over with a roar*
> *And disappears, a star, among mountains.*

Like the other army poems, "Transient Barracks" lives in its particularities, and the mode is still one of presentation; yet its style differs significantly from the grave declarativeness of "Absent with Official Leave," "A Front," or "Second Air Force." It is as if that ocarina in the latrine (in another note he tells us that for a time in the Second Air Force a man was assigned to play the ocarina to improve morale) were responsible for the playful sound effect of "Summer. Sunset. Someone" in the opening line. As for the "G.I. can of beets" (a "G.I. can" is a large garbage can), James Dickey was enamored enough of the image to use it to title an essay in which he traced a line of what he called "literalist" poets (including Hardy, Frost, Edwin Arlington Robinson, Philip Larkin) and contrasted them with "Magic-Language" poets (Hopkins, Hart Crane, Stevens, Berryman). Yet there is a sense in which the G.I. can of beets is too good to be true, too "literal" to be quite literal—there may be altogether more "magic" to Jarrell's writing than at first appears.

The poem continues:

The day-room radio, switched on next door,
Says, "The thing about you is, you're real."
The man sees his own face, black against lather,
In the steamed, starred mirror: it is real.
And the others—the boy in underwear
Hunting for something in his barracks-bags
With a money-belt around his middle—
The voice from the doorway: "Where's the C.Q.?"
"Who wants to know?" "He's gone to the movies."
"Tell him Red wants him to sign his clearance"—
These are. Are what? Are.

Dickey quotes the lines in his essay and says, "It's real, all right," only to suggest that such poetry has its limitations, since it may be too exclusively in bondage to the literal, the empirical, to "the details of an actual situation." For him, fine as some passages are, Jarrell's "romance with the ordinary" usually fails to touch the "magical" side of language.

I would counter by insisting that, magical or not, good poetry does something surprising and pleasing with language, and that these lines from "Transient Barracks" (and indeed the whole poem) play with the ordinary, the "real," in ways that are fresh and that prefigure what Jarrell would bring to full accomplishment in his late poems. The song—if it is a song—heard on the radio, with its quite possibly banal insistence that "you're *real*" (that word given a throbbing emphasis); the man looking at his face in the mirror—a situation bristling with unreality—and thinking, or so the narrator thinks, "it is real"; then the voices with their ordinary questions and answers, their rhythms unmistakable—all these prepare us for momentous comment by the narrator. And what is the comment? "These are. Are what? Are"—five monosyllabic grunts in the direction of an inexpressible reality. My point is that Jarrell is not writing "simply" here, is not writing literally, but rather that the poetry consists of a very complicated, humorously sympathetic play with notions of the real, and that this play leads to original, even memorable effects in the poetic line and to an empathy more convincing than in many of the other war poems. So, in this transient barracks, something more than transience may be said to have taken shape in the poem's figure.

A similar claim can be urged for what he made of his wartime service. In a longer letter to Tate early in 1945, he rehearsed the progress of his military career and said about the seven months he had stayed at Chanute Field, just previous to moving west:

> I felt so strongly about everything I saw (the atmosphere was entirely one of lying, meaningless brutality and officiousness, stupidity not beyond belief but conception—the one word for everything in the army is *petty*) that, stiff, sore, and sleepy, I'd sit up at night in the day room—all the other lights were out—writing poems, surrounded by people playing pool or writing home or reading comic-strip magazines.

He may have bent over backward here to assure Tate that the army was no picnic, but the remarkable thing is that he wrote a poem at Chanute like "Absent with Official Leave." In other words, Jarrell was able to put brutality, officiousness, stupidity, and overall army pettiness behind him, and to write his poems out of motives and feelings much less monolithic, more humanly mixed, than those he named to Tate.

FIVE

New York and The Nation

LITTLE *Friend, Little Friend*, Jarrell's second book of poems (the title refers to a bomber's name for his fighter escort pilot), was published in October of 1945 by Dial Press, under the instigation of Philip Rahv. It is by far the handsomest of his books of poems, bound in dark purplish-blue cloth of a very fine weave, with its front cover stamped with eleven black stars and its spine stamped in vivid orange yellow. Although not widely reviewed, it received intelligent and appreciative commentary from Delmore Schwartz in *The Nation* and Theodore Spencer in *The Saturday Review of Literature*. Schwartz emphasized Jarrell's advance beyond the poems in *Blood for a Stranger*; he had lived through a subject —the army, the war—of which his earlier poems had only a premonition, thus were relatively thin and abstract. What made many of the new poems memorable was their comparative thickness of texture, in which, for example, we are given a pilot whose plane has been hit:

> Strapped at the center of the blazing wheel,
> His flesh ice-white against the shattered mask,
> He tears at the easy clasp, his sobbing breaths
> Misting the fresh blood lightening to flame,

Darkening to smoke; trapped there in pain
And fire and breathlessness, he struggles free
Into the sunlight of the upper sky—

The beginning of "A Pilot from the Carrier" was the sort of thing
Theodore Spencer admired for its presentation, as he did the poet's
attempt to move beyond the helpless individual by placing him in
the grip of vast impersonal machines. But when Jarrell tried to be
analytic or didactic about "the State" in these new poems, there
was the sense of *déjà vu*, of going over ground already traversed
in his first book. And, Spencer noted, when on occasion he attempted to be satirical—as in "The State" or "Gunner" (in which
the dead soldier asks, "Did the medals go home to my cat?")—
the result was embarrassing.

Yet, as Delmore Schwartz pointed out, satire was mainly absent
from these poems; the dreaded Jarrell, expert at making overwhelming wisecracks about other poets, himself wrote poems that
were mainly solemn. If and when they became witty, Schwartz went
on to add, "what a modernist Pope we might have." What Schwartz
didn't go on to wonder about was how Pope would have handled
World War II. As previously noted, Jarrell's attempt *not* to see the
war and the army mainly as (in Shapiro's phrase) a "gigantic slapstick" made certain kinds of wit—of the authoritative, "brilliant,"
Popean sort—impossible or undesirable. On the other hand, in
Little Friend, Little Friend there are passages, though not whole
poems, in which something like wit may be observed; in which
Jarrell's perception of the incongruity of things, of what had happened to him and his fellow human beings, comes sharply to life.
"Losses" speculates about what it means to kill and be killed in
war:

We read our mail and counted up our missions—
In bombers named for girls, we burned
The cities we had learned about in school—
Till our lives wore out; our bodies lay among
The people we had killed and never seen.

129

> *When we lasted long enough they gave us medals;*
> *When we died they said, "Our casualties were low."*
> *They said, "Here are the maps"; we burned the cities.*

Avoiding the directly satiric as well as the solemnity of didacticism, the poem achieves freshness and surprise by its deadpan juxtaposition of things that don't, yet do, belong together. "In bombers named for girls, we burned / The cities we had learned about in school" is writing that has the force of wit, and it is present in these poems more often than Schwartz recognized.

In one of his letters, Robert Frost speaks of the importance for poets of having what he calls a "strongbox" full of poems to be tapped when the occasion arises. By the time *Little Friend* was published, Jarrell at age thirty-one had filled such a box, and at the beginning of 1946 he wrote Lowell that he already had his next book finished (*Losses*, published two years later) and four or five poems for the one after that. Moreover, although he continued to write war poems of the sort that made up *Little Friend*, he also wrote or finished a longish poem, "The Märchen," which Tate published in *Sewanee* in the spring of 1946, and which laid out some of the mythic-folktale elements that would be increasingly important in his poetry. Altogether in 1945 he published twenty-five poems in the usual places; beyond that he wrote two verse chronicles, the first of which ("Poetry in War and Peace") contains the previously discussed remarks about Marianne Moore that reveal his sense of himself as a writer about war. The other prose pieces also have that war—just ending—in mind. Besides the tribute to Ernie Pyle, a review of a book of poems about Jews by A. M. Klein registered Jarrell's consciousness of the death camps. And the second of his published essays on Auden demonstrated, in its conclusion, how forcefully contemporary events had left their mark on him.

Asserting that what he called Auden's recent submission to, rather than rebellion against, the universe really meant that "the universe is his own shadow on the wall beside his bed," Jarrell quoted from Auden's review of a new edition of Grimm's tales. In it Auden urged that parents read them again and again to their children, so that the salutary, non-rationalist nature of the tales would banish such bogeys as "the Society for the Scientific Diet, the Association of Positivist Parents, the League for the Promotion of Worthwhile Leisure, the Coöperative Camp for Prudent Progressives"—these and other "bores and scoundrels can go jump in the lake." Rather than amusement at so Audenesque a summoning up of Bad Things, Jarrell expressed dismay:

> Such a sentence shows that its writer has saved his own soul, but has lost the whole world—has forgotten even the nature of that world: for this was written, not in 1913, but within the months that held the mass executions in the German camps, the fire raids, Warsaw and Dresden and Manila; within the months that were preparing the bombs for Hiroshima and Nagasaki; within the last twelve months of the Second World War.

Speaking of Auden's list of "bores and scoundrels" he asks, "Were *these* your enemies, reader? They were not mine," and wonders whether Auden supposed "that the S.S. men at Lublin and Birkenau had not been told the tales by their parents." With a final apprehensive looking ahead to the world of the future, he predicts that, if there are people in that world and if they should be asked, "What did you do in all those wars?" then their only answer would be " 'I lived through them.' But some of us will answer, 'I was saved.' " It is a surprisingly humbling moment, suggesting in part how far Jarrell had come from his enchanted response to Auden's early poetry. Auden, of course, had changed and not—in Jarrell's estimation—for the better. But so, at least for a time, had Jarrell changed, and so had the world.

From November 1943, when he arrived at Davis-Monthan Field, until his final discharge from the army at a separation center back in Austin in February 1946, Jarrell's real life appears to have been lived in his writing: in his poems, his essays and reviews, his letters to others—especially to Robert Lowell—about poetry. In a sense one could say this about any period in his career, but once settled with Mackie and Kitten, first in a small one-room accommodation in crowded and expensive Tucson, later in a larger apartment, he had no need to write anybody in detail about what he did every day as a celestial navigation tower operator. Except for a long retrospective letter to Tate, filling him in on his career in the service thus far, the relatively few letters available from this 1943–45 period scarcely refer to ordinary life: Mackie has a job working for the Red Cross; he is playing lots of tennis, reaching the final rounds of Tucson tournaments. At one point he is threatened with being coopted to help write a history of the Second Air Force, but manages to get out of it. In September 1945, after V-J Day, when his job as a trainer at the B-29 base was no longer necessary, there was, he thought, a real possibility of his being sent overseas. But it never materialized; instead, he worked for a time as assistant to the base's legal officer investigating complaints, some of them most curious: "Saturday I had to go to a border jail, get statements from witnesses about a soldier who fell out of bed and fractured his skull, and measure the bed. It was 4 feet high and 24 inches wide"—this, from a letter to Margaret Marshall, was signed, "Your crime reporter." Eventually his thirty-eight months of service made him eligible for discharge.

Like anyone who looks forward to such an event, he was filled with projects to undertake when released—in his case mainly literary ones. He had signed on to do a book on Hart Crane for Henry Holt's American Men of Letters series. The second Auden article was to be followed by another (later they were to be part of a book on Auden), which would deal with the sources of Auden's ideas in such theologians as St. Paul, Luther, Calvin, Kierkegaard, Barth, "and the other Neo-Calvinists, etc." He wrote Lowell that for months he had read almost nothing but great quantities of theology, and he proposed to write a book about Paul (in addition to those on Crane and Auden). Besides continuing to write poems—one of them was to be about the bombing of Nagasaki, which especially horrified him—he planned to write about many other things, among them the notorious incident in which General George Patton had slapped a soldier.

How carefully and seriously he arranged these projects in his head may be questioned, since part of the whole extravagance involved some epistolary showing off to his friends Lowell and Tate. Certainly his career as a teacher appears to have been far from the front of his mind; he told Lowell in August 1945 that he was filling out a Guggenheim application and heard that he stood a good chance of getting a fellowship since the head of the foundation had mentioned his name to Ransom. After teaching for a year back at Texas, he hoped to use the fellowship money for two years of living and writing in New York. A further scheme (mentioned only once in the letters) involved using the G.I. Bill to take a year of psychiatry and anthropology courses at Columbia from Abram Kardiner and Ralph Linton. In his work plan submitted to the Guggenheim committee, he said that after his discharge he planned to write more poems and prose about the war, as well as critical books about Auden and Crane, each of whose poetry, he said, was of the greatest "symptomatic" importance.

The Guggenheim application was successful, but more of a surprise than the fellowship award was an invitation from Margaret Marshall to replace her temporarily as literary editor of *The Nation*. He had reviewed poetry for the magazine just before the war and had published there his manifesto on modern poetry, "The End of the Line." Marshall had also been extremely receptive to publishing poems he sent her, including longer ones from *Little Friend* like "Siegfried," "The Wide Prospect," and "Burning the Letters." In the fall of 1945, Marshall invited him to write a poetry chronicle for *The Nation* and then, since she was planning to take a year's leave, suggested that he replace her soon after he was discharged, his tenure to begin April 1, 1946. The timing couldn't have been better: Jarrell was discharged in February, and after he endured a bout of influenza (during which, mistakenly, he was told that an X-ray showed fresh tubercular lesions—in fact they had healed long ago), he and Mackie stayed with the latter's mother in Austin, then visited Anna Regan in Nashville, proceeding from there to New York, where Marshall had obligingly found them a temporary apartment.

Jarrell responded to Margaret Marshall's invitation with an especially interesting and revealing letter in which he set out to describe himself to her and to say why he would be good at the job she proposed. The letter is worth dwelling on because, for all the difficulty or impossibility of telling the truth about oneself to someone else, it seems to me a fine example of the effort to do just that. Thoreau's belief that "with thinking we may be beside ourselves in a sane sense" comes to mind when the following is encountered in Jarrell's self-summing-up:

> I believe that my tastes are reasonably wise and "objective," rather than narrow and personal. I certainly don't like, or have connections with, any particular sort of writing or any particular variety of literary opinion. (Several of my best friends have happened to become editors, and it seemed to me that their dogmatic convictions and idiosyncrasies and general sectarian leanings hurt their work a lot.)

Attractive about this is that qualifying "reasonably" before "wise," and the claim to be "objective," even as the word is placed in quotation marks. His insistence that he is not committed to a particular sort of writing or literary opinion is that of a man who has invested everything in the effort not to be parochial in his tastes or authoritarian in his critical allegiances. At the same time, he is obviously seeking to distinguish himself from friends in power— Tate at *Sewanee*; Ransom at *Kenyon*; Brooks and Warren (though now no longer) at *The Southern Review*—whose conservative politics and generally "Southern" frame of mind he found uncongenial. He believed that his deep commitment to wide reading, to a pluralism of tastes and inclinations, would secure him from bondage to sects and cults. And indeed when—just before he headed for

New York—Tate wrote him a warning letter about "New York cliques" (doubtless of leftist persuasion), Jarrell replied by telling him that not knowing those cliques "will grieve and bother me just as much as not knowing the more prominent representatives of the Red and Green factions that bet on the chariot-races in Byzantium." He was proud, he said, that he had never met anyone on the staff of *The Nation.* So much for Tate the intriguer and controversialist, attempting to act as guide and mentor once more without success.

But there is more here than biting the fatherly hands that fed him. The following sentences to Marshall about the kind of student he had been and the kind of reader he was have the ring both of conviction and of discovery, as if he were finding out more about himself in the act of composing the letter. He tells her he was educated as a psychologist "with great quantities of philosophy and the sciences—especially physiology":

> I have a lot of funny interests and I've read a great deal in all of them. I read very fast, get year-long crazes about particular fields, and read steadily in them, with big shining eyes. Besides the things that I write about and am obviously interested in —you know what they are—I've been particularly interested in Gestalt psychology, ethnology and "folk" literature, economics (especially Marxist), symbolic logic and modern epistemology, theology and its origins, and a few even queerer things.

These "interests," he says, are of no practical value to him but will serve him well as an editor responsible for seeing that more than merely literary books get reviewed. Just as he didn't want to be categorized as conservative or Southern, so he wished to elude the English-major stereotype, someone who knew all about poems and fiction but couldn't handle economics or symbolic logic. From his reports on his own reading, the above capsulization looks accurate enough.

A more complicated, possibly troublesome question arises in the letter when he makes a stab at characterizing himself as a person by identifying the kind of temperament he thinks he possesses. In one sense he knows it is impossible to do this, to be "objective," yet he goes ahead anyway, informing Marshall that he has "an even, cheerful, and optimistic disposition: what I write is thera-peutically the opposite, I guess." Unlike many writers, he says, he doesn't feel essentially different from "ordinary" people—and here surely he speaks out of what his army experience, coming to its close, had taught him. This self-description lays out most crisply the basic configuration, or split, in his character: the even, cheerful person who soldiered along, adapting himself successfully to thirty-eight months in the army, and the darker spirit who knew that life was unendurable and that poetry, in telling the truth about this fact, was only a palliative. My inclination is not to understand or "accept" this split as an indication of a character at troubled odds with itself, but to take it rather as a measure of Jarrell's sanity. All of us, to one degree or another, look at life in these irreconcilable ways, even as, day by day, we entertain both of them and continue to function. That eventually Jarrell's sanity broke down does not seem to be a warrant for turning the remarks he made to Margaret Marshall about his own cheerful disposition into the stuff of self-delusion.

In practical terms, what must have convinced Marshall she had made a good choice was Jarrell's assurance that he would be able to get along with his new colleagues, especially since, after the army, "*any* civilian organization will seem a miracle of efficiency and good sense and humane charm to me." But he also admired *The Nation*'s regular contributors to the Arts section, and thought their presence made the magazine superior to *The New Republic*. This is in no sense unwarranted flattery of Marshall, since in 1946 the back pages of *The Nation* were indeed a superior operation. Bernard Haggin's music criticism was arguably as informed, stren-uous, and discriminating as any written in the country; James Agee on film and Clement Greenberg on art, like Haggin on music, can still be read as brilliant reports on what was happening week by week; some of Lionel Trilling's best essays and reviews appeared in the magazine; while for all Delmore Schwartz's limitations as a poet and fictionist (in Jarrell's judgment), he was a good critic.

Under the magazine's editor, Freda Kirchwey, a number of strongly leftist presences, including J. Alvarez del Vayo and Carey MacWilliams, dominated *The Nation*'s front section. But the back pages were animated by the spirit of criticism rather than the propagation of any party line. Though in his year's tenure as literary editor Jarrell brought in interesting new contributors of poetry and criticism, Marshall had set a fearfully high standard for him to live up to. To take one example: the Midwinter Book Review issue of February 1946 contained essays by Hannah Arendt and Perry Miller, some "Notes By the Way" (as Marshall called her own column), poems by Lowell, reviews by Stuart Chase, Reinhold Niebuhr, Jarrell, and Trilling; plus drama, music, and art columns by Joseph Wood Krutch, Haggin, and Greenberg, respectively. The regular weekly offerings were of equal quality, though shorter. In fact, the only one of *The Nation*'s regular contributors whose writing Jarrell disliked was Diana Trilling, the head fiction reviewer, whose summer vacation he looked forward to, since, he said, he would be able to assign novels to someone else.

He continued to use the excellent stable of reviewers Marshall had assembled, and expanded it by drawing upon the likes of Empson, Marianne Moore, Robert Fitzgerald, Ransom, and Berryman. He published a piece on Ernie Pyle by Bill Mauldin. He invented good combinations of reviewer and book, like Blackmur on Robert Penn Warren's *Rime of the Ancient Mariner* essay, or like Empson on Robert Graves, Lowell on Wallace Stevens, Moore on Elizabeth Bishop, Eleanor Clark on Malcolm Lowry, Ransom on Henry James's *The American Scene*. He published as many Lowell poems—ones about to appear in *Lord Weary's Castle*—as he could get his hands on; he published William Carlos Williams and Louis MacNeice and Bishop and Graves's "To Juan at the Winter Solstice." He ran a special music issue with MacNeice's poem "Slow Movement," an article on Ernest Newman by Haggin, and intel-

137

ligent contributions by Morton Dauwen Zabel and Charles Farrell. Readers of *The Nation* were doing better than perhaps they could have known at the time.

The music issue represented more than a pious gesture on Jarrell's part toward one of the magazine's departments. His love of classical—what was then called "serious"—music shows up frequently in the letters, especially those written while he was in the army. (Remember also his remark to Cecile Starr about how he "knew all the Beethoven symphonies.") In a letter to Mackie from Sheppard Field, he suggested that his friend at the University of Texas, Guy Steffan, might be willing to donate his copy of Mozart's "Prague" Symphony to the record library at the barracks, and added that she might send along their own, badly executed Busch Quartet recording of Beethoven's Opus 127: "We'd really be doing a service to any soldiers with classical tastes—classical as distinguished from *Scheherazade* and the *Nutcracker Suite*." His interest in that particular Mozart symphony and Beethoven quartet mark him as a fairly sophisticated listener, one who had gone beyond not just popular Rimsky-Korsakov and Tchaikovsky items but also more well-known pieces by Mozart and Beethoven. There was also, as mentioned earlier, his ecstatic response to the Schumann piano concerto ("the national anthem of my own particular war," he called it), not a recondite piece, certainly, but one that only experienced ears can properly hear.

He played no instrument, and although in his early days at Texas he speaks of taking piano lessons, nothing much came of them. Mary Jarrell writes entertainingly about the first time she laid eyes on him in the student lounge at the writers' conference in Boulder, Colorado, where he was playing a three-fingered trill, someplace above high C on the piano. It turned out, she said, that it was all he knew, and that inevitably he would play it on every piano he got near. Later, when they were married, he would occasionally burst out against his parents' neglect of his musical education: "You'd have *thought* somebody'd have *seen* to it that I got pi *ano* lessons!" Mary Jarrell also confirms that the piano was his favorite instrument, its music his favorite sound. And she declares herself surprised that critics of Jarrell's poetry haven't paid more attention to the number of poems in which musical pieces or forms, names of musicians and composers crop up, with a frequency comparable to their appearance in Auden's work. While his engagement with piano music remained steady, his devotion as a listener to late romanticism—to Mahler, and particularly to Richard Strauss—increased as, after his visit to Salzburg in 1948, his romance with the German language and with Austria flourished. Near the end of his life he grew increasingly interested in Wagner.

In his enthusiastic letter to Margaret Marshall about the *Nation* job, he mentioned that, among others, he admired the writings of B. H. Haggin, and in a letter a month or so after his stint had begun he said he had been particularly enjoying talking on the phone to Haggin and to James Agee about their columns. He soon met Haggin in the flesh, at one of those parties neither of them was fond of, and Haggin remembered that Jarrell approached him with outstretched hands, beaming (his characteristic facial posture toward him, Haggin said) and declaring, "I'm one of your greatest admirers." It was a good match: both of them revered Bernard Shaw's music criticism for its combination of wit, acerbity, and fiercely argued judgments. Though Haggin also listened to jazz, he and Jarrell were devoted mainly to the classical canon of the eighteenth and nineteenth centuries; both cared primarily about experiencing individual composers or performing artists in all their richness and detail. When Jarrell later reviewed Haggin's collection of essays and reviews from *The Nation*, he referred to him as "a sort of exemplary monster of independence, of honesty, of scrupulous and merciless frankness." In pointing to Haggin's consuming interest in "saying precisely what he thinks about a composer or performer, in representing as accurately as possible the quality and value of what he hears," we note that this is precisely what Jarrell had been doing in the poetry chronicles written over the past ten years. Furthermore, the fact that Haggin felt the need to

139

write many "unfavorable" pieces—principled, argued objections to often highly successful performers and composers and other critics—was equally for Jarrell an essential part of the function of criticism, an "aesthetic" function that, as with the Shaw they both admired, was also a moral one.

Haggin also wrote about ballet for *The Nation* and was particularly enthusiastic about George Balanchine's work at City Center. From this period stemmed Jarrell's love of the dance—or rather, not so much "the dance" as the dancers and dancing in what would become the New York City Ballet. Margaret Marshall was also a balletgoer, and in December 1951, when Jarrell was spending a year at Princeton and making brief visits to New York, he writes of going with her and Haggin to the City Center. The letter is filled with praise for Tanaquil Le Clercq, comparing her favorably with Danilova in the bride's role in Balanchine's *Le Baiser de la Fée*. How much technical expertise he picked up about the dance is uncertain, but his high pleasure surely is not: "Gee, gee! I almost died of bliss at Tanaquil Le Clercq's best moments (she's so young that when you see her a year later she's much better)." (He felt similar enthusiasm for Lotte Lehmann, his favorite lieder singer, whom he also heard in the company of Haggin.) Jarrell admired the grace, the beauty, the glamour of Balanchine's dancers, particularly his female leads. Apparently, the only thing that could keep him away from a Saturday matinee at City Center was his passion for sports cars. Earlier in 1951, he wrote Hannah Arendt: "I am going to do something rather notably absurd Saturday; instead of going to a matinee (ballet) I am going to Bridgehampton, Long Island, to see the sports car races—all sorts of strange and wonderful and exotic cars."

His feelings about living in New York City were in one sense quite uncomplicated. Two months after he and Mackie began living there (they had now found a permanent apartment on Hudson Street in the Village—"small, expensive, with ingeniously horrid furniture; but with clean walls and shiny kitchen and bathroom"), he was writing Warren that New York was "the worst place to live

I've ever seen" and informing Ransom that it was like an extension of the army. Other letters reveal similar sentiments, nor did the place grow on him with time and increased familiarity. Yet in more ways than one it was extremely important to his identity as a poet, even more so than as a critic. His exposure to music and ballet, encouraged and tutored by Haggin, began to lead him toward kinds of human expressiveness that neither the sober content nor the austere "music" of the army poems had room for. His admiration for the female performer; his developing responsiveness to Balanchine's artistry, which centrally involved the ballerina; his growing fondness for turn-of-the-century Germano-Austrian romantic music (by 1951 he was a lover of Schönberg's *Verklärte Nacht*), which exceeded Haggin's more severely discriminating taste— these inclinations would show themselves, though not always in coherent or satisfying shapes, in the poems written between 1948 and their publication in *The Seven-League Crutches* in 1951.

Besides the friendship with Haggin, he became close to Hannah Arendt, who was then working for Schocken Books and who asked him to translate some German poems, even though his knowledge of German was meager. He also edited the reviews she wrote for *The Nation*, and this led to lunches together, an invitation to her home, and eventually to visits that continued over the next five years, especially during his time at Princeton. Arendt is eloquent about what Jarrell meant to her, especially what he did to open up English poetry for her by reading it aloud, showing her, in her words, "a whole new world of sound and meter [. . .] the specific gravity of English words, whose relative weight, as in all languages, is ultimately determined by poetic usage and standards." As she summed it up, "Whatever I know of English poetry, and perhaps of the genius of the language, I owe to him." There is no mystery about why Jarrell was interested in this extraordinary woman— who would not have been?—but seen in terms of the year in New York, their friendship figures as another aspect of the broadening, the "internationalizing" of his sensibility. He was to publish, in 1947, "Jews at Haifa," a poem about refugees turned back from

Israel and sent instead to a resettlement camp at Cyprus. It paints an exact, unsparing portrait of

> *The hundreds at the rail*
> *Lapped in the blue blaze of this sea*
> *Who stare till their looks fail*
> *At the earth that they are promised; silently*
> *See the sand-bagged machine-guns,*
> *The red-kneed soldiers blinking in the sun.*

This kind of sympathetic observation is not new to Jarrell's poetry, but it could only have been strengthened and extended by knowing Arendt, who was herself about to publish *The Origins of Totalitarianism*. When it appeared in 1951, he wrote her a teasing, loving letter about a photograph of her on the dust jacket which (he said) made her look like "a shy, sincere, serious schoolgirl; you ought to be wearing a dark blue uniform-blouse with *Koenigsburg Gymnasium* lettered on it. It's very touching, but I'll never dare make an unkind remark to you: you would, plainly, burst into tears." Plainly she wouldn't, and that was part of her charm for him.

As for other friends, Lowell and Jean Stafford were living in Maine that year, but he and Jarrell kept in close touch, at one point Jarrell inviting Lowell to accompany him and Mackie to a party given by *The Nation* which—with reference to Lowell's being on the wagon—would be "too dignified for you to need to drink." He added, "I don't drink either." So the comedy of a visit he and Lowell paid John Berryman, who was teaching in Princeton at the time, was heightened in Berryman's account of it by his assertion that on that occasion Jarrell had a hangover, "and that was very amazing because Jarrell did not drink. He's the only poet that I've ever known in the universe who simply did not drink." (This amazing fact was pretty nearly true, although he later qualified his distaste for alcohol enough to admit the occasional German white wine.) The hangover, so Berryman claimed Jarrell claimed, was caused by a poisoned canapé eaten at one of the cocktail parties he had to endure in New York, perhaps the just-mentioned *Nation* event. So at Berryman's house Jarrell proceeded to be "miserable and witty," walking up and down and composing out loud a new Lowell poem with all its stage properties, an activity Lowell did not find amusing. Finally he and Berryman calmed Jarrell down to the point where he ceased making up the "wonderful apocryphal poem by Lowell": "We stationed him on the couch, and I gave him a book of photographs of the Russian ballet (he was very keen on ballet). While the rest of us had dinner, he lay there and made witty remarks about the photographs of the Russian ballet."

Berryman had the last word on this event, and a finely stylized one it was, making things out to be more perfectly comic than they could quite have been in reality. The reality was of course that there were three competitors in the room, three omnivorous poetic imaginations, each surely intent on swallowing up the other two. Both Jarrell and Berryman idolized Haggin; but as Eileen Simpson has pointed out, Berryman's Haggin was not Jarrell's. Lowell was about to publish *Lord Weary's Castle*, his *succès d'estime* and the beginning of a distinguished career; given Jarrell's detailed criticism of the poems in that book (we will come to it shortly), he could think of himself as Lowell's mentor and critical conscience—if not, as Pound was to Eliot, *il miglior fabbro*. Meanwhile, Berryman was to publish *The Dispossessed* (1948), poems Jarrell would review and praise, though with just a hint of patronizing charity toward their weaknesses. And Jarrell himself—"a terror as a reviewer" and "blazing with ambition," as Berryman wrote on different occasions—was still, on the basis of his first two books of poems, something less than fully arrived as a poet. So the room at Princeton bristled with competition, implication, and witty aggression.

The period from war's end through Jarrell's year at *The Nation* does more than merely provide further evidence that he was "a terror as a reviewer"—something he had already demonstrated conclusively in his prewar work in the magazines, especially his *New Republic* exchanges with Cowley and, later, David Daiches in defense of his principles and practice. Little was to be added to that reputation by further demolitions of more poets and their most recent books. About his postwar identity as a powerful figure in the poetry world, R. W. Flint observes:

> To say that he had been a disturbing figure during his years as poetry editor of *The Nation* would be a rash understatement. Not since Poe had an American poet of his distinction laid down the law in quite such a carnival spirit. He reached maturity at the climax of the New Critical era, whose excesses he both relished and deplored with brilliant finality, and could not have been the kind of poet he was had he not been an equally good critic.

It was only one year at *The Nation*, but no matter; Flint is claiming that not even Eliot or Pound—the one an institution, the other institutionalized—could compare with Jarrell, at least insofar as what Flint went on to call "the bacchic exhilaration of his rejections and dislikes." What he neglects to point out is that Jarrell's laying down of the law during his literary editorship consisted not in annihilating bad poets (he ceased to write chronicles for the magazine while he was in charge) but rather in making the strongest case for three American poets whose new books seemed to him to represent the most significant voices in post-modernist poetry: Lowell, Elizabeth Bishop, and William Carlos Williams.

The postwar moment may have had something to do with his impulse to promote these poets—two of them on the basis of their first books, the third on a career that, in Jarrell's eyes, was fully coming into its own. In doing so, Jarrell—who on the basis of *Little Friend, Little Friend* had himself been named by one reviewer as in the front rank of "the new generation of American poets" and second only to Lowell—did something not in his own best interests. It was unusual, that is, for a young poet to elevate his major competitors while perforce keeping silent about his own work; clearly what Flint called his "exhilaration" came out not merely in his dislikes but—really for the first time—in the intensity of his likings. His enthusiasm for *Lord Weary's Castle*, Bishop's *North & South*, and the first book of Williams's *Paterson* was not controlled or even influenced by some strategy whereby he would draw the map of postwar post-Eliotic work. Five years previously he had said that modern poetry had reached "the end of the line"; that it couldn't be any more "modern"—dislocative, experimental, idiosyncratic —than it had become. Auden's method was a way out of modernism, and to write like him, Jarrell felt, was a way of avoiding writing modernist poetry. But that was in the past; Auden no longer seemed someone to be imitated. Lowell, Bishop, and Williams offered three ways of writing poetry which proved there was something at the end of the line after all—or after it.

His efforts on behalf of Lowell's work predated the appearance of *Lord Weary* and are a fascinating study in one poet's attempt to refine and improve the work of a fellow poet and friend. In 1943 he had written Mackie from Chanute Field that Lowell had some poems in the recent *Sewanee* ("original and goodish, though unsatisfactory and queer") which made the two Berryman poems that followed look feeble in comparison. By the end of the next year, however, when Lowell brought out *Land of Unlikeness* in a small edition published by the Cummington Press, with an introduction by Tate, he decided that the poems' originality far outweighed their unsatisfactoriness, and reviewing the book, he called Lowell at his best "a serious, objective, and extraordinarily accomplished poet." "The Drunken Fisherman," one of the few poems from *Land of Unlikeness* which passed virtually unchanged into *Lord Weary*, was judged by Jarrell to be the best poem of any in the books he was reviewing (they included collections by Williams and Marianne Moore). Lowell, he said, was a "really traditional" poet whose basic strength was the language itself.

Jarrell never really demonstrated, in his short review, the force of these assertions, but he was clearly impressed, even awed, by Lowell's "obstinacy of temperament extreme enough to seem a form of violence." Just as he was able to destroy a bad poet with jokes, he could bring a good one to memorable life through humorous one-liners, like the following one about Lowell: "Among the usual rout of Catholic converts he looks like another John the Baptist, all zeal and hair." With a crack at Lowell's and his own erstwhile mentor, now viewed from the perspective of Davis-Monthan Field, he noted that "airplanes [Lowell] treats as Tate does, only more so—he gives the impression of having encountered them in Mother Shipton." But the review's conclusion is unambiguous and boldly forthright in its commitment: "Some of the best poems of the next years ought to be written by him."

Nobody except academic students of Lowell or Jarrell is likely to hunt up a scarce copy of *Land of Unlikeness* (250 copies were printed) to see whether all this fuss was justified. And in fact the book contains almost none of the poems—"The Quaker Graveyard in Nantucket," "Colloquy in Black Rock," "Mr. Edwards and the Spider," and others—for which *Lord Weary* became noted (indeed, a number of its earliest poems were never reprinted). But Jarrell had caught something irresistibly spellbinding in the poet's voice, to be heard here and there in *Land of Unlikeness* and about to burst forth in the splendors of the Quaker Graveyard poem. When in the summer of 1945 Lowell sent him the manuscript of *Lord Weary*, Jarrell seized the occasion as if to make sure his prophecy about Lowell would come true. "I had rather read your poems than anybody else in the world who is writing now," he began in the least uncertain of terms. The letters that followed during the fall never wavered from that commitment: "I think it's terribly important for you to get your book absolutely perfect so far as inclusions, omissions, or little changes are concerned, for this reason: it will be the best first book of poems since Auden's *Poems*, and might, with luck or sense on people's part, be a wonderful success." The critic who had been a scourge to so many books of poetry now found himself utterly taken by Lowell: "You know how little contemporary poetry I like: if I'm affected this way—unless I've gone crazy—it must be the real thing." Only such a conviction could have brought forth the comparison to Auden's book, published fifteen years previously—the magical *Poems* (1930) that he so much admired.

Randall Jarrell, two and a half years old

Eight years old. In Long Beach, California

About fourteen years old

In a high-school production of Arms and the Man

Randall Jarrell, at twenty-four

Randall and Mackie Jarrell, with Kitten

In the army, 1943. Chanute Field, Illinois

Randall Jarrell, Robert Lowell, and Peter Taylor, 1948

Elisabeth Eisler

Randall Jarrell, at Princeton, 1951

In Manhattan, spring 1954

With Mary Jarrell, Alleyne (center), and Beatrice (right), summer 1954.
Laguna Beach, California.

(*Above and facing*)   *In Washington, D.C., June 1957*

Randall Jarrell, June 1958

Teaching. The University of North Carolina at Greensboro, 1963

Randall and Mary Jarrell in Rome, 1963

Yet for all his enthusiasm, he was not blind to Lowell's limitations and he identified them in terms that, retrospectively, refer not merely to the early poems but to Lowell's later career. He faulted Lowell for not putting enough "people" in the poems—for not representing enough the "actions of men"—and for being too "harsh and severe," a shortcoming which, in Jarrell's eyes, Lowell was already alleviating. By criticizing particular phrases, lines, and passages from Lowell's poems, Jarrell hoped and helped to make them less mannered, less pompously solemn. He encouraged Lowell to tone down or rid himself entirely of the "extreme rhetoric" that marred (for example) some recent additions to "The Quaker Graveyard"—phrases like "fiery deluge, corrosive smoulder of its mould," or "time's lubricious feathers." These and other excesses (he pointed out to Lowell) were "awfully contrived and rhetorical, a tour de force but awkward too," and as with most of the suggestions his friend made, Lowell removed the offending lines. This is not to suggest that Lowell was lazy about revising his own work, since he did so continually until his death; nor can one claim that Jarrell's various suggestions made the difference between the success or failure of *Lord Weary's Castle*. But the value of such real, detailed, passionate criticism was inestimable to Lowell. He himself paid tribute to it when, in his memoir of Jarrell, he called him the only man he had ever met "who could make other writers feel that their work was more important to him than his own." "What he did," Lowell continued, "was to make others feel that their realizing themselves was as close to him as his own self-realization, and that he cared as much about making the nature and goodness of someone else's work understood as he cared about making his own understood." It was true disinterestedness—the belief that poetry was so important that whether you or someone else was writing it did not matter. In encouraging Lowell to make his poems "start from a real point of departure in contemporary real life," Jarrell spoke out of what he himself had just accomplished in some of the poems in *Little Friend*. As for the Arnoldian repeated insistence on "real," it was followed by another of Arnold's favorite tags when

147

Jarrell wrote Lowell: "I think you write more in the great tradition, the grand style, the real *middle* of English poetry, than anybody since Yeats." One wonders for a moment what difference it would have made to Jarrell if his own poems had been given the benefit of a comparably searching and ambitious criticism, offered by a critic who could place him historically and who had, above all else, the will to believe in the poems' value. (Admittedly this would have been a forbidding task, since, as Peter Taylor recalls, any attempt to make suggestions to Jarrell about his work invariably met with disbelief and dismissal.)

It remained only for the private reader-critic of Lowell's manuscript to go public, which Jarrell did on the publication of *Lord Weary* in what was probably the most influential review he ever wrote. "From the Kingdom of Necessity" freely cannibalized his earlier review of *Land of Unlikeness*, especially its best jokes; but it went on at greater length, combining a valuable discussion of Lowell's "odd and imaginative Catholicism," and the way it governed his poems, with an analysis of his poetic technique. He had written Lowell that the book could be the best first book of poems since Auden's, and already other reviewers, in their praise, had backed him up. He had also told Lowell that his poems were "in the great tradition," a claim he now affirmed by insisting that Lowell's intensity was equaled by his organization:

> Inside its elaborate stanzas the poem is put together like a mosaic: the shifts of movement, the varied pauses, the alternation in the length of sentences, and the counterpoint between lines and sentences are the outer form of a subject matter that has been given a dramatic, dialectical internal organization; and it is hard to exaggerate the strength and life, the constant richness and surprise of metaphor and sound and motion, of the language itself.

Such organization was much closer to traditional English poetry than to the "semi-imagist" organization of modernist verse, although Lowell complicated the traditional by "stream-of-consciousness, dream, or dramatic-monologue types of structure." Summing up, Jarrell called Lowell's work—rather confusingly, it must be said—"a unique fusion of modernist and traditional poetry [. . .] essentially a post- or anti-modernist poetry, and as such is certain to be influential."

One sees Jarrell straining these at best inadequate terms so as to render his sense of Lowell's originality and the way his individual talent took its place in Eliot's "tradition," thereby altering that tradition. He praised Lowell's more recent work for moving toward a less constricted and less rhetorical descriptiveness, toward a more "dramatic" speech, like the "clear, open, and speech-like" voice in "Katherine's Dream" (part III of "Between the Porch and the Altar"). Though he could hardly foresee the poems Lowell would be writing in a decade and would publish in *Life Studies*, Jarrell encouraged in him the openness he was increasingly to achieve in his own poetry.

David Kalstone put the matter succinctly when he pointed out that Jarrell was interested in poetry "that accommodated more of the human voice and its contradictions—hence his attraction, from early on, to dramatic monologues." No wonder, then, that he advised Lowell to moderate harshness and severity in the interests of more mixed attitudes toward life and other people. Of Jarrell's mentors, neither Tate nor Warren showed any such mixed response to things. The grim violence of Tate's attitude toward both life and language was something Jarrell had rejected; while, after reading Warren's *Selected Poems* (1944), he wrote to Amy Breyer deBlasio that "the world and everything in it, in them, is so purely Original Sin, horror, loathing, morbidness, final evil, that to somebody who knows Red it's plain he manages his life by pushing all the evil in it out into the poems and novels. All his theory says is that the world is nothing but evil, whereas the practice he lives by says exactly the opposite."

For all his admiration of Warren's life and character, Jarrell had a moral objection to his poetry, and "moral" is also the word that should be used in speaking of his high estimate of the books published in mid-1946 by Williams and Bishop. The "beauty, delicacy, and intelligence" he found in the best parts of *Paterson (Book I)* had importantly to do with its "musical" organization of themes, which organization he described in his review. But it had also, inseparably, to do with the human complication of Williams's voice, heard in *Paterson* in ways that for Jarrell were "beautiful and un-expected"; as in the opening of the third part of Book I:

> *How strange you are, you idiot!*
> *So you think because the rose*
> *is red that you shall have the mastery?*
> *The rose is green and will bloom,*
> *overtopping you, green, livid*
> *green when you shall no more speak, or*
> *taste, or even be. My whole life*
> *has hung too long upon a partial victory.*

Or the following voice from the second part:

> *Only of late, late! begun to know, to*
> *know clearly (as through clear ice) whence*
> *I draw my breath or how to employ it*
> *clearly—if not well:*
>
> *Clearly!*
> *speaks the red-breast his behest. Clearly!*
> *clearly!*

Jarrell quoted this red-breast passage in order to show how im-portant were Williams's repetitions in unifying the various themes of his long poem. But those repetitions were also satisfying for the way they expressed a human voice searching and seeking, moved and excited by the things it is now able to say, the new words it has discovered. This blend of motives and elements Jarrell found morally satisfying; it was "wonderful and unlikely that this extraor-dinary mixture of the most delicate lyricism of perception and feeling with the hardest and homeliest actuality should ever have come into being!" And it is what, for him, constituted Williams's

Americanness: "There has never been a poem more American," he asserted, predicting—what later he would have to take back—that *Paterson* when completed would be the "best very long poem that any American has written."

After this effusion over the "geological event" of *Paterson*, he wrote two long paragraphs of exclamatory appreciation of Bishop's *North & South*. Jarrell had met Bishop during the year in New York and invited her to a dinner to which he also invited Lowell, whom she had not met; thus a triumvirate was formed, each member of which, over the years, boosted the others' work. In his brief notice of *North & South*, Jarrell did nothing that could pass for analysis of the poems but, rather, engaged in a practice he would often adopt when the poet under consideration was someone he wanted to praise. The "method"—though it is hardly that—consisted of a liberal use of adjectives and nouns to suggest the qualities present in Bishop's poems. His favorites—"The Fish" and "Roosters"—are "calmly beautiful, deeply sympathetic"; others are "charming" or "beautiful fragments"; generally the poems are "pleasant and sympathetic," and show "restraint, calm, and proportion" in their workmanship and organization. Bishop's art is "unusually personal and honest in its wit, perception, and sensitivity," and "all her poems have written underneath, *I have seen it*." His major claim is:

> She is morally so attractive [. . .] because she understands so well that the wickedness and confusion of the age can explain and extenuate other people's wickedness and confusion, but not, for you, your own; that morality, for the individual, is usually a small, personal, statistical, but heartbreaking or heartwarming affair of omissions and commissions the greatest of which will seem infinitesimal, ludicrously beneath notice, to those who govern, rationalize, and deplore.

The sequence of clauses continues, the pressure mounting until it is artfully released as he quotes the end of "The Fish" and—as Bishop did the fish—lets us go.

It might be noted that such "positive" recommendation relies on generalized adjectives like "sympathetic" and "honest" to convey the quality of a poet's work. A few years after the review, having bought a copy of *North & South* to give someone as a gift, he reread the poems and wrote Bishop that the best of them were "just wonderful [. . .] especially for the tone and moral attitude, or whatever you'd call it"—a similarly vague recommendation. And when, in the concluding paragraph of his introduction to Williams's *Selected Poems* (1949), Jarrell called those poems "honest, exact, and original," and praised their "generosity and sympathy, their moral and human attractiveness," he was resorting to currency that doesn't really distinguish them from Bishop's or Ransom's, both of which he characterized with similar terms. To what extent he was aware of this limitation and whether he thought of it as a problem for the critic of poetry, one can't say; but in the Williams introduction he set forth as a principle in writing about contemporaries the following caveat:

> The most important thing that criticism can do for a poet, while he is alive, is to establish that atmosphere of interested respect which gets his poems a reasonably careful reading.

For Williams—as surely for Lowell and Bishop—such an atmosphere was just beginning to be established, and Jarrell enriched it.

We will defer more extended dealing with the rhetorical procedure employed in his major appreciative essays on Whitman, Frost, Stevens, Moore, and others. Here it can be said that his notion of the best way to establish "interested respect" for the poets he cared about usually did not involve detailed exegesis of individual poems—of the sort that New Critics like Tate and Warren and Brooks were so good at, and that he himself practiced brilliantly in his thesis on Housman. Rather his "method" was a good deal more hit-and-run. He mentions or quotes attractive bits from poems by Bishop or Williams as examples of the "moral and human attractiveness" he finds in their work generally, or at its best. Implicitly or directly, he challenges readers to see for themselves whether the case as stated is in fact the case—in other words, he insists that we actually *read* the poet in question. David Kalstone refers to Jarrell's motive during the postwar years, when he wrote his most influential critical reviews and essays, as "outflanking the New Critics." But that may be to put it a little more strategically than necessary and to emphasize insufficiently the temperamental difference between him and his more academic peers. Jarrell's hunger for or yearning after the "real" in life or in poems was not to be satisfied by the universities—here he agreed somewhat with Williams's anti-intellectualism. But it could be satisfied by teaching, so long as that teaching was inseparable from reading and from the sense of what mattered to people with ordinary resources of sympathy and honesty. If modernism had reached the end of the line, then it made sense to look for old-fashioned qualities and virtues in poems that were alive, that were "real." Such a program could be grass-roots reactionary or philistine; but Jarrell's wit and learning and humor made it something else again.

While in New York he supplemented his salary at *The Nation* by giving a writing course during the academic year at Sarah Lawrence, where Robert Fitzgerald and Mary McCarthy were also teaching. The president of Sarah Lawrence, Harold Taylor, had read Jarrell's war poems, been impressed by them as well as by his critical writings, and invited him up to give a talk, after which he extended Jarrell a one-year invitation to fill in for an absent colleague. In Taylor's memory, Jarrell wasn't much in evidence at Sarah Lawrence, heading back for New York after he had taught his class; but in fact the writer was making mental notes on the place, and on its president, who would be celebrated—if that is the word—as Dwight Robbins, head of the fictional Benton College of *Pictures from an Institution*. (Taylor would also figure in McCarthy's novel *The Groves of Academe*, causing him—as he put it years later—to think twice before appointing visiting "novelist-teachers with a predisposition to carve people up.")

There is something fitting in Jarrell's moving from Sarah Lawrence to another women's college, the Woman's College of the University of North Carolina in Greensboro, where, except for brief stints elsewhere, he taught happily for the rest of his life. The invitation from Greensboro was instigated by Peter Taylor, who had moved there from New York in the fall of 1946. Earlier in that year, the friendship between him and Jarrell had deepened during the few months they were both living in New York City. In his reminiscence of Jarrell, Taylor recalled that, when in 1947 he told a friend that Jarrell was coming down to Greensboro to be interviewed, the friend predicted that he would be stifled in such a "Southern female seminary." But Taylor noted that the "very advanced, very experimental institution" where Jarrell taught while living in New York—Sarah Lawrence—conducted its education through conferences and required no grades from the instructor. There was something unreal about this (like living in New York) and Taylor says shrewdly that Jarrell, with his passion for the "real" as it showed itself in the poems of Williams or Bishop or Lowell —and in his own work—was exactly suited to Greensboro, North Carolina. Its "seminary atmosphere" was preferable to the liberated world of Sarah Lawrence; the only thing the two institutions had in common was the presence of some bright young women, an important continuity. To Margaret Marshall, on the eve of her return to *The Nation*, Jarrell wrote that he had been impressed by the Greensboro campus, large enough to contain both "an abandoned golf-course and a pine forest on it. But," he concluded, "New York makes you a sucker for anywhere else."

Perhaps so; still, he had benefited hugely from his year there, mainly in the widening and in some cases the deepening of his intellectual and personal friendships: Haggin and Agee; Hannah Arendt and her husband, Heinrich Blücher; Robert Fitzgerald, Rahv and the *Partisan* group; Bishop and Lowell and Williams; Peter and Eleanor Taylor, whom he would follow to Greensboro. For a man who had spent his army years in isolated spots, and who previous to that had been pretty much pinned down in Texas, New York must have felt like the place where everybody, even

Auden, at some point came to live. About the city he would never say—as he did about Europe after his first trip there in 1948— that it had changed his life. Yet in living there he opened himself up to the possibility held out at the end of his poem "The Märchen," published that spring of 1946: "Neither to rule nor die? to change, to change!"

SIX

A Country Life

IN August of 1947, Jarrell invited Lowell, then Poetry Consultant to the Library of Congress, to visit the Jarrells and the Taylors in Greensboro:

> We ought to be moving into our house—I'm sure Peter's written all the details—in the first week in September. We'll have two extra bedrooms; you'd better come and stay a lot— we'll put a cot in the doorway between the two, so you'll get full value from both. This is a nice tennis town, and I've been playing a great deal. We really are getting to feel pre-war, non-New-York, just one more version of pastoral.

The pastoral idea was inspired partly by their living temporarily in the house of Marc Friedlaender, an English department colleague who owned what Jarrell described to Haggin (whom he also invited to come and stay) as "a tremendous modernist house—15 or 20 rooms—in a pine-forest, twenty yards from a lake." Getting to feel "pre-war," as he put it to Lowell, had partly to do—since New York felt like an extension of the army—with recovering the rural aspects of his life at Kenyon and at Texas; he once referred to his and Mackie's house outside Austin as a "cottage in the country." So this "version of pastoral" is not only a jokey allusion to William

156

Empson's book but a way of imagining his life as consisting of homely circumstance, pine forest, and recreation, with plenty of time and space to read and write. Even when classes began, the pressure felt minimal. He wrote Lowell in November that by contrast with Sarah Lawrence, where people tried unsuccessfully to get him to go to meetings, "Greensboro leaves one alone just wonderfully—we've had to go out to dinner only once, and in six weeks of school we've had one meeting of any kind."

The new house to which Lowell was invited was a duplex purchased by the Jarrells and Taylors at 1924 Spring Garden Street. If not so pleasantly rural a retreat as the Friedlaenders', it was conveniently near the Woman's College and afforded the two couples a chance to develop their friendship. Eleanor Taylor remembers Jarrell "ensconced on the couch in their living room with an afghan over his legs, looking out the window behind the couch (where Kitten was often perched), a coal fire going in the grate, with his writing in his lap—the athlete in invalid's trappings—or, perhaps, the wolf in grandmother's nightgown." She was struck by how he had no use for work—the sort of work necessary to get the duplex into shape: "Once we found [him] painting a room, and Randall said almost tearfully, 'I don't *like* it. I just happen to be good at it!' " Evidently he was not so good at mowing a lawn, since the rye grass the Taylors persuaded him to plant (by telling him it didn't need to be cut) was allowed to grow rank and untroubled.

He had mixed feelings about the quality of his students at the Woman's College. Soon after classes began in the fall, he wrote Hannah Arendt that he had several good students in his modern poetry and poetry writing classes: "The first day one of them, to my great amazement, turned in a faithful imitation of Robert Lowell. But the only thing to do with the freshmen here is to write a ballet with a Chorus of Peasant Girls for them." A couple of years later, momentarily fed up with his students, he wrote to Margaret Marshall that "the average North Carolina girl talks as if she were an imbecile with an ambition to be an idiot." And in a note from the same month to Bishop, he said that he had been reading lots of anthropology "and now amuse myself by looking at the North Carolina faces and deciding they're full of Paleolithic survivals or else fell against a wall early in life." These killer remarks, of the sort that would go into a novel he was soon to write, were obviously designed to amuse his sophisticated Northern correspondents— Arendt, Lowell, and Bishop. But he was not merely sarcastic, as would be shown by "A Girl in a Library" (published in 1951), in which he took the North Carolina female intelligence, voice, and face, and turned it into what was—if not a ballet—the richest, most varied dramatic narrative he had yet composed.

He came to teach at Greensboro with his third book of poetry, *Losses*, set for publication (by his original publisher, Harcourt) in March 1948, and with what he saw as two-thirds of an additional book. Or so he had written Lowell the previous summer, with the · probable knowledge that he had not attained the reputation Lowell had gained through *Lord Weary's Castle*—a reputation significantly boosted by Jarrell's own review. *Lord Weary* won Lowell the Pulitzer Prize and an award from the National Institute of Arts and Letters; also an invitation to serve as Poetry Consultant to the Library of Congress and a Guggenheim Fellowship. Neither saw anything wrong with reviewing the other's books, and Lowell was slated to write about *Losses*, then begged off on grounds that he was engaged in a complicated and painful dispute involving charges he had brought against the director of the Yaddo writers' colony at Saratoga. Stephen Spender did review *Losses*, in *The Nation*, calling Jarrell's language as "distinctive in its way" as Lowell's and also praising him for being "preoccupied with the question of the nature of man." But a more interesting review than Spender's (or than Robert Fitzgerald's brief one in *The New Republic*) was a mainly adverse assessment in *Poetry* by the British poet W. S. Graham.

Graham felt that Jarrell's name both as poet and critic by now carried enough prestige that it was fair to point to what Graham saw as a great gulf between reputation and achievement. He first complained about the notes Jarrell had provided for some of the poems, as if such "painstaking documentation"—of the meaning of a military term or the identity of a speaker—could provide a helpful connection between the reporting of poetic experience and its verifiability in the "real" world. More important, Graham detected in Jarrell's work a fear of "formal, consciously 'made' poetry," with the result that the poetry seemed diffuse, the prosody old-fashioned: "Always the texture of the poem is as loose and casual as possible, as though attempting to hide the fact that the words follow each other in an order chosen for any conscious poetic end." Finally he objected, as Jarrell had tellingly with Auden, to the presence of so many capitalized Lifes and Deaths; to what Graham called—in "Burning the Letters," the war poem Jarrell thought his best—"a deafening organ-peal of the pseudo-profound." By contrast, the side of Jarrell that appealed to him was one that—as Graham first pointed out—was influenced by Robert Frost, echoes of whose "deceptively homely but polished verse" could be heard in the more successful poems from *Losses*, which also showed traces of Hardy.

Graham's criticism marked the first time anyone had stood up and said what there was to be said *against* Jarrell's poetry. His two main complaints—that Jarrell's texture and prosody were too casual and that in his efforts to speak grandly about life and death Jarrell was sometimes too solemn for his own good—remain lively issues for anyone coming to terms with the poetry. Although Hayden Carruth, in a reply to Graham's review, attributed the English poet's dissatisfaction to the fact that he didn't understand American cadences, the explanation is doubtful—especially since Graham had admired Jarrell's work in the past and admired parts of *Losses*. One should rather acknowledge this critic's wisdom in identifying a strain of the vatic profundity Jarrell had been such a merciless critic of in other writers. And in citing Frost's name, Graham put his finger on the poet whose influence was beginning to be felt in Jarrell's work.

Jarrell had come relatively late to an appreciation of Frost's poetry. In his Kenyon days he had been contemptuous of Frost; rereading him in 1947—as he prepared to review *Steeple Bush* and deliver a summer lecture on Frost at Indiana University—he changed his mind. Or, rather, he became concerned to distinguish Frost's best work from that of what he called, wittily, "the Farmer-Poet [. . .] a sort of Olympian Will Rogers out of *Tanglewood Tales*." In his own career, Jarrell had long aspired to get more "speech" into his poems, but didn't think of Frost as a poet notable for such effects. It is likely that his conversations with Lowell, who was himself attempting to loosen up his forms so as to accommodate the sound of someone talking, spurred the interest in Frost. But there were other, less purely technical reasons for the interest, which would be expressed in the brilliant 1952 essay "To the Laodiceans" that found in Frost the moral and human attractiveness Jarrell had already praised in Bishop and Williams.

Williams, like Frost, was also a postwar discovery for Jarrell, whose laudatory review of *Paterson (Book I)* led to an invitation from Williams and James Laughlin, his publisher, to write an introduction to a *Selected Poems*. Jarrell wrote mockingly to Lowell about how Tate had told him that "he was glad you and I were back to writing about 'the really good poets' after Williams and Frost—that we made too great claims for 'Bill Williams.' " Evident is both his irreverence toward Tate's lordliness and his embracing of the "Americanness" of Frost and Williams, of a colloquial "plain American that cats and dogs can read" (a phrase from Marianne Moore that Jarrell liked to quote). When *Losses* was published, he had a copy sent to Williams, whose response was, Jarrell said, the most interesting thing anybody had ever written about his poetry (the letter has not survived). In reply, he sent Williams a just-finished long poem, "The Night Before the Night Before Christmas," and a letter explaining that, as to technique, he rarely wrote in "regular ballad forms" anymore; rather, "by having irregular line lengths, a good deal of irregularity of scansion, and lots of rhyming, not just perfect regular rhymes, musical forms, repetitions, 'paragraphing,' speech-like effects, and so on, you can make a long poem seem a lot shorter and liver." That he seriously miscalculated in the overlong and at times incoherent poem he sent to Williams is less important than the kind of stylistic attempt he was making.

In other words, the "loosening effect on the poetic line" that W. S. Graham deplored in most of the poems from *Losses* was exactly what Jarrell was in practice trying to achieve. (Graham objected specifically to the trailing-off sequence of dots [. . .] that Jarrell grew even more fond of in later work and that served to break up any rhythmical tautness.) Of course it does not dispose of a critic's objection to the poet's style to say that, in fact, the poet was working to achieve just such a style; and in addition, Graham found looseness of phrasing and word order in some of the "tight," regularly structured war poems. Still, there is enough "formal, consciously 'made' poetry" (Graham's words for what he found lacking in *Losses*) to suggest that Jarrell knew he could write that sort of poem pretty well and was determined to risk himself in a less protected manner than what became standard academic–*New Yorker* verse in the 1950s. For example, Graham thought the most successful poem in the book was "A Camp in the Prussian Forest," and evidently others agreed with him, since it became one of Jarrell's most reprinted poems. No doubt its subject matter—the death camps—has had more to do with its popularity than any aesthetic considerations.

> *I walk beside the prisoners to the road.*
> *Load on puffed load,*
> *Their corpses, stacked like sodden wood,*
> *Lie barred or galled with blood*
>
> *By the charred warehouse. No one comes today*
> *In the old way*
> *To knock the fillings from their teeth;*
> *The dark, coned, common wreath*
>
> *Is plaited for their grave—a kind of grief.*
> *The living leaf*

Clings to the planted profitable
Pine if it is able;

The boughs sigh, mile on green, calm, breathing mile,
From this dead file
The planners ruled for them. . . . One year
They sent a million here:

Here men were drunk like water, burnt like wood.
The fat of good
And evil, the breast's star of hope
Were rendered into soap.

I paint the star I sawed from yellow pine—
And plant the sign
In soil that does not yet refuse
Its usual Jews

Their first asylum. But the white, dwarfed star—
This dead white star—
Hides nothing, pays for nothing; smoke
Fouls it, a yellow joke,

The needles of the wreath are chalked with ash,
A filmy trash
Litters the black woods with the death
Of men; and one last breath

Curls from the monstrous chimney. . . . I laugh aloud
Again and again;
The star laughs from its rotting shroud
Of flesh. O star of men!

Jarrell's note to the poem tells us that the Nazis forced the Jews
to wear a yellow star; that the Star of David, which the narrator

has presumably constructed a homemade version of, marks a Jew's grave; and that the poem is spoken by an American soldier after the capture of this death camp.

Surely the first thing to remark about "A Camp in the Prussian Forest" is its lucidity. Compared to most of the poems in *Blood for a Stranger* and *Little Friend, Little Friend*, it is uncluttered with verbiage and rhetoric, clear in its argument, modest in its vocabulary and the pitch of its voice. There is a pattern to the alternating iambic line lengths, and the rhymes are artfully disposed, with a different rhyme pattern to the concluding stanza. Through enjambment, the voice achieves forward movement, thrusting us along a tight syntactical curve ("The living leaf / Clings to the planted profitable / Pine if it is able") over lines and sometimes over one stanza to the next. It is a thoroughly professional performance as well as an imaginable and dignified way of speaking about an unspeakable subject. Its virtues were not lost on Graham or the anthologists.

Yet who speaks in it? Jarrell's note identifying the speaker as an American soldier seems wishful thinking, for nothing in the poem demands such a presumption. Or rather, there is nothing in the cut of the speech (and is it "speech" anyway?) that identifies it as emanating from an American soldier. We hear instead an impersonal "I" who knows and feels deeply about the death camp, the Jews, the Prussian forest, and whose only response to the horror of it all is the exclamatory irony of the poem's final words: "O star of men!" And if we try to imagine a real soldier, there on the scene and reporting to us what he did and said—"I laugh aloud / Again and again"—it begins to sound ludicrous, since there is something too stagy about this imagined figure, standing there, looking at the "monstrous chimney" whose "last breath" is expiring. In other words, "A Camp in the Prussian Forest" is an extremely "regular" poem that doesn't attempt to exploit the irregularities—of rhyme, of "paragraphing," of the "speech-like effects" he spoke of in his letter to Williams. In its statement of a decorous grief it demonstrates, rather, how capable and controlled Jarrell's poetry could be. And other poems in *Losses* reveal a similar formality, like "The Breath of Night," "Jews at Haifa," "A Field Hospital," and "A Ward in the States."

One speculates that he might have gone on producing these short lyrics, all of them spoken or narrated by an omniscient impersonal authority who thinks about things in large, even cosmic terms. Hearing the "owl's soft cry [in] the forest," the speaker in "The Breath of Night" concludes:

> *Here too, though death is hushed, though joy*
> *Obscures, like night, their wars,*
> *The beings of this world are swept*
> *By the Strife that moves the stars.*

Or, in lines quoted earlier from "Jews at Haifa," he contemplates Jewish survivors, turned back from the promised land,

> *Who stare till their looks fail*
> *At the earth that they are promised; silently*
> *See the sand-bagged machine-guns,*
> *The red-kneed soldiers blinking in the sun.*

Intelligent, sympathetic, free of quirks and perversities—in contrast to Lowell's poems of that period, which were full of such things —"Jews at Haifa" is the sort of poem Jarrell learned to write and then decided was not, somehow, expressive of enough in him and in his country; there were sources of life and kinds of speech—a range of, however vaguely, "American" energies—which could not be tapped by the poet who spoke as a godlike, understanding presence. So he determined to explore other stylistic directions.

Such exploration took place in the opening poem of *Losses*, "Lady Bates," which was written after he moved to Greensboro and adopted a Southern setting in place of what had been for the last few years mainly a military-international one. Lady Bates (the "Lady" is a given name, not a nickname) is a little black girl who died—we are not told how—by "mistake," and the poem offers an ironic and affectionate celebration of her brief, undistinguished life. "Poor black trash, / The wind has blown you away forever," says the narrator at one point, his idiom both rueful and irreverent about one more of our human losses. The opening section (or "paragraph," as he called the blocks of which his longer poems were composed) of "Lady Bates" establishes its overall tone and posture toward the dead girl:

> *The lightning of a summer*
> *Storm wakes, in her clay cave*
> *At the end of the weeds, past the mock-orange tree—*
> *Where she would come barefooted, curled-up-footed*
> *Over the green, grained, rotting fruit*
> *To eat blackberries, a scratched handful—*
> *The little Lady Bates.*
> *You have played too long today.*
> *Open your eyes, Lady.*
>   *Is it a dream*
> *Like the ones your mother used to talk away*
> *When you were little and thought dreams were real?*
> *Here dreams are real.*
> *There are no more dreams, no more real—*
> *There is no more night, there is no more day.*

"Lady Bates" was one of the poems Williams liked best in *Losses*, perhaps because it conforms to no preestablished form or stanza into which the "content" is poured. Instead, the voice seems to be spontaneously discovering what it has to say, which direction it will take, and to what lengths a particular line or sentence will go. Its few rhymes arise as though by chance, improvisation, even whim ("today," "away," "day"; the repetition of "dream" and "real," with the latter as end word three lines running). And the variable lines—especially at the beginning, where they pile up clauses that both look ahead to and delay first mention of the child's name until the seventh line—give a further air of improvisation, of a poetic voice that is making up what it can say about its subject.

This is a poetry of statement, of relaxed assertion; or rather, the trick is to make it *seem* relaxed, with all the tensions and ambiguities of modernist poetry unpacked, leveled out into an open, unclenched hand:

> *They looked for you east, they looked for you west,*
> *And they lost you here in the cuckoo's nest*
> *Eating the sweet white heart of the grass. . . .*
> *You died before you had even had your hair straightened*
> *Or waited on anybody's table but your own.*

The humor is bittersweet, the voice detached yet pitying. Like one of Williams's own "pure products of America" who "go crazy," Lady Bates—"A black, barefooted, pigtailed, trifling ghost"— never had a chance, until her spirit met up with a poet. But then neither did the ball turret gunner or the Jews who were exterminated in the Prussian forest. Jarrell looked for "losses" as the core experience of his poetry. He had no time for the winner, the conqueror, the successful or productive life; these were somehow outside the realm of poetry's truest business.

Longer than most of the poems he had previously written, "Lady Bates" is a departure not only from the relative formality of earlier work but also from strong decorum—a rigid sense of what goes with what, what should or shouldn't be said. For example, in a small allegory we are told what happens to the dead girl's soul:

> *Day and Night met in the twilight by your tomb*
> *And shot craps for you; and Day said, pointing to your soul,*
> *"This* bad *young colored lady,"*
> *And Night said, "Poor little nigger girl."*

A few lines later the poem ends, as a third speaker, Death, commands Lady never to awake: " 'You can't move, can you? / You can't move. . . . / You're fast asleep, you're fast asleep.' " What does one make of such writing? Yvor Winters, who heard Jarrell's recording of it for the Library of Congress, pronounced his style of reading "very dramatic, very emotional, and very bad." (It is doubtful that Winters liked the poem any better than its recitation.)

A less hostile description of Jarrell's reading voice might note that its expressive pauses and hesitations seem an attempt to suggest strong qualities of feeling behind the speaking voice. Given Jarrell's rather choked and high-pitched delivery, the results *are* less than appealing; yet it is clear that he knows what he wants to do with his pauses and questionings, and has not just, suddenly and un-accountably, written a "bad" poem. To Winters, who knew exactly what form should consist of in poetry, "Lady Bates" was formless. But it is unlikely that we can be similarly of one mind about it. "Lady Bates" has no interest in imposing itself on us as a com-manding piece of rhetoric that emanated from a poet in full control of things. It is more wayward and private, even dreamlike in its hushed folktale aura, and a harbinger of much to come in the poems.

The appearance in the fall of 1947 of Frost's *A Masque of Mercy* gave Jarrell an excuse to write a review that would put the case for what (in the review's title) he called "The Other Robert Frost"—the subtle, strange, wonderful poet who, for all his popular acclaim, had not yet been truly seen for the severe artist he was. He would return to the task of describing this Frost, at greater length, in his essay "To the Laodiceans"; for the moment he was content, with-out much particular demonstration, to throw out in challengingly assertive terms his claim for the poet's enormous virtues:

> Frost's seriousness and honesty; the bare sorrow with which, sometimes, things are accepted as they are, neither exagger-ated nor explained away; the many, many poems in which there are real people with their real speech and real thoughts and real emotions—all this, in conjunction with so much sub-tlety and exactness, such classical understatement and re-straint, makes the reader feel that he is not in a book but in a world, and a world that has in common with his own some of the things that are most important in both.

This repeated emphasis on the "real" as an honorific term, and also the praise of subtlety, understatement, and restraint, were not

detached observations about another poet's style; in their enthusiastic heartfeltness they show us a writer very much concerned
with doing likewise in his own poems. Whatever the virtues of
Jarrell's early Audenesque rhetoric, or his grimly repetitive insistence on matters of life and death in the war poems from *Little
Friend* (and in those from *Losses* like "The Dead Wingman," "Pilots, Man Your Planes," and "Burning the Letters"), the poems
were short on "real speech" and lacked the "understatement" of
things exactly rendered so as to bring the reader into a shared
world of objects held in common.

Frost's example informs Jarrell's writing in the three poems from
Losses written so near publication date that they were not published
in magazines beforehand. They have a common concern with representing ordinariness, with what a later poem of his called "the
dailiness of life." "When I Was Home Last Christmas . . ." is a
short, sad remembrance of a dead love affair; "Moving" is a longer,
fluctuating consideration of the past, seen through the eyes and
spoken in the voice of a young girl who is leaving her town and
school ("I shall never again sing / Good morning, Dear Teacher,
to my own dear teacher"). In "A Country Life," the subtlest—
eventually to the point of obscurity—of these poems, we observe
him doing new things with the poetic line, as it works to create a
speaking voice new to his work:

> *A bird that I don't know,*
> *Hunched on his light-pole like a scarecrow,*
> *Looks sideways out into the wheat*
> *The wind waves under the waves of heat.*
> *The field is yellow as egg-bread dough*
> *Except where (just as though they'd let*
> *It live for looks) a locust billows*
> *In leaf-green and shade-violet,*
> *A standing mercy.*
> *The bird calls twice, "Red clay, red clay";*
> *Or else he's saying, "Directly, directly."*

If someone came by I could ask,
Around here all of them must know—
And why they live so and die so—
Or why, for once, the lagging heron
Flaps from the little creek's parched cresses
Across the harsh-grassed, gullied meadow
To the black, rowed evergreens below.

The poem goes on to inquire about the meaning of "a country life," of any life ("And why they live so and die so—") whose "random, clutched-for, homefelt blisses" seem no more nor less than "The circumstances of an accident." But the important thing to note is Jarrell's successful attempt, in the first part of the poem, to effect a more tentative, less overwhelming manner than was his wont in earlier "metaphysical" poems about ultimate concerns. The opening line establishes a speaker who can't name what's in front of him and later can't identify what the unknown bird is saying; who "could ask" someone else—someone familiar (as the speaker is not) with this landscape, this "country life"—if only someone would come along (no one does). The line lengths and the pacing are irregular, never providing a definitive rhythm, always sounding a little "off" to the ear; they help create a somewhat meandering voice, with its parenthetical observation, its "Or else," and its generally modest scope of knowledge. This is Jarrell's way of humanizing and making more ingratiating his address to the reader by raising questions the poem cannot answer:

The farthest farmer in a field,
A gaunt plant grown, for seed, by farmers,
Has felt a longing, lorn urbanity
Jailed in his breast; and, just as I,
Has grunted, in his old perplexity,
A standing plea.

Nobody would mistake this for Frost, but I think it no accident that the poem's title and its inhabitants (a bird, a farmer in a field) give a nod in the direction of the poet Jarrell was becoming increasingly involved with, even as he took up a country life in semi-rural circumstances in Greensboro, North Carolina.

It is hard for the critic effectively to present poems like "Lady Bates" and "A Country Life" because, not very much read and too long to quote entire, they work—when they do work—by involving us in an associative, speculative movement that avoids strong climaxes and summary moments when everything comes together into significance. Like so many of Jarrell's earlier poems, they feel uneven in tone, always on the verge of vagueness or obscurity. Having Frost in mind in "A Country Life" doesn't keep Jarrell, at the end of the poem, from drifting toward the profound, or false-profound, as he imagines the "naked clay" that awaits country lives, all our lives:

> *After some words, the body is forsaken. . . .*
> *The shadows lengthen, and a dreaming hope*
> *Breathes, from the vague mound,* Life;
> *From the grove under the spire*
> *Stars shine, and a wandering light*
> *Is kindled for the mourner, man.*
> *The angel kneeling with the wreath*
> *Sees, in the moonlight, graves.*

It's not just the mound that is vague in these closing lines but the entire situation—hardly a situation, in fact, but a series of intoned, "deep" words (*"Life,"* "spire," "light," "man"), all brought on by one of those ellipses or breakings-off (after "forsaken") of which Jarrell became enamored. There is simply not enough pressure on the line, or on the individual words, to make the writing seem otherwise than soft, flaccid, and all-too-inspiring. Frostian subtlety and understatement have been supplanted by something hollower.

Writing about *Losses* in *Partisan Review*, Leslie Fiedler taxed Jarrell with not having a style, a voice of his own. He noted the variety of subjects taken on by the poems, but asked, "Whose is the speaking voice?" In fact, although Fiedler's question was a good one, the poems in *Losses* show a widening of possible dictions. The literary-critical climate in postwar America was dominated by New Criticism and its sense that above all else the poem must be unified, must exhibit an achieved tension among its parts, must show form and content inextricably tied up with each other. The speaking voice of its ideal poem would be detached, ironic, witty, or mordant, and committed to a less than sanguine view of human character and possibility. Lowell's *Lord Weary's Castle* conformed, at least in outline, to such principles, but the newer poems in *Losses* were cut from a different cloth. As previously noted, neither Frost nor Williams won the seal of approval of the New Critic par excellence, Allen Tate; yet—or is it therefore?—they were the modern poets Jarrell was most engaged with at the close of the 1940s. What happened next was that, having committed himself to admiring and using these two very American models, something quite different intruded on his consciousness when, just after the publication of *Losses*, he discovered Europe and fell in love with one of its citizens.

In a letter to Lowell in February 1948, before *Losses* was published and during Lowell's tenure as Poetry Consultant to the Library of Congress, Jarrell suggested that they might give a party for Frost that spring, when all three men would be in Greensboro for the college's Spring Arts Forum. He told Lowell that he was planning to teach Frost that summer, along with Eliot (not in the least an obvious twosome in 1948), at the Salzburg Seminar in American Civilization. This seminar, then in its second year, was a six-week gathering of American teachers and European students sponsored by the American government and the Harvard Student Council. Jarrell hoped that Lowell might be able to accompany him to Salzburg (there was provision for an "assistant"), but because of Lowell's record as a conscientious objector, the State Department refused to issue him a passport. (Mackie, who might conceivably have served as such an assistant, did not go to Salzburg but visited her family in Texas.)

F. O. Matthiessen had taught at the first of the Salzburg gatherings the previous summer, and in the book he immediately wrote about it—*From the Heart of Europe* (1948)—he provided an eloquent, if rather sentimental, testimony as to how moving an experience it was to come together and talk about literature with a wide range of European students at a time when the Second World War was fresh in everyone's mind, and the future of Europe and the world in jeopardy. When Jarrell, a few months after his return to America, attended a meeting of the American seminar participants, he found Matthiessen agreeable but found Matthiessen's account of life at Leopoldskron—the castle where the seminar took place—remote from his own experience. "It wasn't our Leopoldskron. Or our Europe, either," he remarked in a letter written to Elisabeth Eisler, the young woman with whom he had fallen in love that summer in Salzburg.

In a description of Elisabeth Eisler, Mary Jarrell (who met her some years after Jarrell's death) called her "a talented Viennese ceramist," "twenty-eight, half-Jewish, charmingly feminine," "with her short red curly hair, pink-and-white complexion, and round-eyed, round-cheeked face." She had lived with her parents in Vienna through World War II, and her participation in the seminar was the first time she had been away from them since before the war. Enrolled in Jarrell's poetry class, she entered into a friendship with him which indeed marked his weeks at Leopoldskron with something quite other than the intensely shared political and literary camaraderie that Matthiessen had found so exciting. The two walked and talked and read books together; he read poetry to her, she made sketches of him, but—out of deference to Jarrell's marriage, Mary Jarrell insists—they did not become lovers. When they parted at the end of the summer (Jarrell stayed on at Leopoldskron for a time after Eisler left), it was with the intention of continuing to be friends while resuming their lives apart.

Some people have had trouble believing that the relationship was a platonic one—as, presumably, Jarrell told Mary it was. To me it is quite understandable, considering his sexual behavior generally, that it should have been exactly that. Someone once remarked about Fred Astaire that he was interested in women rather than sex, and this seems an accurate way to characterize the graceful, unearthly insouciance of the hero of *Top Hat* and *Swing Time*. There was something of Astaire in Jarrell, whom his friend Lowell described, in words quoted earlier, as possessing a body "a little ghostly in its immunity to soil, entanglements, and rebellion." Next to him, Lowell said, one felt "too corrupt and companionable." It was an apt remark from Lowell, who, while married, companionably slept with other women and even decided he wanted to marry some of them. Elisabeth Eisler was only six years younger than Jarrell, but younger enough to be a candidate for the kind of artistic instruction he enjoyed giving members of the opposite sex, like Sara or Cecile Starr, or like the twelve-year-old Svetlana Leontief, whom he also met and grew fond of during that summer in Salzburg. For him, Eisler represented the Old World, the past, everything that had suddenly changed his life. He was to express that change in various amusing ways: to Arendt he wrote: "Nothing but the army had ever made as much impression on me as Europe"; while to James Laughlin he said: "Europe had about as much effect on me as the Coliseum had on Daisy Miller." To Lowell he put it this way: "My reaction to Europe was roughly this: Had I actually not been there my whole *life*? Why, how'd I get *along*? (Voice is supposed to rise in incredulous wonder.)" One can be assured his voice did rise to just such a pitch.

In the letters he wrote Elisabeth Eisler that fall of 1948, after he returned to Greensboro, he spoke as a man in a distant land, attempting to explain himself, his American life and surroundings, to someone with whom he had shared a very different kind of reality. Mary Jarrell writes that, though they had parted in Salzburg with the resolve to correspond as "friends" merely, soon after Jarrell resettled in Greensboro he wrote Eisler: "I can't be anyone's husband but yours." This single sentence is all that is quoted from the letter, but is perhaps enough to suggest that he was torn between responsible commitment to his present marriage and his continuing life at Greensboro, on the one hand, and the new, truly romantic feelings he felt not just for Eisler but for Salzburg, Europe, the past, and—indeed—poetry, on the other. On his trip to Boston that fall for the meeting of seminar teachers, he visited Hannah Arendt and Heinrich Blücher in New York, and Arendt remarked to her husband that Jarrell's poetry had affinities with Rilke's, even that he somewhat resembled Rilke facially. Jarrell was deeply pleased by this observation, and wrote Eisler afterward about the evening: "They compared me to Rilke because they were Europeans and cared for poetry more—you can't imagine how few Americans care for poetry." His sentimental identification of Europe with poetry, America with the philistine disregard of it, is all the more blatant for its willingness to forget that the Europeans involved here happened to be highly cultured intellectuals who, in Arendt's case certainly, cared about Jarrell's poetry partly because it reminded her of her beloved Rilke. The interesting thing is that, at the same time he wrote Eisler and invited her into the "good" European-poetry-lovers crowd, he was also finishing the essay on Williams he had been putting off all summer, in which he expressed a sympathy for American people, places, and landscape quite at odds with his horrified recoil from Americans as people who don't read poetry.

In writing to Elisabeth Eisler, Jarrell often sounds less like a lover than an affectionate tutor or a lovable, rather strange uncle. He dwells on his own facial expression as if fascinated and rather surprised by it: "My mouth is wide-open, curled in an odd way, as if I were Mowgli calling to some wolves," he says about a dashing picture of himself taken at Salzburg, teaching in a cable-knit sweater. Describing Greensboro and his house, he manages to throw a little enchantment over things: "I'm writing you from the music room, but, alas, there wasn't any letter from you this morning. The sunlight's very beautiful—in a little I'll go and play tennis." Tomorrow, he says, he is going to a football game, "so I will have an 'American face' then—but not a critic's face, an innocent enthusiastic face, the sort I have when I read the funny-papers." Here he might be talking to a little girl who has been charmed by such a clever funny man. His preference for the innocent, enthusiastic football face over the critic's face reflects his struggles with the introduction to Williams's poems and, really for the first time, his doubts about the activity of writing criticism—which activity he compared to rain falling in the ocean: "You're wasted, and the ocean's as salty as ever" (he is thinking of Housman's lines: "It rains into the sea / And still the sea is salt"). He would prefer to write nothing but poetry, presumably an activity in which the "innocent enthusiastic face" could shine out: "But mostly it's better, really, to make things yourself, not to write about what other people have made—if you can make anything yourself." She, of course, was a maker too—not a writer of critical prose.

As in previous letters to Amy Breyer deBlasio and to Allen Tate, Jarrell attempts a self-characterization for Elisabeth Eisler—which, like the earlier ones, is marked by forthrightness. He tries to be coolly objective about himself, even though his reading in psychoanalytic literature told him such objectivity was impossible. He tells Eisler he works hard at his poetry and avoids all sorts of "little duties," i.e., is not much help to his wife. He is cold to and bored by a great many people, sometimes gets cross and makes "critical" remarks (this goes along with nervousness); he is "pretty selfish" —especially about writing poems—and argues hard, is willing to change his mind but says it's difficult to persuade him toward such a change. He likes to be taken care of, is "quite optimistic," is "childish in many ways, but this is as much good as bad." In sum:

> I lead an odd, independent, unsocial life remarkably unlike most other people's lives, the life of someone whose principal work-and-amusement is writing, and reading and thinking about things. And this isn't nice for one's wife unless she has some great interest to take up most of her time.

In a similar vein: "I guess I can sum up my bad points by saying I can't, even if I try, be dutiful and make my life careful and methodical and unselfish and self-sacrificing. Even if I tried, I wouldn't succeed."

Naturally this sort of confession is disarming—fending off criticism by admitting to one's faults in advance. At the same time, there is no huffing and puffing here, no hysteria or pomposity; you feel that at age thirty-four he is hardening into a certain kind of person and becoming more aware of the mold. The references to the wife to whom he's not much help and less than sparkling company not only reflect a divergence in his and Mackie's interests but also may be an attempt to warn Eisler that, should she have visions of ever becoming his wife, she should know what this would involve. One thing that he could do for a woman probably better than anyone else was to provide her with a reading list, and at Eisler's request he offered a list of favorites from Twain to Céline, by way of Henry Adams, Christina Stead, Evelyn Waugh, *Antony and Cleopatra* (his favorite Shakespeare, he said), Blake, Hemingway, and many more. He also encouraged Eisler's literary sensibilities by finding "beautiful" phrases in her letters which he later made use of in his own poems.

His divided feelings about Eisler were resolved, though uneasily so, when at the end of 1948 he decided to stay with his marriage and told her that henceforth they should write each other no more than "normal friendly letters." His "responsibilities" toward wife, friends, and career in the United States were, he said, what he had forgotten the previous summer, and that forgetting "made me behave very badly toward them. Because I let myself feel what I shouldn't have, I made things so that anything I did made someone suffer." He promises to be her "dearest friend" and to help her in any way he can, but no more than that. Over the next two years they continued to correspond and, as is surely understandable, the unease never left him. In what Mary Jarrell says is the last letter Eisler had or kept from him, written in the fall of 1950, his closing words were a plea to forgive him for not writing, "and forgive me for everything else—I feel endlessly guilty toward you." This guilt and related feelings pervaded the poems he wrote during those immediate post-Salzburg years.

Elisabeth Eisler had a successful career as an artist, never married, and lived with her parents until she died in 1975.

In the academic year 1948–49 Jarrell finally accepted the Guggenheim Fellowship he had been awarded two years earlier but had decided to postpone—first because of his *Nation* job, then because he had to teach the first year of his new job at the Woman's College. That fall he taught a single class (which met only once a week) and attempted to get on with writing poems, while finishing his promised introduction to Williams's *Selected Poems* and starting the book on Hart Crane. (He eventually gave up the Crane project and paid back the advance.) In October he wrote Eisler that he had taken his class outside, sat under some trees by a pond, and analyzed Tennyson's "Ulysses"—"full of Faustian yearnings for knowledge, a great believer in science and progress and evolution, miserably bored with Ithaca and Penelope and Telemachus, and full of *good* reasons for leaving—but oratorical like Ulysses." The description not only went to the heart of Tennyson's poem but in the phrase "full of *good* reasons for leaving" went to the heart of Jarrell, who was weighing marital domesticity in pastoral Greensboro against the call of Europe and his correspondent. Like the Frost he was reading—and like Ulysses in the poem—Jarrell stayed home and traveled far in his imagination. That fall he worked on a poem, initially titled "It Is Like Any Other," which used some of Eisler's phrases and which when finished became "The Orient Express," the opening poem in what would be his next book, *The Seven-League Crutches.*

"The Orient Express" (he traveled on the train from Paris to Salzburg) is a poem that may seem flat on first and even later readings; lacking fireworks or striking lines, its tonality is deliberately gray and muted. Without creating a compelling speaking voice—there is really no person present—it explores or meditates on questions of an ultimate sort: how does the world appear to us? what, if anything, is behind that world? how do we "take" it or believe in it? The subject of "The Orient Express" is, in a key word from the poem, "precariousness," as first perceived from a moving train:

> One looks from the train
> Almost as one looked as a child. In the sunlight
> What I see still seems to me plain,
> I am safe; but at evening
> As the lands darken, a questioning
> Precariousness comes over everything.

The poem moves to the child in bed, under a quilt—a powerful and recurrent image in Jarrell's poetry:

> Once after a day of rain
> I lay longing to be cold; and after a while
> I was cold again, and hunched shivering
> Under the quilt's many colors, gray
> With the dull ending of the winter day.
> Outside me there were a few shapes
> Of chairs and tables, things from a primer;
> Outside the window
> There were the chairs and tables of the world. . . .
> I saw that the world
> That had seemed to me the plain
> Gray mask of all that was strange
> Behind it—of all that was—was all.

In an atmosphere reminiscent of "90 North," we are taken from the gray quilt to the plain gray mask of the world, as the child, in a moment of unillusioned perception, sees the world for what it is: not a mask behind which is hidden something "strange" but itself "all"—"the chairs and tables of the world" in their impenetrable otherness. After a space the meditation grows increasingly murky:

> But it is beyond belief.
> One thinks, "Behind everything

> *An unforced joy, an unwilling*
> *Sadness (a willing sadness, a forced joy)*
> *Moves changelessly"; one looks from the train*
> *And there is something, the same thing*
> *Behind everything: all these little villages,*
> *A passing woman, a field of grain,*
> *The man who says good-bye to his wife—*
> *A path through a wood full of lives, and the train*
> *Passing, after all unchangeable*
> *And not now ever to stop, like a heart—*

The ground shifts uneasily beneath us. Evidently, what is "beyond belief" at the outset of this section is the child's earlier perception that there is nothing "behind" the world. Now as "one looks from the train," the strangeness behind things returns; the villages, the woman, the field of grain reveal—and conceal—themselves as the train passes.

Paraphrasing lines that refuse to come into clear focus results in a feeling of vertigo, and this feeling is not dispelled by the poem's final lines, which come after another break:

> *It is like any other work of art.*
> *It is and never can be changed.*
> *Behind everything there is always*
> *The unknown unwanted life.*

What is the "it" here? What does it mean to assert that "life" is always "behind everything"? The poet's own utterance presents itself to us in a manner as enigmatically declarative as the world seen from the passing train. Soon after he had written "The Orient Express," Jarrell remarked in a letter to Elizabeth Bishop that "Rilke certainly is monstrously self-indulgent a lot of the time." If Rilke can be truly charged with self-indulgence, so can a poem like "The Orient Express"—which I single out as typical of several of the ones Jarrell wrote soon after *Losses* was published in 1948. Yet Lowell, no bad judge of poetry, had this to say about the poem when he reviewed *The Seven-League Crutches* in 1951:

> Among the new poems, "The Orient Express," a sequel, I think, to "Dover Beach," is a brilliantly expert combination of regular and irregular lines, buried rhymes, and sestinalike repeated rhymes, in which shifts in tone and rhythm are played off against the deadening roll of the train.

This is ingenious, though Lowell didn't take time in his review to show how those irregular lines and rhymes, played off against the roll of the train, add up to a successor to Arnold's classic. At any rate, the provocative claim takes no account of our uncertainty about just what the poem is saying. Its attempt to evoke inexpressible feelings about matters that lie beyond the reach of language risks portentousness; we question whether the poem is finally profound or profoundly self-indulgent. In any case, this question indicates more about the sort of poem Jarrell had become increasingly interested in writing than any positive or negative answer to the question would reveal.

Whatever the "unknown unwanted life" that lies behind "everything" in "The Orient Express" can be said to consist of, it was something Jarrell wanted to get more of into his poems. By the end of the 1940s he was convinced that to do so demanded a loosening up or reconstitution of poetic form; the stanzas and structures that had served him in earlier books of poems felt like impediments to expression. Meanwhile, Williams's example, particularly *Paterson*, acted as a stimulus toward composition by the musical phrase (in Pound's words) and toward the incorporation of more disparate kinds of materials and juxtapositions—a more "American-grain" texture, as in "Lady Bates." Even more important, Frost was there to urge him toward "the sound of sense," toward "talk" as the principle of poems.

What seems truly incongruous, though, is that, after the Salzburg summer of 1948, Europe should have been so manifestly added to these influences and examples. Europe was the past, history, tradition; it was also the country of the Märchen and the land of Freud, where the buried life was buried all the more richly for its mythical, legendary status. Even before he left the army he had written "The Märchen," his homage to Grimm's tales that begins memorably with a depiction of the forest:

> *Listening, listening; it is never still.*
> *This is the forest: long ago the lives*
> *Edged armed into its tides (the axes were its stone*
> *Lashed with the skins of dwellers to its boughs);*
> *We felled our islands there, at last, with iron.*
> *The sunlight fell to them, according to our wish,*
> *And we believed, till nightfall, in that wish;*
> *And we believed, till nightfall, in our lives.*

But at nightfall something very different begins, and Jarrell attempted in a number of poems he wrote after Salzburg to speak for the forest, the nightfall, the "dream-work" that the human imagination had projected to lie "behind everything." In the words of his subtitle to "Hohensalzburg," written that fall of 1948, he would provide some "Fantastic Variations on a Theme of Romantic Character"—the subtitle of Richard Strauss's *Don Quixote*, except with "Romantic" substituted for "Knightly."

Some of these fantastic variations may be observed not only in "Hohensalzburg" but also in "An English Garden in Austria," or "A Rhapsody on Irish Themes," or "A Quilt-Pattern," "The Night Before the Night Before Christmas," and in shorter poems like "A Soul," "The Black Swan," "The Sleeping Beauty," "La Belle au Bois Dormant," and "The Venetian Blind." I should explain my reasons for dealing cursorily with what, for Jarrell, were treatments of subjects and themes about which he cared deeply and were furthermore written at a time when he was an experienced poet who had begun to write his finest prose essays in criticism. A case might be made that these poems represent him at his most ambitious, at a point when he was attempting to bring together disparate materials, strikingly juxtaposed, within the fluid structure of an associative meditation. "The Night Before the Night Before Christmas," for example, begins with an adolescent girl who lives with her ill brother; both her mother and her pet squirrel have died awhile back. After reading to her brother before bedtime, she reads to herself from *Das Kapital*, and then, falling asleep, is presented as follows:

> *There is something deep*
> *Under her will, against her will,*
> *That keeps murmuring to her, "It's so";*
> *And she murmurs, almost asleep:*
> *"Unjust—no, it's not* so.
> *If he were educated . . ."*
> *She sees six squirrels in a row*
> *Thinking in chorus, in slow, low,*
> *Hissing, radiator-steam-valve voices:*
> *"Wherefore Art Thou, Romeo?"*
> *The big squirrel says, "No.*
> *No, that is not* just *it.*
> *Try it again."*
> *Their skein-silk lashes*
> *Tremble, and they look sidelong up at her—*
> *And cry, softly, in their sly,*
> *Dumb, scared, malicious pain . . .*
> *And try it again.*

Suzanne Ferguson, who has written illuminatingly about many of the poems from *The Seven-League Crutches*, finds that "The Night Before . . ." embodies Jarrell's most extensive character development outside his novel, *Pictures from an Institution*. For almost 400 lines the girl's consciousness is tracked by the poet:

> *Her wandering mind*
> *Comes to what was a joy,*
> *What is a sorrow—*
> *A cave opening into the dark*

Earth, down to the dead:
What, played with day after day,
Stroked, called to, fed
In the small, wild, straggling park—
Told of, night after night, to the boy
Who listened, longing, among the games
Strewn on his rumpled bed—
      was gone, one winter day.

Still, one must ask about this poem—as about many of the poems written at this time—whether there is enough technique to make us able convincingly to infer a "character" from line to line. Or whether, as it appears to me, the verse is simply not powerful or interesting enough to command our belief in the subjects it projects. In "The Truth" (also from *The Seven-League Crutches*), a little boy whose father was killed in the bombing of London recalls the horrible night in these words:

And it was light then—light at night.
I heard Stalky bark outside.
But really it was Mother crying—
She coughed so hard she cried.
She kept shaking Sister,
She shook her and shook her.
I thought Sister had had her nightmare.
But he wasn't barking, he had died.
There was dirt all over Sister.
It was all streaks, like mud. I cried.
She didn't, but she was older.

Admittedly, it is a boy who is presumed to speak here, but the manner seems *faux naïf*; it works so hard at being simple and unadorned that it sounds flat.

Sometimes the "depth" of a poem, its supposedly complex content, is put into question by the relative thinness of the verse through which it is conveyed. In "A Quilt-Pattern," for example, a psychological poem that focuses on "the child's redreaming of *Hansel and Gretel* [. . .] *in terms of his mother and himself* " (as Jarrell explained to Sister Bernetta Quinn), the meaning is deep enough, apparently, to require a page of interpretation by the poet. But the verse itself is spare to the point—as with "The Night Before . . ."—of inanition:

> He breaks a finger
> From the window and lifts it to his—
> "Who is nibbling at me?" says the house.
> The dream says, "The wind,
> The heaven-born wind";
> The boy says, "It is a mouse."
> He sucks at the finger; and the house of bread
> Calls to him in its slow singing voice:
> "Feed, feed! Are you fat now?
> Hold out your finger."
> The boy holds out the bone of the finger.
> It moves, but the house says, "No, you don't know.
> Eat a little longer."

Since there is so little excitement on the surface of the poetry, we may well be tempted—in desperation if nothing else—to head for deeper, interpretive waters. Conversely, there are other poems of this period in which the problem is not flatness but an over-abundance of juxtapositions and associations. "An English Garden in Austria" and "A Rhapsody on Irish Themes" are so crammed with historical and legendary allusions that Jarrell had to provide lengthy notes for them; they feel cluttered, insufficiently removed from the head of the clever poet bursting with names and places, with other poems and stories.

Since one of the aims of this book is to enhance Jarrell's reputation as a poet whose work is currently not sufficiently appreciated, it may seem folly to pass over or criticize adversely poems such as those so summarily treated above. And it is true that the poetry from this period—most of it collected in *The Seven-League*

Crutches—has attracted the attention of critics concerned to reveal hidden, unobvious aspects of his art. As early as 1952, in a review of the book, Parker Tyler analyzed its "dramatic lyrism" as a form of what psychologists called "projection." Jarrell's poetry, Tyler argued, was "of the chthonic depths" and made use centrally of anthropological and magical materials, the sacred wood, the Freudian trio of ego-id-superego, matters of guilt and sacrifice, and archetypal journeys, all of which for Tyler constituted "one of the most mature and rewarding bodies of verse produced in our time." More recently, in her study *The Black Goddess*, Helen Hagenbüchle doggedly pursued the role of the "archetypal feminine" as it revealed itself in Jarrell's poetry, arguing that his childhood experience of a "jealous and all-powerful mother" was the crucial influence on the poems he would write, in which that mother was identified with Death and the Unconscious: "The same Oedipal love-hate that marked the poet's relationship with his mother also characterizes his attitude towards these archetypal powers." Hagenbüchle points out that Jarrell was a psychology major who read extensively in psychoanalytic literature and even—as in "A Quilt-Pattern"—deliberately constructed poems around psychoanalytic themes.

Such ways of talking about Jarrell's poetry are plausible and resourceful attempts at interpretation of work in which the archetypal and unconscious forces seem most dense. (That Anna Jarrell figured in her son's memory and imagination as a "jealous and all-powerful mother" is, however, debatable.) But whether reading the poems in these terms will make that work available to a wider audience of readers seems to me unlikely, especially if such readers (I am one of them myself) are less than convinced by the application of such analytic concepts and categories. Indeed, Jarrell may need to be rescued from his own analytic schemes, especially if most of the poems that result from them—like "A Quilt-Pattern" and "The Night Before the Night Before Christmas"—are as poetically unsatisfying as, to me, they seem. The notion I should put forth— one that is supported by his later poems—is that no special vocabulary or system of concepts need or should be employed to analyze his art when that art is both at its freest and its most controlled. Such an art finds its triumphant embodiment in the earlier-mentioned "A Girl in a Library," which we will consider in the next chapter in conjunction with some of the prose pieces contemporary with it.

SEVEN

The Life of Criticism

T HE years 1950–52 were truly the *anni mirabili* of Jarrell as a
writer of prose. During that period, and especially after his
fourth book, *The Seven-League Crutches*, appeared in 1951, verse
came to him slowly; his next book of poems, *The Woman at the
Washington Zoo*, would not appear until 1960. More than once he
echoed this complaint from a letter—"Oh, oh, OHH! I don't like
to write criticism"—even as he was engaged in writing the most
valuable and daring criticism of his career. A brief chronological
sketch of its highlights reveals first—glancing back to the second
part of 1948—Jarrell's appreciation of John Ransom and his introduction to Williams's *Selected Poems*, foreshadowings of work to
come. One of his two 1950 poetry chronicles for *Partisan* contained
noteworthy pages on E. E. Cummings. In the summer of that year,
at the Harvard Summer School conference on the Defense of
Poetry, he delivered his brilliant lecture-lament "The Obscurity
of the Poet," published in *Partisan* the following winter. His essay
on Stevens ("Reflections on Wallace Stevens") followed in *Partisan*
that spring, and in the fall of 1951 he reviewed three important
books of poetry: second volumes by Lowell and by Richard Wilbur,
and the later—to him disappointing—books of Williams's *Paterson*.
That same fall, his "rediscovery" of Whitman appeared in *Kenyon*,

while his lengthy and amusing diatribe "The Age of Criticism" followed the next spring in *Partisan*. Closing it all off, in the fall of 1952, came the masterly essay on Frost, "To the Laodiceans," a longish review of Williams's two volumes of collected poems, and an appreciation of Marianne Moore.

These essays and reviews, plus short bits from earlier chronicles, made up most of *Poetry and the Age*, which appeared in 1953. And although they were never published, he delivered a series of written-out lectures on Auden during the spring of his year at Princeton that taken together comprise a virtual book. As if all this critical activity—in addition to his teaching at Greensboro and Princeton—weren't sufficient to keep him busy, he revised his "comedy" novel-to-be, *Pictures from an Institution*, portions of which came out in magazines in 1953 before book publication the following year. Finally, during the year at Princeton, separated from Mackie and living by himself, he wrote a great number of letters to the woman who would become his second wife, Mary von Schrader. In their humorous portrayal of the poet's life at an institution, they rival the letters written home to Mackie after Jarrell enlisted.

It was an extraordinary prose period, then, in which the poet regularly lamented his dereliction from poetry while he became— in "The Obscurity of the Poet" and "The Age of Criticism" especially—ever more eloquent about the modern poet's isolation. In his Harvard Summer School talk (after which he participated in a discussion with Lowell, Harry Levin, and others), he argued that it was too simple to say that in America the modern poet was unread because he was obscure. He was unread, in part, because 48 percent of Americans (according to a recent university survey) reported that they had read no book whatsoever the previous year. There was nothing particularly unfamiliar in Jarrell's description of a world "whose newspapers and magazines and books and motion pictures and radio stations and television stations have destroyed, in a great many people, even the capacity for understanding real poetry, real art of any kind": indeed, this was what his audience of poetry readers doubtless expected to hear. What proved fresh and original, especially to listeners familiar with his poetry reviews, was the way his cultural points were not so much substantiated as they were woven into extended satirical fantasies.

It is worth pausing over one of them as illustrative of the prose's satiric density. The following passage attacks the belief that, unlike previous literature, modern verse is obscure and therefore can't be read by goodhearted, ordinary people. Rather, Jarrell argues, it is the poet's identity that has become obscure:

> Any American poet under a certain age, a fairly advanced age—the age, one is tempted to say, of Bernard Shaw—has inherited a situation in which no one looks at him and in which, consequently, everyone complains that he is invisible: for that corner into which no one looks is always dark. And people who have inherited the custom of not reading poets justify it by referring to the obscurity of the poems they have never read—since most people decide that poets are obscure very much as legislators decide that books are pornographic: by glancing at a few fragments someone has strung together to disgust them.

That much would have been sufficient, to have made a just point, in a relatively sober way. But Jarrell is only warming up:

> When a person says accusingly that he can't understand Eliot, his tone implies that most of his happiest hours are spent at the fireside among worn copies of the *Agamemnon, Phèdre,* and the Symbolic Books of William Blake.

In fact, this person, if he is reading at all, is pushing through the pages of *Forever Amber,* and Jarrell goes about filling out a character for him, confiding in us—as might the unwitting person himself—

> that all his happiest memories of Shakespeare seem to come from a high school production of *As You Like It* in which he

played the wrestler Charles; and that he has, by some obscure process of free association, combined James Russell, Amy, and Robert Lowell into one majestic whole: a bearded cigar-smoking ambassador to the Vatican who, after accompanying Theodore Roosevelt on his first African expedition, came home to dictate on his deathbed the "Concord Hymn." Many a man, because Ezra Pound is too obscure for him, has shut forever the pages of *Paradise Lost*; or so one would gather, from the theory and practice such people combine.

To say this is excessive is to say hardly anything, as before our eyes (and before the delighted ears of the Harvard audience whose laughter punctuates the recording of the talk) one grotesque "fact" leads to another, like the person's wistful memory of having played the wrestler Charles, himself remembered for one brief unbrilliant moment before he is borne away. Rather than putting forth a case to be argued with or qualified, Jarrell moves the whole thing onto another plane, one of satiric fantasy in which each unbeatable witty line calls forth another, to the point where the reader-listener's powers of resistance are dissolved. Such is the quality of the entertainment that one forgets to deplore the obscurity of the poet, just as—in the similarly entertaining *Pictures from an Institution*—one doesn't lament the state of things at Benton College. Lowell described the lecture, to Elizabeth Bishop, as "a tremendous philippic [. . .] against our culture that has no time or taste for poetry—something that would have made Jonathan Edwards sound like Montaigne."

Like the novel he was writing at that time, "The Obscurity of the Poet" is full of verbal surprises, turns of clever thought that become almost more interesting than its ostensible subject. By way of illustrating poetry's insignificance in the lives of well-to-do Americans in 1950, Jarrell tells of meeting a man on a boat to Europe who asked him "with uninterested politeness" what American poets he liked best, to which Jarrell answered that he liked Robert Frost and T. S. Eliot:

Then this man—this father who every night danced with his daughter with the well-taught, dated, decorous attractiveness of the hero of an old *Saturday Evening Post* serial by E. Phillips Oppenheim; who had had the best professional in Los Angeles teach his wife and daughter the tennis strokes he himself talked of with wearying authority; who never in his life had gone through a doorway before anyone over the age of seven—this well-dressed, well-mannered, travelled, urbane, educated gentleman said placidly: "I don't believe I've heard of them."

This is delightful, all the way down to the mock-careful specificity of "over the age of seven." But isn't it also too good to be true? Wouldn't this well-mannered, urbane gentleman at least have heard Frost on *Meet the Press* or read an article in *Time* about Eliot's new obscure play, *The Cocktail Party*?

The point of being pedantic and trying to catch the poet-critic in stretching things beyond believability is that "The Obscurity of the Poet" represents Jarrell at the confident height of his powers as an analyst of poetry's place in the modern world—the American world, at any rate. His style of analysis is less analytical than literary and satirical, a "creative" exaggeration in which each sentence is designed to surprise and amuse its audience by improvising on and outdoing the previous sentence. It is, in Lowell's word, a "tremendous" though brittle performance that could have been given only by someone thoroughly convinced of his own authority in the postwar American poetry scene. While he fell short of Lowell's reputation as *the* younger poet, he was surely *the* younger critic of modern poetry, and on his way to becoming a formidable commentator on contemporary culture. Two years previously, he wrote about Williams that one felt about him as one felt about Whitman: "*Why, he'd say anything*—creditable or discreditable, sayable or unsayable, so long as he believes it." Reading "The Obscurity of the Poet," one has a similar feeling that Jarrell can and does say anything as long as he not only believes it but believes that it will amuse his audience and himself. It will be recalled that, in his early married days at Texas, his wife teased him by calling him an "arrogant and pretentious creature," to which Jarrell would reply, "Wittier than *anybody*!" Later, in 1951, he wrote to his wife-to-be, apropos of his behavior during a visit to the Cape that summer by the Peter Taylors, "I've never been funnier and more appealing." Few of us would dare to say such a thing about ourselves, but rather would tone down the account—especially to someone we hoped to marry—so as to escape accusations of arrogance and pretension. Jarrell's certainty that he's never been "funnier and more appealing" partly had to do with his ease with and trust in the Taylors' responses. But beyond that, it was continuous with his confident performance in the Harvard lecture. Full of appealing fun about a subject deeply serious to him, the lecture was a vindication of Frost's claim about himself that he was never more serious than when joking.

Frost's humor was often rather harsh, close to mockery and deflationary ridicule, similar to the sort of thing Jarrell had been handing out in his reviews. Yet as I have noted, humor was notably absent from Jarrell's poems, many of which went straight for seriousness and in the process fell into woodenness and solemnity. Although the poems in *The Seven-League Crutches* were more open in their manner, longer and often more conversationally relaxed, they were not remarkable for their humorous bite—unlike virtually every sentence in "The Obscurity of the Poet." Yet there were signs that humor was surfacing in the poems. A year or so after Salzburg he had written "Deutsch Durch Freud," a poem that begins "I believe my favorite country's German" and goes on to explore what it means for him *not* to know that language well enough. Full of little jokes on himself and others, it is a relaxed performance that he excluded from *The Seven-League Crutches*, probably because he thought it too frivolous (it appeared eventually in *The Woman at the Washington Zoo*). Now, in the spring of 1951, he published together in *Poetry* "A Conversation with the Devil" and "A Girl in a Library." The "conversation" poem, a Faustian, rather overlong conversation between poet and devil, is about writing poetry and the audience for whom one writes; it echoes his concerns in the Harvard lecture, and also allows him to practice a rambling Frostian narrative line. It opens with as easy an address to the reader as he would ever compose:

> *Indulgent, or candid, or uncommon reader*
> *—I've some: a wife, a nun, a ghost or two—*
> *If I write for anyone, I wrote for you;*
> *So whisper, when I die,* We was too few;
> *Write over me (if you can write; I hardly knew)*
> *That I—that I—but anything will do,*
> *I'm satisfied. . . . And yet—*
>   *and yet, you* were *too few:*
> *Should I perhaps have written for your brothers,*
> *Those artful, common, unindulgent others?*

There is a serious worry here about the nature of the audience for his poems (the "nun" mentioned is a real one, Sister Bernetta Quinn, who had just published a lengthy essay on his work), but the accents in which it is couched are facetious—as when he wonders, parenthetically, whether his indulgent readers can write. These readers are invited to write a sort of Brooklyn Dodgers epitaph: *"We was too few."* "And yet, you *were* too few," replies the poet in the sincere voice he hopes to usher in through the repeated phrase "And yet."

That phrase also occurs at a crucial point in the much more considerable companion poem to "A Conversation with the Devil." "A Girl in a Library" is perhaps the best poem Jarrell had written in the seventeen years since he was first published as a student at Vanderbilt. He placed it first in his *Selected Poems* (it now stands at the front of *The Complete Poems*), and it brings together all the important things he had been writing about—with the exception of war—into a narrative that is ingenious, highly amusing, and poignant. The title itself identifies two aspects of life in which he was inordinately interested. In his letters he had been cruel toward "the average North Carolina girl," characterizing her speech as that of "an imbecile with an ambition to be an idiot" and complaining that, for his freshman students, he would have to write "a ballet with a Chorus of Peasant Girls." "A Girl in a Library" mocks its subject's way of speaking and living, but then goes on to give her something beyond a chorus role, singling her out for more extended and troubled consideration. The first section of "A Girl in a Library" is a Jarrellian set piece that ends with a bang:

An object among dreams, you sit here with your shoes off
And curl your legs up under you; your eyes
Close for a moment, your face moves toward sleep . . .
You are very human.
                    But my mind, gone out in tenderness,
Shrinks from its object with a thoughtful sigh.
This is a waist the spirit breaks its arm on.
The gods themselves, against you, struggle in vain.
This broad low strong-boned brow; these heavy eyes;
These calves, grown muscular with certainties;
This nose, three medium-sized pink strawberries
—But I exaggerate. In a little you will leave:
I'll hear, half squeal, half shriek, your laugh of greeting—
Then, decrescendo, *bars of that strange speech*
In which each sound sets out to seek each other,
Murders its own father, marries its own mother,
And ends as one grand transcendental vowel.

Already the range of tone and attitude taken toward the girl is wide, extending from a "tenderness" prepared to risk banality ("You are very human"), to the jokes about how solidly this "very human" girl is built, to the self-delighted creation of her speech as an Oedipal tragedy that ends up in some kind of Emersonian or perhaps Lisztian unity. (He speaks elsewhere of Wallace Stevens's "transcendental, all too transcendental études.") The most disingenuous thing the poet says is that he exaggerates, immediately after which he proceeds to a high exaggeration of what he hears in her voice.

The poem goes on to treat the girl, in her muscular "certainties," as a helpless undreaming female caught in a trap:

> *If someone questioned you,* What doest thou here?
> *You'd knit your brows like an orangoutang*
> *(But not so sadly; not so thoughtfully)*
> *And answer with a pure heart, guilelessly:*
> I'm studying. . . .
> > > *If only you were not!*
> *Assignments,*
> > *recipes,*
> > > *the* Official Rulebook
> Of Basketball—*ah, let them go; you needn't mind.*
> *The soul has no assignments, neither cooks*
> *Nor referees: it wastes its time.*

Writing about the poem, Wendy Lesser says that it shows two contradictory sides of Jarrell's personality, and that in it he "allows himself to waver back and forth [. . .] violently between the mockery that characterizes his essays and the unrepentant sentimentality that colors most of his poems"—between, in other words, the "masculine" and "feminine" sides of his character. A prime example of the latter side immediately follows the previously quoted passage:

> *Here in this enclave there are centuries*
> *For you to waste: the short and narrow stream*
> *Of Life meanders into a thousand valleys*
> *Of all that was, or might have been, or is to be.*
> *The books, just leafed through, whisper endlessly . . .*
> *Yet it is hard. One sees in your blurred eyes*
> *The "uneasy half-soul" Kipling saw in dogs'.*
> *One sees it, in the glass, in one's own eyes.*
> *In rooms alone, in galleries, in libraries,*
> *In tears, in searchings of the heart, in staggering joys*
> *We memorize once more our old creation,*

> *Humanity: with what yawns the unwilling*
> *Flesh puts on its spirit, O my sister!*

Wendy Lesser refers to the poem's air of "virulent self-contra-
diction," yet it seems to me that this is the sort of virulence and
contradiction good poetry thrives on. From his two earlier library
poems, we know that Jarrell loved them as "enclaves" where anything but "Home Ec." and "Phys. Ed." assignments belonged;
places not for studying but for reading oneself into the "thousand
valleys / Of all that was, or might have been, or is to be." This
sturdy, fleshly representative of the Southern college girl can't live
up to such a recipe, of course, can't waste her soul's time properly.
But, the poem wonders, can anyone live up to it? A quite unvirulent
reaching out occurs as the poet notes that the " 'uneasy half-soul' "
he sees in the girl's eyes is also visible in his own:

> *In rooms alone, in galleries, in libraries,*
> *In tears, in searchings of the heart, in staggering joys.*

None of us is good enough for the "spirit" our unwilling flesh tries
to dress itself up in, and so in a Whitman- or Baudelaire-like
apostrophe to the sleeping girl he salutes her as a relative—"O
my sister!" It is as if the poet has surprised himself with a discovery
about his subject that mitigates the satiric detachment with which
the poem began.

Not that the satire disappears. At this point the heroine of Push-
kin's *Eugene Onegin*, Tatyana Larina, appears, and the narrator tells
her about the girl in clever accents that prefigure those of *Pictures
from an Institution*: "For nineteen years she's faced reality: / They
look alike already." (In the novel President Robbins is so well
adjusted to the environment that you can't tell one from the other.)
She is a perfect "fit" with the nature of things:

> *They say, man wouldn't be*
> *The best thing in this world—and isn't he?—*
> *If he were not too good for it. But she*
> *—She's good enough for it.*

"And yet" (the two words that follow this passage) sometimes in her "pink strapless formal" he sees her as modulated "Into a form of joy, a Lydian mode." It becomes apparent that what keeps this narrative energetic is its affectionate, indeed loving veering toward the girl, then away from her in satiric mockery. Jarrell doesn't just "allow himself," in Lesser's formulation, to "waver back and forth" from one to the other, but actively cultivates such movement as his narrative principle.

The climax though not the end of "A Girl in a Library" is ushered in with a prediction that when "in the last light sleep of dawn" the messenger-angel comes to address the sleeping girl, she will not awake, will continue to concentrate on getting her "bachelor's degree / In Home Ec.," while missing the angel. The narrator laments to Tatyana:

> *Oh, Tatyana,*
> *The Angel comes: better to squawk like a chicken*
> *Than to say with truth, "But I'm a good girl,"*
> *And Meet his Challenge with a last firm strange*
> *Uncomprehending smile; and—then, then!—see*
> *The blind date that has stood you up: your life.*
> *(For all this, if it isn't, perhaps, life,*
> *Has yet, at least, a language of its own*
> *Different from the books'; worse than the books'.)*
> *And yet, the ways we miss our lives are life.*
> *Yet . . . yet . . .*
> > *to have one's life add up to yet!*

It would be an exaggeration, though a justifiable one, to say that here is the sort of poetry that, after seventeen years of publishing poems, Jarrell had been meant to write. Its very hesitancies and stumblings, its overemphases (" 'But I'm a *good* girl' "), dashes, and ellipses, its ironic capitalizings and slanginess (he provided an explanatory note for future generations on "the blind date that has stood you up")—all these linguistic practices have been enlisted not in the service of a coherent position on things, to be achieved within the precise boundaries of a formal structure, but in the interests rather of openness, uncertainty, even confusion. What must Allen Tate have said when he encountered the poem? Surely he could not have been pleased; and indeed it risks the charge of mawkishness a few lines later, when the voice says, in a line separated above and below by white spaces: "I love you—and yet—and yet—I love you."

The attempt to hold mockery and love, satire and sympathy together in the same poem puts a great strain on the speaking voice. On the one hand, that voice makes splendidly witty formulations, like the one in which the girl's voice kills its father and marries its mother; on the other, it engages in insistent, potentially cloying repetitions of "I love you," of "And yet." Jarrell wanted both to capsulize "life" in one brilliant phrase after another and to celebrate it by confessing his speechlessness in the face of it. Words fail him, or just about, and that failure implicitly asks to be understood by the sympathetic reader as proof of true feeling. Whatever one thinks about the mixed style in which these impulses are expressed, it was highly unusual for its time, 1951. A glance through John Ciardi's anthology of contemporary poets—which includes Jarrell and which was published the previous year—confirms one's sense of the postwar period as a time when poems became increasingly well wrought, autotelic, full of ironic tension, unified through paradoxical resolutions. Jarrell's achievement in "A Girl in a Library" is historically significant, since such New Critical terms don't take us far in describing its style. But its more important significance has to do with the amount of "life"—the illusion of a world going on—he managed to get into the experience of a poem. In reviewing *The Seven-League Crutches*, Lowell compared its treatment of the girl with Pope's of Belinda in "The Rape of the Lock," and singled it out as the poem in which Jarrell "perhaps best uses both his own qualities and his sense of popular culture." This is a useful way of pointing at, in Henry James's phrase, the poem's felt life.

As Jarrell prepared *The Seven-League Crutches* for publication in the fall of 1951 (it was to be his last venture with Harcourt, Brace), recognition of a public and academic sort came to him. The 1950 address to the Harvard Summer School conference on poetry was followed, in the succeeding spring, by an award of a thousand dollars from the National Institute of Arts and Letters; Jarrell attended the awards ceremony in New York City. By that time he had also received and accepted an invitation to teach at Princeton the next academic year, 1951–52. During his tenure at *The Nation*, he had received a letter from R. P. Blackmur asking for his opinion about the state of contemporary literary magazines, to which he made a lengthy and careful response. Blackmur, whose criticism Jarrell had long admired and whose book of poems *The Good European* he had reviewed in 1948, served as visiting critic at the Greensboro Arts Forum in the spring of 1950. Since both he and John Berryman were teaching in the writing program at Princeton, Jarrell would be assured of two colleagues distinguished by their commitment to writing and to poetry, as well as by their relative isolation from more traditional elements in the English department. In the meantime, he accepted a three-week stint at the Rocky Mountain Writers' Conference held in July 1951 in Boulder, Colorado. While Mackie stayed in the East, in a house they had rented at Dennis on Cape Cod, Jarrell went West and once again fell in love.

In her edition of Jarrell's letters, Mary von Schrader Jarrell tells us that, as a recently divorced woman with two young daughters (she had resumed her father's name), she attended the Boulder conference with her mother. When she met Jarrell and told him which writing classes she was enrolled in, he suggested she drop them and come to his poetry class instead. There followed an idyllic three weeks in which they discussed poetry—Jarrell once more filling the role of tutor—listened to Mahler and Richard Strauss, or talked sports cars, a recent passion of his. Bidding him goodbye at the airport as he prepared to fly back East, Mary said she would understand if, having returned to his real life, he changed his mind and chose not to continue their relationship. But Jarrell silenced her by saying, "No-no-no! Re-dikkl-us! *You* are my real life. I'll write you every day. And you write me. I love you, cross my heart, and I'm going to marry you."

Later that summer he wrote Hannah Arendt from the Cape that truthfully he had liked Colorado as much as Salzburg—a strong statement to make (especially to Arendt) and testimony of how his life had been changed. His life had changed three years before when he fell in love with Elisabeth Eisler in Salzburg, but he decided nonetheless to hold on to his marriage. That marriage did not survive the second shock provided by Mary von Schrader. Sometime after separating from Mackie at the end of the summer, he wrote to Arendt that he was seeking a divorce, told her it had almost happened three years before and that both he and Mackie had been becoming "more and more different in every way for a long time." To Lowell, who was fond of Mackie, he wrote that they "had almost none of the same interests": "She more and more disapproved of me and I more and more felt impatient about her —it was bad for us and getting worse." He added that "you can't write about such things very well." Perhaps not, but reading the letters he wrote from Texas in the years directly after their marriage, as well as those written to his wife while he was in service, one is surprised at this declaration of how they shared "almost none of the same interests." Those letters bespoke a closeness between them; but one surmises that in the years at Greensboro, from 1947 to 1951, Mackie's own academic and social interests moved her in directions away from the poet, who was, as he confessed to Elisabeth Eisler, "pretty selfish" and who led "an odd, independent, unsocial life." The kind of exclusive attentiveness he demanded from a woman simply wasn't there in the wife who had other things to do and other interests to pursue. But it was very much there in the two women he met, three years apart, for whom he was able to provide an intellectual and artistic direction that was fresh and exciting. It is likely, in other words, that the romantic possibilities he discovered in Eisler and in Mary von Schrader were as much a cause of as the result of his marital discontent—although as he himself put it, "you can't write about such things very well."

His passionate feelings for Mary are vividly expressed in a letter he wrote her after returning to the Cape in August: "Living has never been at all like living with thee"—there is a sense of exaltation and high privilege in using "thee." He was fascinated by the "astronomical coincidences" of their both having been born in May 1914, just four days apart, and of their once having lived in Long Beach, California, at exactly the same time. "Truly we are one and were always one. *As* you know, there is no difference between us, we are each other's completely." The merging of two people that D. H. Lawrence both yearned after and warned against as impossible had, for Jarrell, already taken place between him and Mary. It was expressed again, in a different way, at the close of a letter in which he asked her about a rock she had found at Boulder and which they referred to as a meteorite. "O star, sister, breathe on me!" he writes, echoing the language of a little poem, "The Meteorite," he had just composed:

> *Star, that looked so long among the stones*
> *And picked from them, half iron and half dirt,*
> *One; and bent and put it to her lips*
> *And breathed upon it till at last it burned*
> *Uncertainly, among the stars its sisters—*
> *Breathe on me still, star, sister.*

The letter in which this poem was enclosed was written when he was back briefly at Greensboro, alone, preparing to leave for the year at Princeton, while Mackie, with Kitten, returned to the University of Texas to work for her Ph.D. In this state of suspended animation, poised between two lives, he thought of a lovely, little-known verse by Thomas Hardy, the opening poem in Hardy's next to last volume, *Human Shows, Far Phantasies.* "Waiting Both"—which, like the meteorite poem, invoked the stars—seemed to say everything about his present condition:

> *A star looks down on me,*
> *And says: "Here I and you*
> *Stand, each in our degree:*

> *What do you mean to do,—*
> *Mean to do?"*
>
> *I say: "For all I know,*
> *Wait, and let Time go by,*
> *Till my change come."—"Just so,"*
> *The star says: "So mean I:—*
> *So mean I."*

The year Jarrell spent at Princeton is well documented, since he wrote constantly to Mary; in fact, he *wrote* constantly, only a few poems, but a great deal of criticism. The letters contain a number of complaints about money (or the lack of it—half his salary went to Mackie), and at one point he writes Hannah Arendt that he'd like to visit her in New York but can't because he's saving up for a Christmas plane trip to California to visit Mary: "I am living as far as I can like Diogenes—I go along the street and say scornfully to the squirrels, and ants too, 'You spendthrifts!' " When an undergraduate invited him to dinner at a Princeton eating club, he took real delight in thinking how he had saved a third of the fare for a trip to New York; when a check for $12.50 arrived from his publisher it was another blessing. To Lowell he confessed that he was "awfully broke," which condition went along with leading "a very quiet industrious lonely life." He lived in Donald Stauffer's large house (Stauffer was a professor of English, on leave that year), rented before he and Mackie separated. So he had plenty of room (he told Lowell) to "read, write [. . .] listen to classical music over the radio, sleep." For the first time he was obliged to exercise his meager culinary skills. "You should see me cooking and eating my dinner," he wrote to Mary; "the kitchen table where I sit is within reach of the icebox and the toaster [. . .] it's all very Functional." He invited Elizabeth Bishop to come and stay with him (she did not) and held out the promise of modest cooking. "I can cook scrambled eggs and toast, with reluctance." To Mary he confided the secret of his success with those eggs: "As there was no egg-beater I just mixed the eggs and cream together in the skillet and it worked like a charm—and since this saves washing and drying (a) the egg-beater and (b) a bowl, I'll go along with it a while longer."

On his own for the first time since the army (where he didn't have to cook his own meals), he wrote joyously to Mary about how he had "fixed up" his bedroom, changed it from the "dreary scholarly mess" it was to a sanctuary where he lived in the midst of precious objects: "photographs of Donatello sculpture, photographs of Mary von Schrader, two of Elisabeth [Eisler]'s drawings, a map of Salzburg on the door, and a big, *big* picture of Kitten" —the list moves from favorite artist through favorite women to the climactic Kitten. A number of other sacred objects, along with his favorite authors—"my own Proust, and Rilke and Hardy and Grimm's Tales," plus his boyhood Bible—served to keep the academic world of Princeton at bay. If he made it all sound orderly, the reality soon turned out to be nothing like this neat enumeration of things, each in its appointed place: "My, my bedroom's mussed up: it looks as if the cyclone that blew Dorothy to Oz had stopped off and spent the weekend here," he wrote Mary later on, sounding like a little boy puzzled by what had happened to his own special place. In fact, it wasn't just the bedroom that was "mussed up": Eileen Simpson (married to Berryman at that time) remembers him surrounded by a really appalling mess everywhere ("my extraordinarily messed-up—like Kenyon—house," as he put it). It was worse, she said, than is suggested by the cliché about feckless bachelors who can't keep a place picked up.

Picked up or not, it was a refuge from the Princeton that early on he decided felt like "an absurd costume-ball set": "I walk through it looking for you to make it real," he wrote Mary. There were certain friends with whom he sometimes lunched or spent evenings: besides Blackmur and the Berrymans—Jarrell analyzed Eileen's handwriting and in exchange she did a Rorschach test on him—there was Robert Fitzgerald, who was running the seminars in literary criticism, and Edward Cone, a professor of music who played Schubert on the piano for Jarrell and, among other things, extended his sense of Liszt's virtues as a composer. (Later that year, he remarked that if he were a music critic he would write an article on Liszt comparable to the one he had just finished on Whitman, seeking in each case to identify wonderful things in their writings that critics had missed in their eagerness to dwell on faults.)

His feelings about Richard Blackmur were complicated, and over the course of the Princeton year he kept trying to work them out. Blackmur had figured prominently in the list of serious, "hard" critics he had drawn up ten years previously in his essay on contemporary poetry criticism, and he had read Blackmur's seminal essays from the 1930s on the modern poets—Eliot, Yeats, Stevens, Moore, Cummings, Pound, Hart Crane—some as they appeared in the little magazines. Blackmur's dense, often opaque style was far away indeed from his own homely and humorous idiom, but when Jarrell came to write about those poets—and eventually he wrote briefly or at length about all of them—Blackmur's judgments and analyses were the most considerable efforts to hand. Along with Blackmur, Lionel Trilling had attended the Greensboro Arts Forum in 1950, and Jarrell subsequently praised the shrewd criticisms of Trilling in Blackmur's essay "The Politics of Human Power."

At Princeton, he heard and partly admired Blackmur's lectures on Stendhal, on Dostoevsky, on James's *The Ambassadors*, but was troubled by his mannered behavior and his manipulative tendencies, also his penchant for shocking people—or trying to—by saying "awful or unseemly things in a relishing-in-his-mouth way" (Jarrell was appalled by Blackmur's not only saying but repeating, "What if my breath does smell bad? The dead smell worse"). He was especially offended by Blackmur drunk—not an uncommon event—and by how, at a party at Edward Cone's, Blackmur "talked very pessimistically, egotistically, and obscenely, a bad combination." As the year proceeded, Jarrell's feelings vacillated. He admired Blackmur's literary acumen, and even had some personal fondness for him (he liked to kid Blackmur, and thought Blackmur enjoyed being kidded, since few people dared to do so), but Blackmur's egotism repelled him: "He thinks he's really good, really hot, and this isn't so good." Of course, Jarrell himself was often accused of arrogance, and one thinks of what Robert Frost once wrote about another poet, W. H. Davies: "His is the kind of egotism another man's egotism can't put up with." In retrospect, Jarrell and Blackmur were on a collision course. They finally collided at the Auden lectures Jarrell gave at the Seminars in Literary Criticism that spring. According to Jarrell, he "demolished" Blackmur, who behaved badly during the question period out of jealousy of the visiting critic. At any rate, the exchange of views—the "demolition"—seems to have cleared the air, since at the final lecture Blackmur was evidently well behaved. Years later, in 1960, when Jarrell was nominated by Lowell for membership in the National Institute of Arts and Letters, Blackmur—along with Elizabeth Bishop—seconded the nomination.

Since Blackmur and Jarrell have each been called the "best poetry critic" of their generation, a comparison is in order. In reviewing Jarrell's *Letters*, Christopher Benfey suggested that he should be called, rather, the "best poetry reviewer" since, unlike Blackmur (or Empson or Northrop Frye, Benfey adds), Jarrell did not change the way we read poets of the past. Yet it is not clear that Blackmur did so either; instead, he provided elaborate and subtle "introductions" at the highest level to what he saw as the major, mainly American, poets of this century. His essays were complicated, speculative forays, instructions in how to approach various difficult poets. For example, his essay on Stevens ("Examples of Wallace Stevens"), written in 1931, approached the poet by way of his odd vocabulary, then went on to make an illuminating comparison of Stevens's poetic difficulty with that of Eliot and Pound. Along the way Blackmur had occasion to quote some lines from one of Stevens's early poems, "Disillusionment of Ten O'Clock":

> *People are not going*
> *To dream of baboons and periwinkles.*
> *Only, here and there, an old sailor,*
> *Drunk and asleep in his boots,*
> *Catches tigers*
> *In red weather.*

About these lines and the poem which they conclude he says:

> There is no doubt about the words or the separate statements.
> Every part of the poem makes literal sense. Yet the combi-
> nation makes a nonsense, and a nonsense much more con-
> vincing than the separate sensible statements. The statement
> about catching tigers in red weather coming after the white
> nightgowns and baboons and periwinkles, has a persuasive
> force out of all relation to the sense of the words [. . .] The
> shock and virtue of nonsense is this: it compels us to scrutinize
> the words in such a way that we see the enormous ambiguity
> in the substance of every phrase, every image, every word [. . .]
> Half our sleeping knowledge is in nonsense; and when put in
> a poem it wakes.

The last sentence especially, in its almost proverbial force, is typical
of Blackmur's profundity. From inspection of details he rises to
generalization about literary psychology and the power and mystery
of language.

Jarrell's remarks about the same poem occur in his "Reflections
on Wallace Stevens," published in the spring before he went to
Princeton. He treats it as one of many examples of Stevens's complaint about the lack of the exotic and the unexpected in America.
It is "Disillusionment of Ten O'Clock," he says, because everybody
has gone to bed early. "The houses are haunted / By white nightgowns" (so the poem begins) because they are the nightgowns of
"Common Man, Economic Man, Rational Man—pure commonplace, no longer either individual or strange or traditional." Further
details from the poem are fitted into this scheme:

206

Here and there a drunken and disreputable *old sailor* still lives in the original reality (he doesn't dream of catching, he *catches*): *sailor* to bring in old-fashioned Europe, old-fashioned Asia, the old-fashioned ocean; *old* to bring in the past, to make him a dying survival. What indictment of the Present has ever compared, for flat finality, with "People are not going / To dream of baboons and periwinkles"? Yet isn't this poem ordinarily considered a rather nonsensical and Learish poem?

Written twenty years after Blackmur's commentary, Jarrell's doesn't seriously argue with or even mention his predecessor; he deflects things in a completely different direction by saying, in effect, "You considered the poem, perhaps having read Blackmur, to be nonsense? Why, not at all—it's a poem about the poverty of living in the New World." Jarrell's final question, tossed off in a colloquial manner (we are to suppose he means an Edward, not a King Learish poem), is as final as Blackmur's pronouncement about nonsense in the way that it—like Blackmur's sentence—does not expect to be argued with.

Jarrell wrote his essay on Stevens just after he had given his "Obscurity of the Poet" talk at Harvard; so his reading of Stevens as a maker of gaudy rhetoric, in compensation for the poverty of American culture, was continuous with the talk. But more important, and what distinguishes him from Blackmur as a critic, is the way his taste comes to the fore and takes over the essay. The occasion for writing on Stevens was the appearance of *The Auroras of Autumn* (1950), which to Jarrell seemed repetitive and overly abstract in comparison with Stevens's earlier *Harmonium*. Individual poems were less and less differentiated from one another, while the "philosophical" habit in the writer became ever more pronounced ("G. E. Moore at the spinet" was his way of characterizing the habit). Thus the "immediacy and precision and particularity, the live touch of things" Jarrell found *Harmonium* so full of had been lost in rhetoric, elaboration, and contrivance: "In *Auroras of Autumn* one sees almost everything through a shining fog, a habitualness not just of style but of machinery, perception, anything: the green spectacles show us a world of green spectacles; and the reader, staring out into this Eden, thinks timidly: 'But it's all so *monotonous*.' "

Such criticisms had been leveled at Stevens before. But Jarrell's complaint has force because it was made only after he had warmly admired *Harmonium* and before he went on to pay tribute to Stevens as "one of the true poets of our century, someone whom the world will keep on reading just as it keeps on listening to Vivaldi or Scarlatti, looking at Tiepolo or Poussin" (the names are carefully chosen). When, four years later, he was given Stevens's *Collected Poems* to review, he found himself deeply moved by the late poems in the section called "The Rock" and admitted that, in writing the earlier essay, he might not have been sufficiently familiar with or sympathetic to *The Auroras of Autumn*. But he refused to take back his adverse verdict: "Whatever is wrong with the poems or with me is as wrong as ever; what they seemed to me once, they seem to me still."

This combination of personal taste with an impersonal concern for critical standards is expressed in related terms when, in "The Age of Criticism," he says memorably: "A real critic has no one but himself to depend on":

> He can never forget that all he has to go by, finally, is his own response, the self that makes and is made up of such responses—and yet he must regard that self as no more than the instrument through which the work of art is seen, so that the work of art will seem everything to him and his own self nothing.

One of the differences between reading a "critic" like Blackmur and a "reviewer" like Jarrell is that—although Blackmur is at least as individualistic as Jarrell—the former writes about Stevens as if his perceptions were not the product of a particular temperament with certain likes and dislikes. Blackmur is concerned, rather, with formulating truths about the function of "nonsense" in Stevens's poetry, or the way it is less "dramatic" than Eliot's. By contrast, Jarrell is occupied with "his own response, the self [. . .] through which the work of art is seen." Thus it makes all the difference to him—and he presumes to his readers—that he finds *The Auroras of Autumn* unsatisfactory as a volume of poetry; his function as a critic is to attempt to say why this is the case.

Viewed from the distance of almost four decades, Jarrell's adverse remarks about the limitations of Stevens's later style might be deemed irrelevant or misplaced, given the adulation with which the poet is now regarded. In fact, the essay is "real" criticism because the challenge it presents still needs to be made: is there a sameness or repetitiveness or derivative quality to be found in Stevens's style in longer poems such as "An Ordinary Evening in New Haven," "The Owl in the Sarcophagus," "The Bouquet," or the volume's title poem? And does that repetitiveness set off, by contrast, the superior originality and "life" both of the earlier *Harmonium* and of the final poems which succeeded *The Auroras of Autumn*? Questions like these, by promoting fresh thought about a body of work, help to keep it alive.

In "Reflections on Wallace Stevens," Jarrell dealt with a poet whose best work, he felt, was superior to that shown in his newest book; in concluding the essay, he spoke out against the notion that good poets get better as they get older—as they pass, say, from forty to sixty. It is more likely, he claims, that either the poet will have stopped writing altogether (one thinks of the late Philip Larkin) or will be turning out—as he thought Stevens was in *The Auroras of Autumn*—"exercises in his own manner." In a memorable final sentence he defined a good poet as "someone who manages, in a lifetime of standing out in thunderstorms, to be struck by lightning five or six times; a dozen or two dozen times and he is great." This emphasis on the rarity of excellence carried with it an insistence that even "great" poets often wrote less-than-great poems. In his own critical writings he determined—consciously or not is difficult to say—that he could produce "real criticism" only by avoiding blanket praise of his subject. Rather, he would make it clear that good poems are difficult of achievement, arrive infrequently, often—over a period of years—cease to arrive, and can be seen truly only by contrast with the ordinary, the derivative, the expected kind of writing that even good poets' works are filled with.

Accordingly, he not only pulled no punches, he doled them out to some of the contemporaries he most admired. "Here I sit surrounded by unkind remarks about the last three parts of Williams' *Paterson*," he wrote Mary von Schrader on a fall afternoon he'd spent watching Princeton rout NYU in football. "I'll bet Williams will want to murder me," he added, then quoted Shaw's remark about the critic: "His hand is against every man and every man's hand is against him." The unkind remarks about *Paterson* would find their place in a review of three poets (the others were Wilbur and Lowell) he was writing for *Partisan*, and in each case praise was measured against blame. He termed Wilbur, whose second book, *Ceremony*, had just appeared, "the best of the quite young poets writing in this country," younger than Lowell and Bishop and himself. But he was mercilessly satiric about how often Wilbur was *too* charming, too pretty, too poetic: "He is like one of those Southern girls to whom everybody north of Baltimore has said, 'Whatever you do, *don't* lose that lovely Southern accent of yours'; after a few years they sound like Amos and Andy."

He thought that Lowell, in the long title poem from *The Mills of the Kavanaughs*, was the victim of his own powerful mannerisms:

> It is too much a succession of nightmares and daydreams that are half-nightmare [. . .] so that there is a sort of monotonous violence and extremity about the poem, as if it were a piece of music that consisted of nothing but climaxes. The people too often seem to be acting *in the manner of* Robert Lowell, rather than plausibly as real people act (or implausibly as real people act).

Again, the emphasis is on the "real" as a final touchstone for good poetry (Wilbur's poetry was often too delicate and charming and skillful to be quite "real"), which quality he found present in Lowell's "Mother Marie Therese" and "Falling Asleep over the Aeneid," also from the volume.

Williams presented a more troublesome problem than Wilbur or Lowell; Jarrell, after having praised the first book of *Paterson* so highly, was chagrined to discover that the poem had gone steadily downhill, until the bottom was reached in Book IV. A worrisome signal occurred in Book II, where Williams began to write about credit and usury: Jarrell pointed out that Williams had always resisted Pound when the latter tried to get him to admire "European things" like Santa Sophia or poetic meter: "Yet he takes Credit and Usury over from Pound and gives them a good home and maintains them in practically the style to which they have been accustomed—his motto seems to be, *I'll adopt your child if only he's ugly enough*." After objecting to a number of things in the later parts of the poem, he reminds us and himself that Williams was one of the best poets alive, and the last one to be—he says— "properly appreciated." Yet he may also now be overvalued, rather than seen truly as "a *very* good but *very* limited poet [. . .] a notably unreasoning, intuitive writer." In the one-sided war Williams waged with Eliot, Jarrell judged Williams to have come off badly, especially when *Four Quartets* was compared to *Paterson*. The "long dreary imaginary war in which America and the Present are fighting against Europe and the Past"—a war which Williams had been actively "volunteering for and organizing"—is deplored by Jarrell on the following interesting grounds: "But go a few hundred years back inside the most American American and it is Europe: Dr. Williams is just as much Darkest Europe as any of us, down there in the middle of his past." Jarrell's own commitment to Europe was so recent and so intense as to have made impossible any full-scale support of Williams in such a struggle. But his judgments about Williams's poetry, as about Stevens's, take on authority because of their two-sidedness; he speaks with passionate intelligence both for and against.

Jarrell turned next to the writing of an essay, requested by Ransom for *The Kenyon Review*, which would eventually become "The

Age of Criticism," but this he put aside as potentially too long and proceeded instead to an appreciation of Walt Whitman. Meanwhile, in his letters he complained (as he did so frequently in the letters written from Princeton) about being a critic ("Oh, writing *criticism*! Booooh! Let's be novelists"). The essay on Whitman became his most aggressive attempt to break down the categories of "creative" and "critical," which he sought to do by extensive quotation from Whitman's poetry, with little of the analytical commentary that New Critics usually provided. He claimed that, to show Whitman for what he is, "one needs simply to quote" rather than explain or argue. So quote he does, making his case for why Whitman is a poet "of the greatest and oddest delicacy and originality and sensitivity, so far as words are concerned." To put the emphasis squarely on Whitman as a user of language, rather than as sage or American Consciousness, was a bold stroke that richly paid off— but only because Jarrell himself was delicate and original and sensitive in the way he extracted lines, passages, phrases in which the poet's greatness revealed itself. Nobody could have read the Whitman essay—or can read it still, for that matter—without marveling at how little of this poet one really *knows*, and how good is much or most of what Jarrell quotes.

As for Whitman's infamous lapses and awkwardness of expression, Jarrell's tack is not only to admit them but to welcome them as—in their badness—"unusually absurd [. . .] really ingeniously bad." Numbers of such expressions are cited, and the reader is invited to become, in a sort of camp way, fond of them. About Whitman's "I am a habitan of Vienna," he says, "One has an immediate vision of him as a sort of French-Canadian halfbreed to whom the Viennese are offering, with trepidation, through the bars of a zoological garden, little mounds of whipped cream." This is both very funny and eerily right about the line, but is of course not "analysis" so much as something a novelist or poet might produce as the only adequate response to Whitman's grotesque phrase.

But the essay also reaches a height of eloquence when Jarrell immortalizes lines by Whitman which, ever and only since his essay celebrated them, have been quoted and requoted. They are from the passage in *Song of Myself* which describes a wrecked steamship and the rescue of its passengers. Beginning with "I understand the large hearts of heroes," it proceeds through a series of "how" clauses focusing on the rescue, then comes back to Whitman the poet:

How the lank loose-gown'd women looked when boated from the side
of their prepared graves,
How the silent old-faced infants and the lifted sick, and the sharp-
lipp'd unshaved men;
All this I swallow, it tastes good, I like it well, it becomes mine,
I am the man, I suffered, I was there.

Jarrell comments:

> In the last lines of this quotation Whitman has reached—as great writers always reach—a point at which criticism seems not only unnecessary but absurd: these lines are so good that even admiration feels like insolence, and one is ashamed of anything that one can find to say about them. How anyone can dismiss or accept patronizingly the man who wrote them, I do not understand.

This is a totally convincing moment, and the whole passage from Whitman such a strong peg on which the charge can be hung that it renders the critic speechless, his profession unnecessary. Yet one almost feels that, if Whitman hadn't existed, this particular critic would have invented him in order to put criticism in its proper, subordinate place. For what in effect these lines and the essay's other examples from *Leaves of Grass* represent in the larger scheme of Jarrell's aspirations and inclinations is Life—the life that great poetry both celebrates and creates, and that serves as a corrector of human pretension. He had recently written Mary about what he saw as Blackmur's overestimation of himself: "You ought to realize that even if you're really good it's just in comparison to other people, that really you're practically a joke compared to what you might be and what somebody could be. *What is man that thou art mindful of him* is just so."

Never mind that, after finishing the Whitman article, he wrote: "I'll bet if Whitman is looking down from Heaven and reading my article he's *pretty pleased.*" Jarrell thought, often, that he himself was "really good." But he tried in his criticism to correct the individual talent by showing it something larger—some example of the human and artistic imagination that would put one's critical ego in its place, a secondary place. It is good to have words fail one, as when the poet says, after all his teasing of the girl in the library, "I love you—and yet—and yet—I love you"—"life" having brought him to this pitch of circularity and repetition. Those who would merely dismiss the girl don't see the life in her, are too academic and "critical" in an insufficiently large-minded way, like those clever people who dismiss Whitman, "the rashest, the most inexplicable and unlikely—the most impossible, one wants to say —of poets." In fact, they are not clever enough, not able to see the forest for the trees: "Baby critics who have barely learned to complain of the lack of ambiguity in *Peter Rabbit* can tell you all that is wrong with *Leaves of Grass.*" Conversely, "real critics" (of his sort, though he doesn't say this) have to spend much of their time, in any age, reiterating obvious truths, as he had sought to do with Whitman: that Milton, for example, and despite what Ezra Pound and F. R. Leavis had said, was a great poet; that (with Matthew Arnold's phrase in mind) Pope was no mere "classic of our prose" but a great poet; that Wordsworth, despite all his flatulence, was a great poet. If one looks grandly and lovingly enough, one will see that "there is something essentially ridiculous about critics, anyway: what is good is good without our saying so, and beneath all our majesty we know this."

The essay on Whitman is, among other things, a lively provoking of New Critics like Ransom and Tate and Blackmur who had avoided dealing with Whitman's poetry. But it was the long essay on Frost, "To the Laodiceans," written during the summer after he had left Princeton, which not only culminated his intense critical output of that year but remains his single most important and best piece of critical appreciation. It finely demonstrates the unique nature of his way with poets and poetry; it is also the place where he complains most eloquently about the impossibility of writing adequate criticism. If, he says, he were talking about Frost's poems with friends, or reading them aloud with students, some sort of justice could be done to them—he could recite and discuss thirty or forty poems "and feel sure about everything." He would not need "to praise or blame or generalize," but would let the poems "speak for themselves," which in Frost they do so well:

> But when one writes a little article about Frost, one feels lamentably sure of how lamentably short of his world the article is going to fall; one can never write about him without wishing that it were a whole book, a book in which one could talk about hundreds of poems and hundreds of other things, and fall short by one's essential and not accidental limitations.

He returns to this anxiety, endemic to the writer of critical essays, when he comes to Frost's longer narratives and dramatic dialogues from *North of Boston* and realizes he has no space to quote them. If he *could* quote all of "Home Burial," "The Witch of Coös," "A Servant to Servants," then "Pharisee and Philistine alike would tiptoe off hand in hand, their shamed eyes starry; anyone who knows these poems well will consider the mere mention of them enough to justify any praise, any extravagance—and anybody who doesn't know them doesn't know some of the summits of our poetry, and is so much to be pitied that it would be foolish to blame him too." So he asks us to regard the poems as having been quoted.

Of course the "extravagance" has been committed before our eyes, since the argument for Frost's greatness is importantly bound up with Jarrell's insistence that he lacks the space to do it justice; that he is really, by the very nature of *writing*, debarred from making the case that should be made—had he but world enough and time—in the classroom or the living room over the course of many hours, and with the authority of the speaking voice at his command.

This insistence is an example of what Derrida and his followers would pounce on as a "privileging" of speech over writing; yet while Jarrell insists on the inadequacy of his written account, he proceeds to his task with an energy greater than any he had brought to bear on previous subjects. The Frost essay is notable for its vigorously original commentary on five of "Frost's best and least familiar poems"—a claim that, in 1951, was surely justified. If "Neither Out Far Nor In Deep," "Provide, Provide," "Design," "The Most of It," and "Directive" now seem to lie at the center of Frost's achievement, they do so largely because of Jarrell's remarks about them. As he lamented about Frost's narratives, these individual commentaries are too long to quote in entirety, but one of them may be briefly inspected as a sample of the most sustained writing on a single poem he was ever to do. In four pages on "Design" he pulls out all the stops, insisting on being "personal" and witty in a manner that, rather than falling silent in awe before the poem, speaks back to it, almost does it one better.

A single example of this virtuosity occurs as he comments on the last five lines of the sonnet's octet depicting spider and moth on the white heal-all:

> *Assorted characters of death and blight*
> *Mixed ready to begin the morning right,*
> *Like the ingredients of a witch's broth—*
> *A snow-drop spider, a flower like froth,*
> *And dead wings carried like a paper kite.*

Jarrell says about these lines:

> The tone of the phrase *assorted characters of death and blight* is beautifully developed in the ironic Breakfast-Club-calisthenics, Radio-Kitchen heartiness of *mixed ready to begin the morning right* (which assures us, so unreassuringly, that this isn't any sort of Strindberg *Spook Sonata*, but hard fact), and concludes in the *ingredients* of the witch's broth, giving the soup a sort of cuddly shimmer that the cauldron in *Macbeth* never had;

the *broth*, even, is brought to life—we realize that witch's broth *is* broth, to be supped with a long spoon. For sweet-sour, smiling awfulness *snow-drop spider* looks unsurpassable, until we come to the almost obscenely horrible (even the mouth-gestures are utilized) *a flower like froth*; this always used to seem to me the case of the absolutely inescapable effect, until a student of mine said that you could tell how beautiful the flower was because the poet compared it to froth; when I said to her, "But—but—but what does froth *remind* you of?" looking desperately into her blue eyes, she replied: "Fudge. It reminds me of making fudge."

Not only had Frost never before been written about in this way, literary criticism had never been written in such a way. Presumably the young woman who thought of fudge would—in the unlikely event that she read the commentary—forgive Jarrell for using her and her blue eyes in the concluding sentence of a paragraph that has gone on for almost two pages. Or perhaps she and her perfectly bizarre response were fictions summoned into being through Jarrell's headlong, unstoppable inventiveness.

As had become his habit, and before proceeding, "in the nice, old-fashioned, looked-down-on phrase," "to appreciate" Frost's poetry, he cast a satirical look at what, in his earlier piece on the poet, he called "the Only Genuine Robert Frost in Captivity." This was the "public" Frost, the farmer-poet who, unlike Eliot and the rest, was "easy." In "To the Laodiceans" he makes up new names for this figure, calling him "the Grey Eminence of Robert Taft, or the Peter Pan of the National Association of Manufacturers," and says that Frost's public self "incarnates all the institutionalized complacency" he had once mocked and fled from, "and later pretended to become a part of and became a part of." This "Yankee Editorialist" is evoked only so that he, or it, can be moved out of the way and attention directed instead to the many marvelous poems that, as it were, the real Frost had written. Much of the essay's power comes from Jarrell's position as the first critic to treat Frost, not as a desirable alternative to obscure moderns like Eliot and Auden and Stevens and Pound, but as a poet whose subtlety and difficulty were at least equal to theirs. But he was also the first critic who, while admiring Frost greatly, presented an extreme and derisive picture of "the public figure's relishing consciousness of himself." Eliot had condescended to Frost; Blackmur had shaken his head over his "bardic" pretensions; critics on the left had deplored his callousness toward the welfare state, his militant individualism. Jarrell did not attempt to refute such charges, but handed them all over to "the Grey Eminence of Robert Taft," then proceeded to consider poem after poem, passage after passage, in which a quite different world was established and known for itself.

He was the first critic to address, if briefly, the sexuality in Frost's poetry, more of which was present, he noted, at the end of "The Pauper Witch of Grafton" (a Frost poem nobody had ever noticed) "than in several hothouses full of Dylan Thomas." He was the first, so far as I know, to point out the amazing memorableness—in the sense of easy to memorize—of poem after poem, which often, he says, the reader won't need to reread, just repeat. "I was floating in a quarry with my chin on a log when I first discovered that I knew 'Provide, Provide,'" he wrote, and later Robert Fitzgerald testified to being there at the quarry that summer of 1952 and hearing Jarrell proclaim his discovery. More important, he identified the "dark Frost" well before Lionel Trilling (whose phrase it was) did so, but also pointed out that in Frost's poetry no more justice is done to the world's awfulness than "to the tenderness and love and delight" that also suffuses the world. At the close of his essay, he boldly called Frost "that rare thing, a complete or representative poet" whose poems seem not so much like "performances," things made out of words, but rather

> things made out of lives and the world that the lives inhabit. For how much this poetry *is* like the world, [. . .] the world with its animals and plants and, most of all, its people: people

working, thinking about things, falling in love, taking naps; in these poems men are not only the glory and jest and riddle of the world, but also the habit of the world, its strange ordinariness, its ordinary strangeness, and they too trudge down the ruts along which the planets move in their courses.

This is writing that, without the solidity of specification in the essay's preceding thirty pages, would be like what Jarrell said the taste of Frost's "Birches" in our mouths was like—"a little brassy, a little sugary." But in context, with so many poems and details behind it—sometimes just touched, at other times considered at length—it has the ring of truth and of wisdom, as if Jarrell himself were closer to "lives" and the world they inhabit than any mere literary critic could pretend to be.

The Frost essay was, finally, the culmination of Jarrell's work as an encomiastic critic, or "appreciator," as he more modestly thought of himself. Although later in the fifties he published accounts of Stevens (for a second time) and of Robert Graves, we never again quite feel him massing all his forces, his taste, his love of poetry, his gift for the wicked phrase, in order to make the largest possible case for a major poet. If we regret, and sometimes we must, that he did not go on to do a comparable treatment of Eliot, or Hardy, or Hart Crane, we merely testify to our desire for more. Lonely at Princeton, anticipating a new life that had not yet begun, he put his soul into a critical effort which would not be duplicated. The succeeding chapter will examine other parts of that effort as found in his polemical essay "The Age of Criticism," his lectures on Auden, and *Pictures from an Institution*.

EIGHT

Criticizing the Institutions

"The Obscurity of the Poet," delivered at Harvard in the summer of 1950, took a tragicomic look at the modern poet's situation in America. When Jarrell came to Princeton a year or so later, he was already working on a companion piece, eventually finished in early 1952, called "The Age of Criticism." Like "The Obscurity of the Poet," it was a rambling meditation-out-loud, composed of "awful and delightful instances" of how we were living in an Alexandrian age that cared more for criticism than for the poems, novels, and plays that criticism was supposed to help us see more clearly. Near the essay's close, he compared it to Ben Jonson's poem "A Fit of Rhyme against Rhyme," calling his own diatribe "A Fit of Criticism against Criticism." Surely the essay received some of its impetus from his close-up observation of the Princeton English department, where the scene was more critically high-powered than at the Woman's College in Greensboro. He wrote Elizabeth Bishop in December that Princeton students rarely thought of writing anything except criticism, and that the poets and storywriters were a small minority; professors and students argued about such issues as whether Herman Melville was an atheist (spurred by Lawrance Thompson's just-published book on Melville's "quarrel with God") and everyone wrote critical essays. With hindsight we can see that Jarrell had been building up to writing this "fit" against criticism ever since, in his thesis on Housman, he chafed under the restraint of "correct" scholarly-critical behavior. After his summer in Salzburg, complaints about having to write criticism instead of poetry occurred more and more frequently, especially in the letters to Elisabeth Eisler, and he often lamented how much more interested magazines and periodicals were in publishing essays and reviews than the poems and stories those essays were presumably in the service of.

Was it, that era after the Second World War, truly "an age of criticism" for literature? As one who graduated from college the year after Jarrell's essay was published, I remember carefully perusing a study of modern literary criticism, Stanley Edgar Hyman's *The Armed Vision*, and finding its heady air bracing indeed. My undergraduate friends who considered themselves "literary" had read, like myself, shockingly little literature, but a great deal of criticism. Names like I. A. Richards, Blackmur, Empson, and Kenneth Burke (Hyman's favorite four, though he also included a number of admiring references to Jarrell) were repeated reverently and invoked frequently as authorities. We felt that we had been taught to read poems—especially poems—rigorously and religiously by studying the "words on the page" to the exclusion of biographical and historical context, and without worrying about what the poet's intention may have been. Our temptation was to be less interested in discovering new poems or new stories than in finding out what Cleanth Brooks had written about Keats's Grecian Urn and then comparing it with Burke's alternative view. Jarrell himself knew perfectly well—indeed, had already noted it in print—that there were a number of talented, "hard" critics who had brought new intensity and imagination to the interpretation of poetry. But he also knew that, like all good things, this development came at a cost; it would not only be aped by a host of lesser writers but threatened to displace interest in the art it sprang from. At one point in the essay, he asks a rhetorical question that even in the asking verges on becoming a real one: "Criticism *does* exist, doesn't it, for the sake of the plays and stories and poems it criticizes?"

But if "The Age of Criticism" can be seen as accurate literary sociology, it needs to be understood more fully and more deeply as a necessary consequence of Jarrell's ambivalent feelings toward the whole critical enterprise: it defines a place or an attitude he had been headed toward for some time. In the closing moment of the essay's final paragraph, he becomes slightly apologetic about what he has done: an essay on criticism should "avoid satire" and "be documented and persuasive and sympathetic, much in sorrow and hardly at all in anger." Yet rather than avoiding satire he had sought it out; and rather than being soberly documentative he committed himself to an exaggeration. A decade or so earlier, in "The End of the Line," he had asserted that modern poetry was an extension of romantic poetry; this brilliant simplification of an extremely complex subject was nonetheless convincing, for all its being a simplification. Now "The Age of Criticism" achieved a simplification in its sweeping portrayal of the age as one in which not only most people, but most critics, didn't read much, or read only approved landmarks, grazing timidly in well-known pastures. The most amusing and exhilarating passage in the essay—perhaps in any of his essays—is almost too long to quote, and yet needs to be for its full impact to be felt. He has summoned up an imaginary cocktail party at which the guests will talk only about certain books, the "right" ones, like *Ulysses* or *The Castle* or *The Brothers Karamazov* or *The Great Gatsby*:

> But if you wanted to talk about Turgenev's novelettes, or *The House of the Dead*, or *Lavengro*, or *Life on the Mississippi*, or *The Old Wives' Tale*, or *The Golovlyov Family*, or Cunninghame Graham's stories, or Saint-Simon's memoirs, or *Lost Illusions*, or *The Beggar's Opera*, or *Eugen Onegin*, or *Little Dorrit*, or the *Burnt Njal Saga*, or *Persuasion*, or *The Inspector-General*, or *Oblomov*, or *Peer Gynt*, or *Far from the Madding Crowd*, or *Out of Africa*, or the *Parallel Lives*, or *A Dreary Story*, or *Debits and Credits*, or *Arabia Deserta*, or *Elective Affinities*, or *Schweik*, or —or any of a thousand good or interesting but Unimportant books, you couldn't expect a very ready knowledge or sympathy

from most of the readers there. They had looked at the big sights, the current sights, hard, with guides and glasses; and those walks in the country, over unfrequented or thrice-familiar territory, all alone—those walks from which most of the joy and good of reading come—were walks that they hadn't gone on very often.

This pretty clearly is not an instance of documentation that "avoids satire" but a creative fantasy whose implications are interesting. Let us substitute the "real" Jarrell for the imagined "you" at the party who wants to talk about all those unread books. Let us also remember that this real Jarrell didn't like to drink, didn't like cocktail parties, didn't like Blackmur's drinking too much and making a fool of himself, surely didn't expect that these parties were good places to have conversations about *Arabia Deserta* or *Elective Affinities*. Let us then imagine a nervous guest at the party who would prefer to have another drink rather than talk to Jarrell, since the latter may ask the guest (a relatively timid reader) whether he has got round yet to those Cunninghame Graham stories he had not read when last asked.

My point in inspecting the party fantasy is to bring out its satiric loading of the dice. The absolutely wonderful list of titles Jarrell concocts as examples of "unfrequented territory" is also absolutely intimidating. Surely, we feel, nobody but he himself could live up to such a list, and therefore—whether or not it stands as a reproach to the age of criticism that has no time for it—the list, indeed the whole conceit in which it figures, is something quite different from an objective, "true" report on literary and cultural matters. Rather, it puts the stakes so high that one cannot play unless one is willing to lose to the man who thought up the game. Another way of putting things is to say that Jarrell couldn't bear to be just another critic, intent on writing useful appreciations and analyses of his favorite poems and novels. He had instead to dramatize his individuality by constructing an age of criticism against which he alone stood out and which he revealed as an ignoble phenomenon.

In fact, and to the extent that the two activities can be distinguished from one another, "The Age of Criticism" is more about reading than about criticism. Its emphasis has everything to do with Jarrell's sense of himself as a heroic reader, a sense which had only increased over the years since he began to borrow all those books from the library. "It is his reading that we judge a critic by, not his writing," he says at one point; a daring and unobvious thing to say, since it would promote an Edmund Wilson—for the breadth and originality of the books and authors he read and wrote about—over a first-rate practical critic of poetry like, say, Cleanth Brooks. The list of books that nobody at the imaginary party would discuss, since they hadn't read them, was on Jarrell's part a species of sublime showing off, a flexing of his reading muscles in delight as he thought of all the odd, out-of-the-way books he had devoured. "Readers, real readers, are almost as wild a species as writers; most critics are so domesticated as to seem institutions—as they stand there between reader and writer, so different from either, they remind one of the Wall standing between Pyramus and Thisbe." It is domestication or timidity, the fear of being wrong in an opinion, against which he speaks: "Taking the chance of making a complete fool of himself—and, sometimes, doing so—is the first demand that is made upon any real critic: he *must* stick his neck out just as the artist does, if he is to be of any real use to art." The reader who had read and wanted to talk about Cunninghame Graham or Doughty or *Lavengro*—in addition to Joyce and Kafka—had also, most commendably, stuck his neck out. But it didn't happen often enough to satisfy Jarrell.

Perhaps, then, "The Age of Criticism" is less about the age than about Jarrell as a "real reader," unlike anyone—even perhaps his worldly self—who walked around in an earthly body. "Real criticism demands of human beings an almost inhuman disinterestedness," he warns. "Criticism demands of the critic a terrible nakedness: a real critic has no one but himself to depend on. He can never forget that all he has to go by, finally, is his own response." This conception of the critic, like his friend Haggin's, and like Bernard Shaw's before him, is a dramatic-heroic one that may have had something to do with Jarrell's sense, expressed years before to Amy Breyer deBlasio, of having in childhood "been as alone as children ever are" and of being convinced he was quite different from everyone else. No one has described this "difference" better than Leslie Fiedler when he spoke of Jarrell as

> resolutely unsystematic, committed to no methodology or aesthetic theory—responsible only to his own responses, hushed only before the mystery of his own taste. And what unfailing taste he possessed; though its roots were in something nearer to madness than to method, given or endured rather than earned or sought, and therefore often offensive, as any talent is offensive, to those who resist believing in predestination.

The placing of the roots of taste closer to madness than method is a keen stroke, as is the notion that this voice could be "hushed" only by its own self-contemplation. Indeed, such a talent might be judged offensive. Jarrell himself worried about how the essay would be taken and whether people would think, "That cannibal's a Wild Man if there ever was one"; whether, really, he had said the right things, had been fair to critics; whether "some *awful* anti-highbrow people will welcome it and quote remarks (torn from context) made about the bad highbrow critics and will apply them to the good highbrow critics." But since he had championed the virtues of sticking one's neck out, it would have been cowardly for him not to have published the essay.

My emphasis here has been so much on Jarrell's personal impatience with writing criticism (as opposed to poems and novels), and on the satiric verve with which he created an age of criticism, that I may have somewhat neglected the essay's literal message— that the age

> needs to care more for stories and novels and poems and plays, and less for criticism; it needs to read more widely, more independently, and more joyfully; and it needs to say to

225

its critics: "Write so as to be of some use to a reader—a reader, that is, of poems and stories, not of criticism."

Whether, in 1951, we really lived in an age of criticism, there is no doubt that we do so now. In foreseeing the "increasingly Alexandrian" character of his age, could Jarrell in his wildest imaginings have anticipated essay titles such as "Canonicity and Theory: Toward a Poststructuralist Pedagogy," or "Internalization and the Other: Wordsworth's 'Arab' Dream and Hegel's Idea of Beauty," or "From Dyadic to Tetradic Tropologies in Narrative Discourse"—papers delivered at a recent meeting of the Modern Language Association? Jarrell's essay was prescient about present conditions in the academy, where younger professors are necessarily critics first—if not *real* critics—before they are teachers, readers, creative writers. And the essays they write are less "about" their ostensible subject than they are the necessary adjuncts to job applications and to professional success. They are surely not written to be "of some use" to a reader who is more interested in poems and stories than in criticism.

At Christmas, he spent three weeks with Mary in Laguna Beach, and upon his return to Princeton, the letters he wrote her were, if anything, even more absolute in their commitment to the coming marriage: "I want to live with you always, all our lives, and never leave you anymore"; and "I love you so much, sister; it doesn't seem to me that I could have been really alive and had a real life before I knew you"; and "Dearest, my own sister, I want so much to be married to thee, to never leave even for a day." He had begun a correspondence three years previously with someone who would be one of his strongest admirers and interpreters, Sister Bernetta Quinn; but the repeated address to Mary as "sister," along with his use of the pronoun "thee" in writing to her, bids to lift their relationship somewhere beyond sex, even beyond "ordinary" love between man and woman. The insistence on their oneness—brother and sister linked forever in mutuality—may also tie in with

Jarrell's interest in fairy tales; he had written a poem about Hansel and Gretel ("A Quilt-Pattern") and may have seen himself and Mary as correspondingly paired. So in the midst of such total and profuse dedication as is found in the "sister" letter quoted from above, it is good to come across the following compliment, paid her in a slightly different voice: "Oh, there was never anything like you—compared to you Florence Nightingale was a perfect bitch."

This sort of humor was an important force for sanity and good sense in Jarrell's dealings with other people. But on occasion he lost it, mainly with regard to matters of sexuality—or rather, with certain indiscreet ways of talking about it. One such occasion arose at Princeton, when a group of guests at Edward Cone's house were listening to Strauss's *Elektra* on an afternoon broadcast from the Metropolitan. Apropos of the moment in the opera when Elektra, realizing that her brother is coming, sings about how ugly and old she will look to him, Jarrell referred to the behavior of one of Cone's guests:

> Do you know that one of those *pigs* listening kept talking about incest and said an accompaniment was "positively lewd," and half the people laughed appreciatively? I didn't say much more than 2 cold disagreeing sentences [. . .] How I hate such people as that man—they spoil everything they touch with little nasty jokes; and, worst of all, he's an intelligent and in many ways nice person.

There is a partial recovery in the final qualification, but one feels how deep a nerve has been touched. At about the same time, he commented on a related kind of social behavior: "It always surprises me at lunch with these Princeton Intellectuals how many petty or sordid or faintly unpleasant or improper subjects come up. Me for Queen Victoria, as far as Public Life is concerned. I don't think these people make much distinction between them—lunch with acquaintances is Private Life for *them*."

On the basis of such responses he has been called a prude, though one person's prudery is another's disdain for the easy snigger. One can hear, for example, the clever Princeton voice declaring Strauss's music "positively lewd"; and one can imagine Jarrell, who cared supremely about great art (as he thought he heard in *Elektra*), bristling at the reductive, oh-so-knowing comment and reacting accordingly. And part of Jarrell's anger may have been that the clever person wasn't clever enough in his remark—wasn't so clever as, say, Jarrell, who not long before had said of his beloved Mahler's *Kindertotenlieder* that "it sounds as if those children had always been dead: and it's just enough like *Das Lied von der Erde* to make you think the children must have been half-Chinese. All the songs sound as if they wanted to stay on one note all the time but didn't quite have the nerve." If one is going to make adverse remarks about a piece of music, they had better be inventively amusing, not just easy name-calling.

As for the unnamed "improper subjects" that nameless "Princeton Intellectuals" brought up at lunch, he wrote about the incident to Mary, saying that it demonstrated the offensive triviality of institutional "society" as opposed to the society of the two of them together: "You're *my* Real Friend. Gee, I'll be glad to move away from this society into Ours." In fact, he recoiled at off-color allusions or gossip about people's private lives, and in doing so he could sound self-righteous and annoyingly pure-hearted. Yet he was as much an individual in this respect as in others. Berryman couldn't get over the fact that he was a poet who didn't drink; while early in Jarrell's acquaintance with Berryman's wife Eileen, he offered to bet her that his waist was even slimmer than hers, an act for which the adjective "vain" is surely inadequate. As she wrote in *Poets in Their Youth*, he was "unique," which means at least that easy terms like "prude" and "vain" should probably be resisted as inadequate characterizations, even as we admit the corresponding inadequacy of "unique."

On occasion in the spring of 1952 he escaped Princeton and his writing desk. In April he flew to Columbus, Mississippi, for an arts festival at which he met Eudora Welty and joined forces with her against a philistine dean of the graduate school who gave a speech

228

about how the really good, i.e., "successful," writers were not "difficult"—unlike the difficult Mr. Jarrell and Miss Welty, presumably. He liked Eudora Welty, describing her talk as "quite sincere, imaginative, serious." A week or so later, he flew to Grinnell College in Iowa to read from his own work and to judge student poetry. The trip was a great success—not the least part of which was having his handwriting analyzed by a woman who judged him to have an "extraordinarily gay and happy temperament," something he liked to hear about himself—and he seems to have realized fully, for the first time, the pleasing power over an audience that a poet might wield. He wrote Mary: "In 'A Girl in a Library' you could *see* the audience sway and be changed at every big change in the motion of the thought of the poem. I've never, almost, felt more strongly what a wonderful thing it is to have made the poems and have moved people so."

The year at Princeton culminated in six lectures on Auden, "written out beforehand" in longhand. At the end of his 1941 essay on the poet, he had made one of his little apologies (like that which was to conclude "The Age of Criticism"), in which he confessed to feeling embarrassed at having done "so much Analysis and so little Appreciation." But, he added, analysis—even of faults—was one way of showing appreciation, and he hoped later on to try another way. The Princeton lectures were by way of keeping his promise, and since the book on Auden he projected was never to be written, they are in fact his last word on the poet who meant so much to his own early work. The lectures have never been published, and the merest summary here may indicate their content and provoke a curious reader to consult them. As lectures they must have been superb: the lucid speaking voice, as always, full of wit, taking much pleasure in pointing out to the audience all the marvelous things—and a few of the not so marvelous—Jarrell had discovered in Auden's poetry over the years. There are appreciative explications of the early long poems *Paid on Both Sides* and *The Orators*; a section on the early poetry and a lengthy, fascinating analysis of the faults in the 1937 poem "Spain"; some lively and critical observations about *Nones*, his most recent book of poems. Portions from Jarrell's earlier essays and reviews also appear, somewhat recast, in the lectures.

Permeating them is a principle stated at the end of his remarks about *Paid on Both Sides*, one that might serve as a motto for his dealings not only with Auden but with any interesting, difficult artist. After noting that he can't prove any of his interpretations, he adds: "The quality of a really unusual and original work of art like this is something you have to get by repeated readings, by real familiarity, just as you can only become really acquainted with an original or extraordinary piece of music by repeated rehearings." The lectures practice what they preach by dwelling on particular poems and passages from poems in the hope of making Auden more accessible to an audience not of specialists but of generally intelligent readers. Jarrell's earlier essays on Auden had slighted individual poems, in an attempt to chart rhetorical devices and changing patterns of beliefs. (With reference to those beliefs, Jarrell now says that if Kafka's works can be called "the attempt to Escape your Father," Auden's should be called "the attempt to Escape your Auden.") While this slight was rectified in the Princeton lectures, there was still plenty of consideration given to Auden's "thought," including an especially original description of what—in Auden's early work—Jarrell calls the "ladder of love," whose each successive level turns out to be "wrong," a delusion. There was also a generous and accurate summation of what this poet had done and what constituted his virtues and limitations:

> Auden really has seen men and their cities, read their books, looked at their pictures, heard their music, thought their thoughts—and almost everything he has done or heard about it is at his command, is immediately available for his poems. A slower and profounder thinker, a man with more empathy for more people, an uneasier and humbler spirit, would not be able to use so much so freely.

This is perhaps as acute a thing as has ever been said about the poet whom Jarrell also saluted as the "greatest living rhetorician," whose striking command of language exceeded anyone's since Joyce: "His rhetorical powers have undergone an extraordinary elaboration and specialization."

Perhaps the most delightful moment in the lectures occurs when Jarrell entertains the notion that one might get behind Auden's poetry by asking what he "really thinks about things." What, in effect, does he do on Sunday after he's been writing poems all week; what, as a private man rather than a poet, does he think about such ultimate matters as love, death, truth? In an apt comparison, Jarrell suggests that asking what Auden really thinks about the world when he stops writing poems is like asking what Winston Churchill is like as a private person. For Churchill isn't like *anything* as a private person! "You might as well ask, 'What is Churchill like as a nursing mother?' " Moments like these made the lectures stimulating for both audience and lecturer, as a passage in a letter to Mary suggests: "I really felt so gay-serious, competent, and inspired while I talked, and was able to think of long elaborate sentences, lovely phrases, attractive informalities, etc.—so that the impromptu parts were better than the written ones."

Before the lectures were concluded, he wrote Mary that in four weeks they would be together in California: "Think of being through with these lectures; and then Princeton; and then My Old Life [. . .] O joy to be the New Jarrell entirely surrounded by daughters and dachshunds, California and you." This "New Jarrell" was partly an allusion to Bernard Haggin's joking about the "New Haggin"—when in fact he was always the same old Haggin—but Jarrell did view his Princeton experience as something he would be glad to put behind him: a species of academicism; the lineaments of an age of criticism he had satirized in his essay. And after the lectures, when his colleague Francis Fergusson remarked that they had been splendid and "about" what they were supposed to be about—Auden's poems—Jarrell was overjoyed. Similarly, during the following summer, when he taught with Fergusson and others (Robert Fitzgerald, Leslie Fiedler, Kenneth Burke, and John Crowe Ransom) at the Indiana School of Letters in Bloomington, his conviction only deepened that, along with becoming the New Jarrell with daughters and dachshunds, it was time to cast off the "old" New Criticism in favor of the kind he and a few others were practicing.

His letters to Mary from Bloomington that summer (after spending time with her in California, he'd flown to Bloomington for the one-month session) document instances of the "Age of Criticism" mentality—as when, at a dinner party, his mentor Ransom ("cute and sweet as ever") spoke enthusiastically about a fifty-page paper he had received from a student writing on one of Eliot's short quatrain poems: "He told it entirely seriously and praisingly as an example of how wonderful students could be nowadays—didn't see a thing incongruous or disproportionate about it." Much more satisfying was swimming in a quarry with Fitzgerald and Fergusson (the summer heat at Bloomington was steadily awful) and cheering them all up by talking what he called " 'Age of Criticism' talk." A further ally—not surprisingly—was Leslie Fiedler, who was very much not a part of any academic establishment and devoted to standing various received doctrines on their head. The faculty villain at the school turned out to be, of all people, Kenneth Burke—himself not even an academic—who gave a talk about criticism that appalled Jarrell and Fitzgerald: "extravagantly mechanical and verbose and senseless and full of absolutely irrelevant free association." As counterweights to Burke, there was not only Jarrell's own "Age of Criticism"—which he delivered as a lecture even though it had already been published—but a lecture by Fiedler with whose every word, Jarrell declared, he agreed. What the stint at Bloomington had taught him, as a sort of final seal on the Princeton year, was that even in an age of criticism he could feel good about "the possibilities of the new generation of critics and writers, the ones that'll finally take the places (some of the places) of the Old Monuments." He even imagined himself and Peter Taylor, along with Fitzgerald and Fiedler, getting control of "a creative-writing set-up at some school" where art would be given its proper priority over criticism and where (it is not an uncommon fantasy) right-thinking people of human sympathies could unite in holding off the forces of darkness. This was probably as visionary as he would ever become. But a similar visionary flare can be glimpsed in a letter to Mary about how commonplace life was without her and how, with her, he felt like a Rilke poem, and that this feeling would help him write such poems: "Seriously, he's got to seem to me a sort of symbol of the real poet of our age—what to write like to be the opposite of the Others." Being the "opposite of the Others"—in his life, his poetry, his criticism—was scarcely a new aspiration, but was one that, as he grew older and moved into years when relatively few original poems would come, proved increasingly a strain as well as a spur. He had a sense of this fact when he wrote Mary from Bloomington about "how lonely you are when you come out on the side of life and risk-taking and thinking works of art are live and mysterious and unaccountable; on the side of everything that can't be institutionalized and handled and graded by Experts."

In his letters from Princeton, Jarrell complained frequently to Mary about his social life, as when he had lunch with Blackmur and found him unequal to the Blackmur who appeared in his lectures. The "social" Blackmur seemed too much a part of the "whole literary-academic, semi-fashionable, established accepting-things-at-their-own-valuation world." He was glad, he told her, to be "marrying a wild tribe" and asserted that he himself was not "institutionalized." (Photographs of Mary and her two daughters don't show any "wild tribe"—Jarrell projected on them his need to be free, outside the institution.) Yet he was not above making use of the institution or Blackmur as a person with connections, and he acted upon his colleague's suggestion that if he was interested in changing publishers he might get in touch with Harry Ford, an editor at Alfred A. Knopf. Harcourt had been Jarrell's publisher, except for *Little Friend, Little Friend*, but had shown, he felt, only the most dutiful interest in his books. Now he had two non-poetry volumes in process of completion: the critical essays that would make up *Poetry and the Age* and a "prose narrative" (as he termed it in a letter to Ford) that would become *Pictures from an Institution*.

The latter appears to have sprung virtually full-grown from his head. In the spring of 1951 he wrote Hannah Arendt that, inspired by her example (*The Origins of Totalitarianism* had just been published), he too had written a "prose book." (Later, as a joke, he disguised *Pictures* by draping it with the dust jacket from her book.) And Peter Taylor recalls feeling disbelief when at one point Jarrell suddenly announced that he had written a novel. In fact, in 1951 the book was still in the process of being extended and would be extended further when a reader at Knopf worried that it was not quite enough of a "novel." Blackmur had written a prompting note to Harry Ford, who then sent Jarrell an extremely winning letter which said that he and others at Knopf would be highly pleased to consider for publication anything he had written; that, in fact, they had been hoping he might do a novel for them, and that Ford's own admiration of Jarrell's poetry went back to *Blood for a Stranger*. Ford singled out "A Girl in a Library" as a poem "which I would like to claim to having read silently and aloud more times than any man alive." Naturally Jarrell was pleased with the letter and with the idea of settling down at a publisher "who enjoys me and whom I enjoy." When Knopf suggested changing *Pictures* to make it more novel-like, he assured Ford that this was fine by him, that it contained several sections which he had decided to expand, and that he agreed "an odd book's an odd problem; after all, if I'd wanted it easily acceptable I shouldn't have given it two heads."

Pictures is indeed a very odd book, and to label it an "academic novel," or a satire directed at progressive education as it was carried on at Sarah Lawrence, is to replace with a type something quite untypical. Its oddity can be measured by comparing it with Mary McCarthy's *The Groves of Academe*, which was published in 1952, by which time Jarrell had written his book in its earlier form. He read McCarthy's novel soon after it appeared—and was shocked to find his own name in a list of poets who weren't invited to the poetry conference at McCarthy's mythical Jocelyn College—but must have sensed what a very different animal his own creation was. For *The Groves of Academe* is a bona fide academic novel, with a strong plot and a cast of interacting characters skillfully manipulated for our amusement by an all-knowing but also fully removed narrator, so as to produce what the book's cover calls a "satire on American intellectual life."

There is little reason to believe that, even if he had wanted to, Jarrell could have sat down and composed the sort of expert entertainment which McCarthy's exemplifies. The necessary subordination of parts, one to another; the patient development of "character" through local details of dress, speech, and physique, so as to make up someone we can imagine as living and breathing; above all, the building of a convincing and continuous narrative line—this was a kind of creation he had done little of in his previous writing. His war poems typically presented their subjects through the reflective sympathy of a concerned voice; more recently, with "A Girl in a Library" and other narratives from *The Seven-League Crutches*, he had allowed his poetic narrators a wider range of tone and wit, and had begun to think of himself—he wrote Mary—as a "dramatic" rather than a "lyric" poet. In his prose, most notably in "The Obscurity of the Poet," he had developed a way of exposition that was exciting in its inclusiveness, its sudden changes of pace and diction, its witty irony. Yet, as noted previously, Jarrell tended toward brilliant one-liners that obliterated "responsible" analysis of his subject—and that equally could destroy characters in a novel.

Pictures was more or less coincident with "The Obscurity of the Poet"; in fact, whether he turned himself to writing novel, lecture, or poem, a single presence was increasingly in the ascendant. Consider again the following lines about the girl in the library:

> *For nineteen years she's faced reality:*
> *They look alike already.*

> *They say, man wouldn't be*
> *The best thing in this world—and isn't he?—*
> *If he were not too good for it. But she*
> *—She's good enough for it.*

They have obvious links to what is perhaps the most-quoted description from *Pictures*, that of boy-wonder President Robbins, who is "so well adjusted to his environment that sometimes you could not tell which was the environment and which was President Robbins." In each passage Jarrell is talking about the depressing "fit" between a person and the outside world ("reality" or "the environment"). *Pictures* also echoes the lecture in repeating Goethe's observation that man wouldn't be the best thing in the world unless he were too good for it; and various other *bon mots* and witty turns of phrase appear in both novel and essay. In other words, Jarrell was blurring the lines between genres, seeing what he could do to write a lecture that wasn't just a lecture, a novel that really couldn't be called a novel exactly, a poem (like "A Girl in a Library" perhaps) that stretched the possibilities of what poems could do.

Just as Pound's *Cantos* are, among other things (and in Pound's own words), "a catalogue, his jewels of conversation," *Pictures* is centrally, as Peter Taylor has pointed out, a catalogue of Jarrell's witty talk, often—especially in the book's earlier parts—of a malicious, at least satiric, bent. Here is Mrs. Robbins, wife of the president of Benton College:

> People did not like Mrs. Robbins, Mrs. Robbins did not like people; and neither was sorry [. . .] She had been a scholar once, and talked somewhat ostentatiously of *her work*, which she tried *to keep up*. To judge from her speech, she was compiling a Dictionary of Un-American English: if lifts and trams ever invade the North American continent, Pamela Robbins is the woman to lead them. Often, when you have met a true Englishwoman—the false ones are sometimes delightful— you feel that God himself could go no further, that way. Mrs. Robbins existed to show what he could do if he tried.

It continues in this vein, one that might be given the title of an ancient radio show, *Can You Top This?* The writing seems to exist mainly for the purpose of outdoing itself, as each sentence takes off with the ambition of going its predecessor one better. One of the best sequences in the book, about President Robbins, must bring to any academic person's mind a college president he or she has known:

> At first President Robbins talked a little stiffly and warily, but then he warmed to himself. He liked to say: "The secret of good conversation is to talk to a man about what *he's* interested in." This was his Field Theory of Conversation. He always found out what your field was (if you hadn't had one I don't know what he would have done; but this had never happened) and then talked to you about it. After a while he had told you what he thought about it, and he would have liked to hear what you thought about it, if there had been time.

If Robbins is treated less severely than his wife, both portrayals serve less to build up "character" through incremental accumulation than to display the narrator's (he may be called Jarrell, surely) boundless resourcefulness as a stand-up entertainer. In this sense, *Pictures* is as theatrical a book as could be written; the showman continuously performs to a (presumably) delighted audience that only demands more of the same.

The publisher's initial worry that the book was insufficiently novel-like has much to do with the intensity of its verbal performance; this is not to say that "real" novels can't be intensely composed pieces of writing, but that the peculiarity of Jarrell's style works against a sense of the book as real—as somehow about "life"—in the way that *Anna Karenina* or even *The Groves of Academe* is real and about life. Those books have reference; *Pictures*, by contrast, especially the first third of it, offers the reader an ongoing feast of bright, ingenious formulations. There is danger of a glut; and if there are books that, in the tired phrase, one can't put down, this is one that—in my own experience—can be put down more than once. Its density makes it slow going, and its sentences have a way of exploding in your face, leaving you nothing to do but start over again. Consider this reflection about being shipwrecked with a hopeless character named Flo Whittaker: "And after you had been on the raft with her for two weeks and on the island with her for two years, sharing mussels, you would have known her no better than you knew her then; but then, how could you have known her better than you knew her then?" Or this about the Whittakers and their difficult young daughter: "Fern was a thorn in the flesh to remind the Whittakers that they had flesh; but they weren't reminded." Again, about Flo: "This is absurd, of course; no one would say such a thing; but Flo did say such things. Saints are necessarily absurd—and Flo was a saint, of a poor kind; almost all saints are saints of a poor kind." The sentences delight in deconstructing themselves, in taking up tired phrases, worn metaphors, and committing—in Robert Frost's definition of poetry—organized violence upon them. Confronted with Gertrude Johnson, a satiric novelist, the narrator confesses that "I felt sheepish—felt like a flock of sheep, that is—as Gertrude sheared from me (with barber's clippers that pulled a little) my poor coat of facts, worked over it with knitted brows, and then, smiling like Morgan le Fay, cast over my bare limbs her big blanket conclusions." About Gertrude he says, with deadpan subversiveness, "Gertrude *knew* better than this, of course, but we all know better than we know better, or act as if we did." Where are we left at the end of such a sentence?

Taken together, these passages from the book's first third may bring to mind Delmore Schwartz's remark, in his review of *Little Friend* some years previously, that if only Jarrell could inject the wit of his prose criticism into his poetry we would have a modernist Pope. By 1951 that wit was showing up in poems like "A Girl in a Library" and "A Conversation with the Devil," while in *Pictures* the sentences have the compacted witty surprise of the couplet from Pope's *Dunciad* that sets before us a young fop back from his grand tour of Europe:

Intrepid then, o'er seas and lands he flew:
Europe he saw, and Europe saw him too.

For all their differences, both writers share an explosive compression and the power to turn the world into words that—in T. S. Eliot's useful phrase—"create the object which they contemplate." The young dunce back from his grand tour, and Flo Whittaker, shipwrecked and impossible as ever, are each sad specimens of the human; yet Pope and Jarrell leave us thinking not about their moral and aesthetic insufficiency but about the splendid sufficiency of the words that immortalized them. To adopt another of Eliot's formulations, the satire is "creative" rather than "critical."

When in the novel's closing chapter Gertrude Johnson and her husband, Sidney, prepare to leave Benton, she says to the narrator and his wife (the latter a shadowy, nameless presence) that there is something attractive about "living in a quiet dull place like this where nothing ever happens." Gertrude has previously revealed to the narrator the plot of her new novel—which he tells us, with ironic capital letters, was a "Real Plot. It could have happened anywhere—anywhere except, perhaps, Benton." On the face of it, these assertions could refer to the strange, unreal little place that is the "institution" of the novel's title. Yet for all its perceived association with real persons and places (Benton as a version of Sarah Lawrence, President Robbins as a version of Harold Taylor, Gertrude Johnson as a version of Mary McCarthy or Jean Stafford, Gottfried and Irene Rosenbaum as affectionate echoes of Hannah Arendt and her husband), the traditional disclaimer after the title page should nonetheless be taken seriously: that it is a work of fiction, and that its details, names, characters "and the Institution are not intended to, and do not, relate to any existing institution or to any real persons living or dead."

Nothing ever happens in Benton, and Gertrude's "Real Plot" could have happened anyplace *but* there, since Jarrell has written a novel in which nothing happens except stylistically—within the sentences. There is no real plot for the reader to hang on to; one thing does not lead to another; no character significantly interacts with another. We hear, for example, about a famous quarrel between Gertrude and President Robbins—just the sort of thing that would be lively reading in a more traditional academic satire. But it barely appears in the pages of *Pictures*. This absence has everything to do with Jarrell's continuous presence, in his sentences, as a performing self. There is really no room for persons or institutions to exist in their own right, as free and independent creations; even admirers of the novel will perhaps admit that its atmosphere is claustrophobic, the air so relentlessly processed that breathing is difficult.

The narrator "is" Jarrell, to the extent that his qualities and characteristics are blatantly those of his animator: he, this narrator, is married, but without children; writes poetry; served in the air force in the Second World War—and even (in a detail that doesn't occur in Jarrell's letters) confides to us that his mates at Chanute Field in Illinois used to call him "Tex" (Jarrell's home at that time was Austin, Texas). He is of course widely read, an extremely sensitive listener to music, with an excellent eye for painting and sculpture. At one point, Gertrude asks him if he hasn't ever thought of writing a novel, and there is an eeriness for us in knowing that that is exactly what Jarrell had been doing since the day when he—though by trade a poet—sat down and began to compose *Pictures*. It is implied that, if he ever did write a novel (he tells Gertrude that his memory isn't good enough for the task), he would not attempt—as Gertrude does—to see through everything, reducing the world and its people to inferior roles. By contrast, Gertrude's books relentlessly analyze everything ("They did not murder to dissect, but dissected to murder"). But the narrator, it seems, can love other people—like the Rosenbaums; he can, even after he has leveled them, see something worthy and endearing in Gertrude or President Robbins. We are asked to believe that, unlike Gertrude, he knows what it is to be a human being, since he can see the way in which Gertrude is, after all, a human being:

But as a writer Gertrude had one fault more radical than all the rest: she did not know—or rather, did not believe—what it was like to be a human being. She was one, intermittently, but while she wasn't she did not remember what it had felt like to be one [. . .] If she was superior to most people in her courage and independence, in her intelligence, in her reckless wit, in her extraordinary powers of observation, in her almost eidetic memory, she was inferior to them in most human qualities; she had not yet arrived even at that elementary forbearance upon which human society is based.

This is one of the passages from *Pictures* that is notable for its absence of the clever turn; here we do not laugh but are invited to assent, in a fairly sober manner, to the "elementary forbearance upon which human society is based," that forbearance our narrator understands and Gertrude doesn't. In other words, as Suzanne Ferguson points out in her fine essay on the book, we are asked to believe that the narrator—that Jarrell—is different from Gertrude in that he "sees also good in the beings whose follies and blindnesses he impales."

Not all readers of *Pictures* have been able to swallow this added moral dimension as easily as they can appreciate the narrator's satirical thrusts. One reviewer of the book when it was published —Thomas Mabry—found himself repelled instead of charmed by what he called "that paragon of virtue, that paradigm of taste, and that paradox of just-us-folksiness, too" who spoke in these pages. "Can anybody be so right, always?" Mabry asked, and answered his own question: "Nobody, apparently, but the 'I' who writes in the pretendedly ingenuous tone of an inspired but naughty Boy Scout." The "moral dimension" was really a case of a clever, superior talent wanting also to insist that it wasn't *merely* clever, wasn't *really* superior in any exclusively elitist sense. Like many nineteenth-century English novelists, Jarrell tried very hard to put together cleverness and goodness in the same person: the person of great satiric gifts is afraid, one might say, of being too clever for his own good, and yearns for the saving touch of ordinary humanness that makes for kinship with others.

But it is not anything the narrator says about himself that convinces us his range of feeling is wiser and more generous than the pure, inhuman satirist represented by Gertrude. Rather, at moments in the later parts of the book, his playing of the "inspired but naughty Boy Scout" disappears—at least in passages—and is replaced by a gentler, more truly reflective consciousness. Things happen to this consciousness; it is acted upon by another's presence, and one senses in the writing that Jarrell has been taken beyond his tightly controlled witty superiority into a different mood, one of appreciative wonder at the nature of things—at human nature. Jarrell the man was prey to such moods. After flying back from his Grinnell poetry reading in May, he wrote Mary about how beautiful things looked as he landed in New York. Princeton was even more beautiful, the trees in bloom, the air cool and clear, and he walked down to the garden by the president's house to admire "the flowers perfected by man, so fresh and wonderful, that I couldn't help thinking that—regardless of all the awful things he does—man is the glory and wonder of the earth." Sophocles' chorus from *Antigone* about the wonders of man strikes him as "so much righter than the Original Sin people," and he concludes, "To fly across the country in the day time is to think a lot about the Works of Man."

This kind of marveling at life's wonders derives its power largely by sounding so unlike Jarrell, the witty scourge of life's imperfections. One example from *Pictures*, a description of Irene Rosenbaum's singing, points up a similar marveling and an attendant humility:

Of all the singers I have ever heard she was the most essentially dramatic: she could not have sung a scale without making it seem a part of someone's life, a thing of human importance. Yet when the song and her voice said: *We are all dying*, something else about her voice—a quality that could not be localized, that all the sounds possessed together and none possessed apart—said to you also: *Whoever dies?* Over feeling and act, the human reality, her voice seemed to open out into a contradicting magic of speculation and belief, into the in- human reality men discover or create. Her voice pushed back the boundaries of the world.

In a manner analogous to Irene's voice, Jarrell's here opens out into something like a "magic of speculation and belief" that pushes back the world's boundaries. A similar quality of feeling suffuses the book's conclusion, as the narrator, having cleaned out his office and preparing to depart from the now empty campus, muses on absences:

> The lunch I hadn't eaten, the shadows I stepped on, and the barred walks shining and empty in the sun, all the absences that were present there, came together into a kind of elegiac listlessness: everything had for me then too faint and strange a life even to need to perish.

It almost reads like a poem, the mood created not just elegiac but one of elegiac listlessness; not just of the perishing of things, but of a strange endurance beyond the need of perishing. Such writing gives substance to James Agee's claim that the book's fun and its insight are "rooted in humaneness."

Jarrell's mixed feelings about what he had done in *Pictures* came out in letters he wrote to Lowell as the book was nearing publication in the spring of 1954, and to Warren after its publication a year later. To Lowell, whom he was trying to tease into also writing a prose book, he said it had been great fun, "not at all a wearing *job*, like criticism, and you don't have the helpless possessed ex- hausted feeling you have with poetry even when that is most fun: all the playful, inventing, noticing, organizing, knowledge-y side of you can really go to work." But to Warren, who had written him in praise of *Pictures*, he confessed that it was very hard to write a book "in which the main structure isn't a plot or story—I don't

243

think I ever will again." He had been working on a translation of Chekhov's *Three Sisters* (as with other languages, his knowledge of Russian was rudimentary at best) and said that he would like to write a play himself but that he needed "to believe in plots first." This "disbelief" in fictional plots, and his own lack of interest and conviction about hammering one together, could be looked on as a forerunner of what, fifteen or so years later, would be called metafiction, the "anti-story" as practiced by a Coover, a Barth, or a Barthelme. But Jarrell knew also, and took the knowledge seriously, that, as he put it, "Man is the animal that likes narration." A novelist who wouldn't or couldn't gratify that taste wasn't really a novelist but rather the writer of a single unique book, like the one he had written.

At roughly the same time as he finished the novel, he began to conceive of himself as more a dramatic than a lyric poet. His poems in *The Seven-League Crutches* had attempted, not always successfully, to incorporate complicated turns, progressions, and doublings back in a speaker's consciousness (his favorite poems by Frost were the dramatic monologues and dialogues from *North of Boston*). And just as he disliked, or at least shied away from, plot as the unifying core of a novel, so did he largely abandon the attempt to fuse opposites into a unified poem such as the New Critics had championed—Tate's "tension" or Brooks's "paradox" being the operative terms. Instead, his allegiance was toward something larger and more vague, to "life" or the "real," whether it was found in the quirky wanderings of the narrative voice in *Pictures* or the irresolute, open-ended moments he tried increasingly to create in his poems, as in "A Girl in a Library":

> And yet, the ways we miss our lives are life.
> Yet . . . yet . . .
> > to have one's life add up to yet!

His allegiance to life was bluntly stated in an admiring letter he wrote Bishop in 1957: "Your poems seem really about real life, and to have as much of what's nice and beautiful and loving about the world as the world lets them have." He told her he had come to like her poems even better than he liked Marianne Moore's, since "life beats art, so to speak, and sense beats eccentricity, and the way things really are beats the most beautiful unreal visions, half-truths, one can fix up by leaving out and indulging oneself." In the fall of 1952, as he and Mary began their married life together, the question Jarrell faced was what sort of "life" would prove to be most real in the poems he wanted to write.

N I N E

The Group of Two

JARRELL and Mary von Schrader were married in November of
1952 on what she describes as a "fine, bright, smog-free eighth
in Pasadena, as dry and glittering as California used to be in the
twenties." They had been living at Laguna Beach since his Princeton year ended in May and, taking advantage of his leave from the
Woman's College, stayed on in Laguna until mid-January, when
they moved to Urbana and a semester's teaching at the University
of Illinois. Immediately after the wedding, the couple headed for
Madera, there to see the sports-car races, and especially Jarrell's
favorite driver, Phil Hill. The interest in sports cars and their
drivers was of a piece with his love for Balanchine's work and his
dancers—a love hard to sustain if one didn't live in New York. In
fact, his essay about the "little cars," which praised drivers like
Phil Hill for their "dazzling skill, individuality, and aesthetic expressiveness," suggests that this later interest was a stand-in for
the earlier one. He compared Hill to Danilova and Tanaquil Le
Clercq, and to Ellsworth Vines on the tennis courts. (In the last
years of his life, as he watched more and more professional football,
Johnny Unitas became his shining example of the athlete-artist.)

If Jarrell's admiration shows a craftsman's respect for the dili-
gence that produces gracefulness, it also reflects a somewhat boyish

246

hero-worship. But his fascination with the world of sports cars went deeper than merely admiring the expert drivers, since he created a mythology around the racing world in which most of the cars "have a gay, light, irresponsible air—they are perfect meringues of cars." The drivers were equally graceful and insouciant:

> Like birds, they run to crests: a rainbow, converted into billed caps, crowns their brown, bouncy, white-toothed faces. They wear stocking caps, hoods, tam-o'-shanters, fast hats like a skier's or a brownie's; now and then there goes by, in stern, exotic navy, a beret—goes by, one among ten thousand, a deerstalker of Harris tweed.

He urges his readers not only to go to the races but if possible to go in a sports car ("When we go in our Oldsmobile we feel like bears at *Phèdre*—good bears, honest bears, but bears"). When the races are over, "the sports-car drivers blink, shake themselves, and go back to Life"—as does a rapt watcher like himself. Mary Jarrell remembers ritual trips-out-together to one town drugstore after another in search of the latest issue of the sports-car bible, *Road and Track*, which, she felt, came "nearer than anything else to satisfying that leitmotiv of yearning" permeating his poems. The yearning was for an entirely different race of beings, as expressed in "A Sick Child," when the boy in bed says, "I want a ship from some near star / To land in the yard, and beings to come out / And think to me: 'So this is where you are! / Come.' " As the poem goes on to say, they never do arrive, but we may presume that such was the promise *Road and Track* held out to him.

The trips to the drugstore—in the morning after breakfast, in the evening after supper—were but one instance of the Jarrells' operation as a "group of two." In her memoir of that title, Mary Jarrell put it most forthrightly:

> To be married to Randall was to be encapsulated with him. He wanted, and we had, a round-the-clock inseparability. We took three meals a day together, every day. I went along to

his classes and he went along on my errands. I watched him play tennis, he picked out my clothes. Sometimes we were brother and sister "like Wordsworth and Dorothy" and other times we were twins, Randall pretended. "The Bobbsey Twins at the Plaza," he'd say up in our room at the Plaza.

Her statement is the more striking for being made in a tone neither of ironic complaint nor of superiority to those couples not "encapsulated" with one another. This was just the way one particular marriage worked. To Mary's daughters, Alleyne and Beatrice, Jarrell was mainly—in Mary's phrase—an affectionate encyclopedia. The younger daughter, Beatrice, to whom he became very close, has characterized him as an "ideal father." The phrase is aptly dual in implication—in the sense not only of perfect but of unreal; he was not a "real" father who made demands on, suffered through, and was thoroughly implicated in the life of his child. To Beatrice, Jarrell was memorable above all else as a reader of stories, the myths and fairy tales that were the "one cure for Everychild's diseases," as he wrote in an earlier poem.

He seems to have had no interest in raising children of his own, a subject never touched on in his letters. That someone so passionately committed to, and thoroughly obsessed by, the child's situation should express no interest in fathering one himself may initially seem surprising, but in fact may have been the condition for such vision about the subject as he possessed. The twentieth-century writer who seems comparably engaged with the child's relationship to his parents—especially to his mother—and to the world is D. H. Lawrence, who was also childless, an "ideal father" insofar as he was filled with ideas about how children and parents should and should not behave. Both Lawrence and Jarrell were great celebrators of life—that thing which Gertrude Johnson in *Pictures* couldn't see, since she was so busy seeing through it. But there is good reason to assume that Jarrell's self-absorption and his total dedication of that self to Art—poetry, music, ballet, paintings, tennis, sports cars—left little room for fatherhood. He liked to be married, liked being married to Mary, and liked being an "affectionate encyclopedia" to her daughters. Real fatherhood was one of the "entanglements"—in Robert Lowell's word—his spirit was immune to.

One entanglement he thoroughly and joyously capitulated to was his beloved cat, Kitten. It is easy, perhaps too easy, to say that he, Kitten, was all the child Jarrell ever needed; having said it, one feels slightly embarrassed, and partly on Jarrell's account. Yet the intensity of his feeling for this black Persian cat was revealed so often and so unabashedly (Kitten is one of the principal characters in the index to Jarrell's letters) that to be simply embarrassed in the face of it is to be unimaginative. When, during his army service, Mackie sent him some pictures she had taken, Jarrell wrote back, saying he was delighted, had looked at them over and over, and that "I want some more of Kitten and some more of you." The order of request is perhaps insignificant, but a later letter, after further pictures had arrived, suggests that Kitten was stiff competition for any mere wife:

> Your pictures of Kitten are wonderful. The best one, one of the best photographs I've ever seen, is the one of Kitten walking in the alley across the street. The dark glowing look he shares with the trees makes it look as if it ought to be called *Kitten in Fairyland* [. . .] The one of Kitten eating alone on the front porch has such a patterned texture (to Kitten's fur, I mean) that it's hard to believe it's not a painting.

Although he goes on to assure Mackie that *she* also looks charming in some of the pictures, his prose doesn't match the fervor with which Kitten's photographs are celebrated. When he received an army medal at one point for his performance as a pistol marksman, he wrote Mackie that he wanted "(I'm serious) Kitten to wear it round his neck on a ribbon on state occasions."

Mary Jarrell describes how overjoyed he was when, after the divorce, Mackie decided not to keep Kitten any longer and sent him back to Jarrell. One of the most charming sections of "The

Group of Two" details the various ways he and Kitten would play together, and one of its most affecting passages recounts the night Kitten was struck and killed by a car, the subsequent burial, and Jarrell's grief-stricken mourning. (Mary Jarrell is not the only one to have noted the eerie similarity between Kitten's and Jarrell's death.) I am aware that delight and sympathy were and are not universal responses to his love of Kitten (there are some funny anti-Kitten stories in circulation, and Jean Stafford thought it a pathetic name for a cat), and the whole situation could be made to look faintly absurd. I don't find it absurd (just as I don't mind an anti-Kitten story), but in fact a central instance of Jarrell's extravagance of spirit as it embraced and would not let go of something precious. The embrace could be a fierce one, as a faculty colleague once found out when he twitted Jarrell about using meat-ration coupons during the war so that Kitten could eat well. Jarrell flashed back with "Why of course! What would you *expect*? He's only a poor cat, and has to eat what he can. People can eat anything. What an absurd remark." The response has the bite and surprise of good poetry as it moves in a direction neither we nor the victim could have anticipated.

When, after having been away for two years, Jarrell, newly married, returned to Greensboro in the fall of 1953, he dug himself in—happily so, at least early on. Robert Watson, who became a colleague that fall, remembers him on registration day, just before the doors had opened to students, reading bits from *The Wind in the Willows* and exclaiming how marvelous it was and how glad he was to be teaching again at the college which was "like Sleeping Beauty." When Sleeping Beauty woke up and gave a party, it was a different story. Watson's testimony is but one of many that confirm how shy and uncomfortable Jarrell was at parties, and how he usually chose to sit on a sofa with his wife and perhaps another person, discussing "books, or paintings, or perhaps sports." With Peter Taylor now at Kenyon, Jarrell's main social companions were Malcolm Hooke, from the French department, and his wife, Lucy.

250

Except for one significant exception—involving Hooke—Jarrell took little or no part in campus politics. The exception (Mary Jarrell gives an account of this complicated affair in the *Letters*) involved a proposed new program of General Education, sponsored by Chancellor Graham and Jarrell's old friend Marc Friedlaender. Members of various departments, including Malcolm Hooke, felt threatened and were opposed to the program, and at the crucial faculty meeting Jarrell rose in defense of his friend Hooke (who had been attacked) and in opposition to the proposed new program. Friedlaender, whose party lost the fight and who thereafter resigned from the Woman's College, recalls that Jarrell's speech was absolutely devastating in its satirical force, all the more devastating since he so rarely exercised his voice in faculty meetings. Yet the speech appears to have been more a defense of his friend than a philosophical objection to General Education. Although later Jarrell would write sensible, capable memoranda about English teaching within the department, he seems to have avoided the role of education philosopher, certainly of curricular wizard.

As the milestone of his fortieth birthday approached, Jarrell wrote in January 1954 to James Agee, who had sent him a congratulatory note about *Pictures*, that he missed the old days when he could read Agee on movies every week. Lamenting the falling off of both *Time* and *The Nation*, Agee's places of publication, he said that he had been busy that past fall translating "(with much Russian assistance)" Chekhov's *Three Sisters*, and added:

> I've written a fair amount of poetry in the last three years, but I was working on *Pictures* so much of the time that I wrote less—and, too, when you write poetry you're writing both against the current of the world and the current of the World of Poetry, a small world much more interested in Wallace Stevens than in Chekhov, Homer, and Wordsworth combined.

With *Poetry and the Age* in its second printing and *Pictures* about to appear (Agee had seen a pre-publication copy), he told Agee that he was basking in visibility, after having been an invisible poet for

251

so long. The irony was an apparent one, since his relative "visibility" had been attained through the medium of critical prose, a
medium he considered inferior to poetry. At any rate, he remained
preoccupied with the poet's obscurity and with the "current of the
world" which perpetuated this obscurity in its disregard for art.

The previous spring, at Illinois, he had delivered a lecture called
"The Taste of the Age," which began by declaring that whatever
age it is, it always tastes bitter. Looking back to Matthew Arnold,
living in the Victorian era, which Jarrell could call, wistfully, "that
Indian Summer of the Western World," he reminded his audience
that Arnold himself looked back with envy on Goethe and his age,
which Arnold had arrived too late for. Jarrell wondered whether
Arnold's "wistful, exacting, articulate despair" was the response
of a particular historical moment, or was what everyone feels about
their own era. Recently he had published a little poem, "In Those
Days," that viewed the impulse on a more personal level:

> *In those days—they were long ago—*
> *The snow was cold, the night was black.*
> *I licked from my cracked lips*
> *A snowflake, as I looked back*
>
> *Through branches, the last uneasy snow.*
> *Your shadow, there in the light, was still.*
> *In a little the light went out.*
> *I went on, stumbling—till at last the hill*
>
> *Hid the house. And, yawning,*
> *In bed in my room, alone,*
> *I would look out: over the quilted*
> *Rooftops, the clear stars shone.*
>
> *How poor and miserable we were,*
> *How seldom together!*
> *And yet after so long one thinks:*
> *In those days everything was better.*

The poem suggests that we treasure the past, however unideal it was, just because it's now behind us. "And yet after so long one thinks"—the phrasing carefully avoids a sentimental declaration that things really *were* better in those days. Yet this poem is rooted in a powerful nostalgia, and one which became increasingly important to his poetry.

"The Taste of the Age"—a title which, like "The Obscurity of the Poet," carries a double sense—is bitter always because we are tasting these days rather than, in imagination, "those days." Jarrell questions why we feel this way about the past:

> Do people feel this way because our time is worse than Arnold's, and Arnold's than Goethe's, and so on back to Paradise? Or because forbidden fruits—the fruits forbidden us by time—are always the sweetest? Or because we can never compare our own age with an earlier age, but only with books about that age?

Good questions, of which the most promising is the second one, which suggests that the past contains forbidden fruits—courtesy of time—that are therefore the sweetest to us because of the feeling, against all reason, that in those days everything was better. So the letter to Agee about writing "against the current of the world" is at another level a statement about how poetry tries to arrest the flux and to create "a momentary stay against confusion" (in Frost's phrase) through the sound and shape of the made poem.

Perhaps the clearest example of Jarrell's efforts to arrest time is "Aging," written as he approached his fortieth birthday:

> *I wake, but before I know it it is done,*
> *The day, I sleep. And of days like these the years,*
> *A life is made. I nod, consenting to my life.*
> *. . . But who can live in these quick-passing hours?*
> *I need to find again, to make a life,*
> *A child's Sunday afternoon, the Pleasure Drive*
> *Where everything went by but time; the Study Hour*
> *Spent at a desk, with folded hands, in waiting.*

> *In those I could make. Did I not make in them*
> *Myself? The Grown One whose time shortens,*
> *Breath quickens, heart beats faster, till at last*
> *It catches, skips. . . . Yet those hours that seemed, were endless*
> *Were still not long enough to have remade*
> *My childish heart: the heart that must have, always,*
> *To make anything of anything, not time,*
> *Not time but—*
>   *but, alas! eternity.*

When, in 1960, *The Woman at the Washington Zoo* was published (it contained "In Those Days" and "Aging"), Donald Hall, reviewing it, raised the question of Jarrell's sentimentality, a question that had surfaced before and would again. "Aging" seems a prime target for such a charge (though Hall didn't refer to it) because of the plangency with which the man laments his inability to stop time, whose "quick-passing hours" make it impossible for him "to make a life." This key verb, "make," calls to mind how the artist, the poet, is traditionally invoked as the maker, who shapes into words what eludes us as we are swept along by life's current. The man imagines that what he needs is something like those childhood experiences that seemed to go on forever—the Sunday-afternoon pleasure drive or the quietly endured study hall. If in those days things weren't exactly "better" (how boring those Sunday drives could be, how thought-killing that study hall was), still there is nothing like them to be found now.

If one accepts I. A. Richards's definition of sentimentality as a response "inappropriate to the situation that calls it forth"—some overreaction to things, single-minded in its direction—then superficially the first stanza of "Aging" is susceptible to the charge. But not really: the capital letters, setting off the Pleasure Drive and Study Hour in a consciously artificial way, serve notice of the vulnerability, indeed childishness, of such a wish, while they prepare for the quite crushing turn on "make" in the first line of the second stanza:

In those I could make. Did I not make in them
Myself? The Grown One whose time shortens,
Breath quickens, heart beats faster, till at last
It catches, skips. . . .

The Grown One is as frail a reed as the longed-for Pleasure Drive, a pathetic, flimsy personification of weakness that moves through time toward death. Here indeed is the ironic fruit of the man-as-maker, all of the moments of whose past life now make up this aging creature trying desperately to talk himself into some acceptable terms for his situation.

In the vocabulary of the New Criticism that Jarrell had grown up with, "Aging" would properly be understood as an ironic rather than a sentimental poem, insofar as it comprehends, plays with, and undercuts the heartfelt wishes of its beleaguered speaker. But not quite or wholly ironic, since the poem is more individual, more "open" than that. Having done its ironic dance, it tries to break out of that dance with a further gesture of longing, another "yet":

Yet those hours that seemed, were endless
Were still not long enough to have remade
My childish heart: the heart that must have, always,
To make anything of anything, not time,
Not time but—
but, alas! eternity.

This ending might well be judged cloying or excessive in its manner, though in fact hardly any attention—approving or disapproving—has been paid to "Aging." Its Jarrellian repetitions, its breaking of the last line with a dash, its quite unmodernist employing of the old-fashioned "alas," followed by an exclamation mark—all are provocations to the charge of sentimentality. On a simple biographical level one could say the poem was a special birthday card written to himself; but it is also a good test, especially in its last three lines, for readers to see whether they find Jarrell's manner appealing and poignant—as I do—or something rather less so.

Clearly enough, "Aging" was written "against the current of the world," but also, presumably, against the current of the world of poetry—an insulated place in which poets reviewed other poets, read aloud from their own works, and taught writing seminars to students who tried to imitate them. And yet he was very much a part of that world—for example, he reviewed Lowell and Lowell returned the compliment; and he was interested enough in Stevens to write a handsome appreciation of his *Collected Poems*. A glance at "the world of poetry" as it looked to Jarrell in mid-1950s America may help to clarify this contradiction by establishing his sense of himself as different from it—at least his desire to be different from it.

In reviewing Richard Wilbur's second book, *Ceremony*, in late 1951, Jarrell praised its skill and delicate grace but also complained that the poet never got "lost either in his subject or in his emotions." Wilbur didn't take enough risks; he never went too far, but never went far enough, and Jarrell concluded by warning Wilbur: "If you never look *just* wrong to your contemporaries you will never look just right to posterity—every writer has to be, to some extent, sometimes, a law unto himself." Five years later, he wrote Bishop that, as a chancellor of the Academy of American Poets, he had nominated her for their $5,000 award, but that she probably wouldn't get it, since "the world of the younger poets, at present, certainly is the world of Richard Wilbur and safer paler mirror-images of Richard Wilbur—who'd have thought that the era of the poet in the Grey Flannel Suit was coming?" He was both alluding to a popular novel of the time and talking about younger poets— those under forty, an age he had just passed. In 1957, a year after he made the remark to Bishop, what would turn out to be an influential paperback anthology of those poets, *The New Poets of England and America*, was published, edited by three of them— Donald Hall, Robert Pack, and Louis Simpson. The book contained work by fifty-two poets under forty (Lowell just slipped in, having been born in 1917), a "gray-flannel" group insofar as it included only six women, no blacks, and no representatives of either the Beats or the New York School (though Allen Ginsberg's *Howl* and John Ashbery's *Some Trees* had been published the previous year). There is no record of Jarrell's response to the anthology, but we may assume he saw it as a verification of what he had been complaining about to Agee and Bishop: too many of the poets didn't take enough chances, didn't risk looking "*just* wrong" to their contemporaries.

Historically, American poetry was about to move from the era of the gray-flannel suit into the era of—in a phrase of Donald Davie's—"the poetry of sincerity." Lowell's explorations of self in the poems that were to make up *Life Studies* would soon appear in magazines; W. D. Snodgrass and Anne Sexton had begun publishing their "confessional" lyrics (Snodgrass's "Heart's Needle" was in the *New Poets* anthology); Robert Creeley and Robert Duncan were offering alternatives to "academic" poetry, while the West Coast Beats flaunted their personalities and satirized "square" culture. What Jarrell missed in Wilbur and those poets who, he was to say later, came out of Wilbur's overcoat was the presence of an "I" in the poem who, as it were, meant business—who attempted to deal with real conflicts in the self by exploring and enacting them in verse. It is not coincidental or irrelevant to these questions about the proper style of poetry that in the summer of 1954 Jarrell grew a full beard, something rarely done in 1950s America. "When I look in the mirror it's just as if the fairies had stolen me away and left Odysseus in my place," he wrote Robert Penn Warren that summer. This forty-year-old Odysseus thought of himself as contending against both the world and the world of contemporary poetry, instead of settling down, as he thought younger poets were all too thoroughly engaged in doing. For, in fact, despite Jarrell's lament in "The Obscurity of the Poet" about the modern age's neglect of poetry, the 1950s were not an unpropitious time to be a poet. Years later, in his memorial tribute to Jarrell, Karl Shapiro noted that both of them had "predicted the Alexandrianism of the age, and like everybody else, we throve on it. We drove our foreign cars to class to teach [. . .] Half of us stopped rebelling and not because of middle age. The age made it so easy to be a poet, or to survive on lobster, the age gave in so sweetly to our imprecations, the age so needed us to help it hate itself." To be sure, Jarrell's own "rebellion" was seldom overt or theatrical; his criticism of institutionalism is to be found, rather, in the absolutely individual nature of his writing—his un-willingness to share the going style of criticism or poetry, novel or polemic.

While turning forty in May of 1954, he was also arranging his *Selected Poems* for publication the following year. At issue were questions not only of inclusion and exclusion but of sequence. Deciding against a chronological ordering, he broke up the book into two main sections, each with a number of smaller categories. The second section was made up of the war poems; the first in-cluded everything else he wanted to republish. He also wrote an expansive nine-page introduction with notes to the poems, com-paring himself as note-writer not only to his contemporaries Mar-ianne Moore and William Empson but also to Wordsworth and Tennyson, who wrote "hundreds of pages of notes and prefaces and reminiscences" for their collections. In preparing the volume he came to terms with twenty years of his work: *Selected Poems*—following directly on the heels of his novel and his book of criticism—put the seal on his reputation not just as a poet but as a man of letters. If such a role was exactly what, in casting himself against the current of the world of poetry, the poet Jarrell should have been uncomfortable with, there was also a sensible "social" side of him that was delighted with his recent success. In August of 1954, when *Pictures* had sold 8,000 copies, he joked to his publishers, "The readers of America—8,000 of them, anyway—are out of their minds." He may have felt a bit that way about *Vogue* when the magazine asked him to write an article on sports cars; but he delivered the article, and wrote Shapiro that "we really are going to buy that Mercedes—*Pictures* has been doing pretty well."

Sometime after *Selected Poems* was published, he discovered a new poet, one who seemed to challenge the "gray-flannel" style he disliked. The *New Poets* anthology contained seven poems by an Englishman named Philip Larkin, taken from *The Less Deceived*, which had not yet been published in America. Larkin was a discovery he shared with Lowell, who wrote to Jarrell in 1957 (enclosing a version of his "Skunk Hour") to say that he had been reading Larkin in recent months and liked him better than anyone since Dylan Thomas, indeed liked him better than Thomas. Larkin was, said Lowell, not only the most interesting of the "movement" poets, but "unlike our smooth younger poets says something." Jarrell wrote in reply that he was "delighted" with Lowell's remark about Larkin, since he himself was "crazy about him." We can understand Larkin's attractiveness to Jarrell as that of an original voice which spoke forcefully, directly, and humorously from a first-person perspective on things of this world. It was a voice concerned to make poetry out of the conflicted thoughts and desires that any man, living and growing older in the world, might have. Yet for Larkin (as John Bayley has suggested) life's most intense experiences only demonstrated—in the words of the title of one of his poems—"the importance of elsewhere." Larkin's art thrived on deprivation, on *not* having in his hands what was so strongly there in his imagination ("Deprivation is for me what daffodils were for Wordsworth" was how Larkin himself put the case). In responding to Larkin, Jarrell responded both to the supple brilliance of a speaking voice that was "like life" and also to the way in which that voice always insisted, and behaved as if, "life" was elsewhere. In the words of his own "Aging," he needed "to make a life" from the seemingly endless hours of his lost childhood, or from the nostalgic memory of "those days" ("In Those Days") when everything was, somehow, better. In other words, "elsewhere" began to enter Jarrell's poetry with more poignant frequency in the middle 1950s, at a time when he had securely established himself in the institutional world of letters.

Two examples of such insistence, "Windows" and "Nestus Gurley," were published in 1954 and 1956 respectively. The earlier poem, written in irregular stanzas—really just clusters of irregular, unrhymed lines—works through slow-paced repetitions intended to mesmerize and disarm the reader. The scene, at first impersonally described, is of snowbound houses whose dark walks lead to closed doors. The houses look "As if they slept, the bedclothes pulled around them," but lights are still burning in some of them. They are the houses of *others*, a fact that deeply engages the rather shadowy "I," who tells us that

> *Those who live there move seldom, and are silent.*
> *Their movements are the movements of a woman darning,*
> *A man nodding into the pages of the paper,*
> *And are portions of a rite—have kept a meaning—*
> *That I, that they know nothing of. What I have never heard*
> *He will read me; what I have never seen*
> *She will show me.*

In *Selected Poems* he placed "A Sick Child" first in a section with a Freudian title, "Dream-Work." The child's plea was that "somewhere there must be / Something that's different from everything. / All that I've never thought of—think of me!" In "Windows" we see that the sick child was father to the man, or rather, to the man-child, who watches and longingly imagines "The windowed ones within their windowy world." Because they have nothing to do with him—are truly elsewhere—they can be made the subject of rich fantasy:

> These *actors, surely, have known nothing of today,*
> *That time of troubles and of me. Of troubles.*
> *Morose and speechless, voluble with elation,*
> *Changing, unsleeping, an unchanging speech,*
> *These have not lived; look up, indifferent,*
> *At me at my window, from the snowy walk*
> *They move along in peace. . . . If only I were they!*
> *Could act out, in longing, the impossibility*
> *That haunts me like happiness!*

260

The poem as it unfolds is an acting out of the impossible wish to be someone else, to be elsewhere—a longing "That haunts me like happiness!" The phrase is pointedly turned: to be haunted by happiness is—and is not—to possess it; it is "like" the thing but not the thing itself.

To be haunted by an impossibility like happiness was the condition Jarrell as a poet aspired to, ever more intensely, over the final ten years of his life. "Windows" is a memorably disturbing, if also slightly too caressing, presentation of that aspiration. It belongs to the "Dream-Work" category of his poems inasmuch as the reader's experience is of a shifting, nebulous sequence of assertions seemingly risen from some place buried under consciousness, as if the normally controlling poet were moved by forces beyond his control. Whether we find the experience movingly rendered or too yieldingly regressive probably depends upon our response to the conclusion in which the fantasy is consummated:

> *Some morning they will come downstairs and find me.*
> *They will start to speak, and then smile speechlessly,*
> *Shifting the plates, and set another place*
> *At a table shining by a silent fire.*
> *When I have eaten they will say, "You have not slept."*
>
> *And from the sofa, mounded in my quilt,*
> *My face on* their *pillow, that is always cool,*
> *I will look up speechlessly into a—*
>
> *It blurs, and there is drawn across my face*
> *As my eyes close, a hand's slow fire-warmed flesh.*
>
> *It moves so slowly that it does not move.*

The appurtenances of many previous Jarrell poems are here ("Absent with Official Leave," "A Sick Child," and "A Quilt-Pattern," among others), as the man-child, "mounded" by his quilt and cool pillow, looks up into the inexpressibly comforting face that is not a face but a hand, and not just an ordinary hand but a sort of unmoved mover who feels like the essence of Mother. It is tempting to read "Windows" in light of Jarrell's childhood, his lack of a stabilizing family and a fully attentive mother. Yet any explanation that bids to fill in the spaces and hesitations of its verse should be resisted, since the poem's voice makes its appeal through a speech that is not quite fully articulated—that suggests there is more in the experience than can be put into language.

"Windows" appears to be a poem of depths, but "Nestus Gurley," which followed two years later, is both deeper and wider in its sympathies, in its humanity, and—most of all—in its tone. In early 1955 Jarrell reviewed Stevens's *Collected Poems*, published just before Stevens's death. The review was an occasion for him to amend the complaint, made in his earlier essay, that Stevens did too much philosophizing in verse. Now he was concerned to celebrate Stevens's achievement in its "plainness and human rightness," and he compared the last poems to Verdi's *Falstaff*—both works the products of men grown old—in the way they gave us "a world in which everything is enlarged and yet no more than itself, transfigured and yet beyond the need of transfiguration." These words might similarly be applied to what Jarrell attempted to realize in his poem about a paperboy named Nestus Gurley (the name taken from a real paperboy in Greensboro), whose twice-daily deliveries are portrayed as a visitation:

> Sometimes waking, sometimes sleeping,
> Late in the afternoon, or early
> In the morning, I hear on the lawn,
> On the walk, on the lawn, the soft quick step,
> The sound half song, half breath: a note or two
> That with a note or two would be a tune.
> It is Nestus Gurley.

The manner is grand, slow-paced, the dailiness of the domestic treated as if it gave off aspects of eternity. And the poem's conclusion is one of the great sequences in Jarrell's work:

When I lie coldly
—Lie, that is, neither with coldness nor with warmth—
In the darkness that is not lit by anything,
In the grave that is not lit by anything
Except our hope: the hope
That is not proofed against anything, but pure
And shining as the first, least star
That is lost in the east on the morning of Judgment—
May I say, recognizing the step
Or tune or breath. . . .
                              recognizing the breath,
May I say, "It is Nestus Gurley."

This breath is literally the breath of life, to be recognized once more on Judgment Day, when the Book of Death is closed. In the delicacy and rightness of its pace, of the poem's own breathing, we may be reminded of Pound's insistence on composition according to the musical phrase rather than the "heave" of pentameter (and yet at least the ghost of pentameter is there, beating away behind the lines), or of Williams's attempt in his "new measure" to breathe more freely and truly. It is exactly "breath" that matters here, as the penultimate line breaks off, then picks up again while building a formal chiastic structure (May I say / breath / breath / May I say) to reassure and delight the ear. One's feelings at the poem's end are, like that hope that will light our graves, not "proofed" against anything, and do not invite themselves to be named squarely. Instead, I should say about them something like what Leavis said about some lines from one of Hardy's poems— that we know from the art what the man was like, and that we can be sure what personal qualities we should have found to admire in Jarrell if we could have known him.

Early in 1956 Jarrell was invited to serve a two-year term as Poetry Consultant to the Library of Congress. After an awkward moment—when an informant told authorities at the Library that

263

he was a Communist (since he had published poems in "leftist" magazines like *The New Republic* and had worked for *The Nation*) —a character reference from the chancellor of the Woman's College cleared him. The Jarrells took up residence in Washington that fall, and Jarrell may have been especially busy, since there had been no Consultant for the past four years. His contributions included the solicitation of original manuscripts from writers (there were tax benefits involved), interviewing and recording poets, and doing generally "lots of newspaper and radio things," as he wrote Elizabeth Bishop near the beginning of his tenure. And, in fact, both his own poetry and criticism took a back seat to official tasks. The last of his series of quarterly essay-reviews for *The Yale Review* appeared that autumn: besides a number of omnibus poetry reviews, the series included his appreciation of Stevens's *Collected Poems* and a long essay on Robert Graves, which, like the essays on Frost and Whitman, was a pioneering effort at discriminating among the poems and suggesting some ways of appreciating the poet. In effect, these essays marked the end of Jarrell's criticism of poetry; in the remainder of his life, only an essay on Frost's "Home Burial" and the retrospective "Fifty Years of American Poetry" really count as such.

He produced only four poems during his two years at the Library, but his output was even thinner than the numbers would suggest. Soon after his arrival in Washington he wrote Bishop that, except for a poem about Donatello's statue of David ("The Bronze David of Donatello") and a just-completed one titled "The Woman at the Washington Zoo," he hadn't written much lately, although he had "done eleven or twelve Rilke translations." Neither of the other two poems he wrote during the Washington period—"Jerome" and "Jamestown"—is among his best work, and in fact a drought had begun that would not be significantly relieved until, in 1963, he experienced the creative surge that resulted in the poems of his final book. His letters don't complain about drying up, but in the summer of 1957, when he was staying on Cape Cod, working on an introduction to an anthology of short stories for

Anchor Books, Mary Jarrell says he even had trouble writing prose. The introduction was eventually written (the anthology appeared in 1958) and he would follow it during the course of the next five years with an introduction to a group of short Russian novels (also published by Anchor), plus separate introductions for three different collections of Kipling stories. He would engage himself in translating the first book of Goethe's *Faust*. He would see into print a collection of "essays and fables," many of them about popular culture (*A Sad Heart at the Supermarket*), and a volume of poetry (*The Woman at the Washington Zoo*). These things were in addition to his job at the Library of Congress, his teaching at Greensboro (resumed in the fall of 1958), his reading, his listening to music and looking at pictures.

This somewhat rough list of his activities in the five or six years beginning with the Washington appointment would constitute, for most of us, a quite reputable and varied output of work; it also suggests that the extraordinary pace Jarrell had maintained from the years when he was a graduate student at Vanderbilt up through, let us say, the publication of *Selected Poems* in 1955 was indeed extraordinary. So the "drought" has to be put into perspective. One might even hazard the judgment that *not* to compose poems quite so fast as previously he had done represented a gain rather than a loss to his art. Compared with Lowell's or Berryman's production, which during the 1960s picked up its pace as each of them turned out poems with what seemed abandon, Jarrell's looks modest. On the other hand, the amount of waste in both Lowell and Berryman is significant, and Jarrell's later work might better compare to Elizabeth Bishop's. (Consider, by contrast with Lowell and Berryman, the even quality and relatively small quantity of the poems she wrote in the years from 1965 until her death in 1979.)

It is also possible that the happiness of his marriage, certainly in the years until he became ill, acted as a check rather than a spur to the writing of poems. Philip Larkin once said in an interview that poetry didn't come out of happiness—one needed to be unhappy to write it. Some of the remarks which occur in Jarrell's essays from the 1950s suggest that, for the first time, he was letting himself go and relaxing into creature comforts. The sports cars, the time spent watching professional football, a holiday in Italy with the Taylors and the Robert Fitzgeralds in the summer of 1958— these and other things were shared activities with his wife ("To be married to Randall was to be encapsulated with him"). In "Love and Poetry," one of two essays he wrote in 1956–57 for *Mademoiselle* (not *The Nation*, please note), he says of some words from Charles Darwin's diary, "*A nice soft wife on a sofa, with good fire and books and music perhaps*": "This is the poetry of marriage; what bachelor can hear it without a pang, what husband hear it without wanting to leave his nasty hard typewriter, light the fire, put *Verklärte Nacht* on the phonograph and sit with his wife—his nice soft wife—on the sofa? Love makes poets of us all." Those outraged by such reactionary talk may feel slightly mollified by a further remark from the same essay in which, after quoting Rilke on love's being a greeting between two solitudes, he writes: "The solitude that another solitude greets, protects, and touches—learns, by love—is no longer able to believe in its own solitariness, and hears with perplexed wonder the voices that tell it that each of us is, now and forever, alone."

Such a perplexed wonder was exactly what Jarrell had the good fortune to experience in his marriage, and its poetry was unlike that written out in lines and stanzas. In the pages of his *Mademoiselle* essay about the pleasures of sports cars (the one referred to earlier was published in *Vogue*), he unabashedly pictured himself and Mary, their new Mercedes, the four cases of Pilsner Urquell they had bought to go with it ("it'd hardly be right for the drivers of a Mercedes to drink domestic beer, do you think?"), and the German general's leather overcoat he had purchased in Austria:

When I wear it and Mary wears a Garbo- or lady-spy-type trench coat and we speed along, all sleek and white and low, with little Negro children calling to us, sweet as song sparrows, "Go, man, go!"—why, then we feel like Toad in *The Wind in the Willows* when he saw his first car.

266

This is another cozy version of the poetry of marriage, no less enthusiastically portrayed than the earlier bliss on the sofa. "That time of troubles and of me," or "the impossibility / That haunts me like happiness," which he wrote about yearningly in "Windows" and in other poems, was undermined by the real domestic happiness he had fallen into.

With his increased visibility as a public literary figure—Poetry Consultant to the Library of Congress—came a growing dissatisfaction with America: the more he saw of it the more appalled he was at what he saw. In the fall of 1957, he wrote Hiram Haydn, who had invited him to join the editorial board of *The American Scholar* (and who, two years later, would leave his position as editor-in-chief at Random House to co-found Atheneum Publishers), that all that summer he had been feeling "depressed about the United States now, and kept thinking of an imaginary piece called *A Sad Heart at the Supermarket*." That essay, eventually published in the spring of 1960, was an extended Arnoldian lament about how the media, television primarily, were providing Americans with a substitute for living. Perhaps his government appointment encouraged him to feel greater responsibility for the civilization in decay around him; but it was also a fairly common response on the part of literary intellectuals in the 1950s who took refuge in the minority culture of Art, while looking out sadly or disapprovingly at mass civilization amusing itself. Still, his "depression" and writing block that summer of 1957 probably were precipitated by more complicated psychological events—of which growing older was a central one—than despair about life in America. When he returned to work at the Library that fall, he was suffering from a painful sacroiliac injury ("I've been quite sick for several weeks," he wrote Lowell in November). Looked at in light of the serious illness he would suffer seven years later, the mental and physical depression of 1957 was a trial run.

Just how hard he worked at his consultant task can be gathered from a report he wrote at the end of his first year, which—in the section devoted to his public appearances—lists a fall trip to the West Coast, where he gave seven poetry readings at various state universities and a lecture on Wallace Stevens in San Francisco. Further lectures and readings were given at ten colleges and universities scattered about the country. There were Phi Beta Kappa addresses at Vanderbilt and Howard; a three-day visit to his old home at the University of Texas, involving lectures, classes, conferences; addresses and poetry readings to innumerable groups of every sort, from the Poetry Society of America to the Houston Council of Teachers of English; taped interviews, broadcasts, televised appearances, newspaper interviews, and all sorts of advice given to the widest range of inquiries. At the end of four pages that describe his activities on behalf of the Library, he finally notes that he also worked on translations of Rilke poems and on the anthology of short stories he was putting together.

In the spring of 1957, he had determined to leave Knopf, feeling—as he had when he came there from Harcourt, Brace— that not enough serious interest was being taken in his poetry. He looked forward to Haydn's publishing his next collection of poems and his *Supermarket* culture pieces. (Both books were eventually published by Atheneum, with Harry Ford as editor.) In the back of his mind was a book on the psychoanalytic foundations of Eliot's poetry, a project for which—he wrote Bishop just after coming to Washington—he had almost finished the notes and which might run as long as six or eight hundred pages if he were to make use of all his material. In light of the never-written book on Hart Crane and the even older Auden project, it is fair to say that there was in Jarrell much of the Coleridgean projector of schemes. Essentially he was a writer of poems and essays and reviews, not of books; but in the late 1950s he became more and more restless, more inclined to flip from one project to another rather than to focus concentratedly on any one of them.

The two years in Washington also included a stint with Peter Taylor at a writers' conference at Antioch in the summer of 1957 and a longer session at the University of Cincinnati the following spring. Ten years after his term as literary editor of *The Nation*, his job at the Library of Congress gave him the chance to use his executive ability in ways that it hadn't been used in Greensboro. The Washington experience also enabled him to get back into closer relations with Lowell and, particularly, with Bishop—to whom he wrote that he hoped to write a long essay on her work. And it gave him a firsthand acquaintance with the world of contemporary poetry and poets—from which, when he returned to teaching at Greensboro, he withdrew with some relief. (Mary Jarrell's account of his meeting the Beats in San Francisco, and of a subsequent six-week visit paid them in Washington by Gregory Corso, is a highly amusing cautionary tale.) For all the stimulation of being at the center of things—if the Poetry Consultant may be thought of as central—as a poet he needed to be somewhere else in order to oppose both the world and the world of poetry (impossible to do the latter if you are the Poetry Consultant). Yet it took him some time after his return to North Carolina to resume his career as a productive poet.

Thus *The Woman at the Washington Zoo*, which brought him his most significant recognition—the National Book Award in 1961—contained relatively little recent work. Its earliest poem was published in 1945, and its later ones, with two exceptions, were finished soon after he moved to Washington in 1956. The title poem and "The Bronze David of Donatello" occupy key positions as first and concluding poems in the volume, and they seem to me, along with those I have touched on already ("In Those Days," "Aging," "Windows," and "Nestus Gurley"), to constitute the book's main achievement. This may be to slight two poems that follow the title poem, "Cinderella" and "The End of the Rainbow," which were placed together probably because they are both about women grown old whose lives have somehow gone wrong. In "Cinderella" the heroine, grown into "A sullen wife and a reluctant mother," sits all day by the fire, her only companion an "imaginary playmate" —a fairy godmother turned crone and gossip, with whom she shares stories about the perfidy of men. "The End of the Rainbow" examines, at inordinate length and diffuseness, an aging female landscape painter with blue-rinsed hair, transplanted from Ipswich to

Southern California, her only companion a Pekinese named Su-Su and certain more communicative imaginary playmates—like the Frog-Prince, who goggles at her from the mail box. Both poems are continuous with the folktale-fanciful imagination Jarrell had displayed most fully in *The Seven-League Crutches*, and I pass over them here because whatever their importance to him in his attempts to give expression to psychic materials deep in his consciousness, they do not seem to me to work very well as poems—that is, as impressively maintained verbal performances. Certainly, and unlike the "life studies" poems Lowell was engaged in writing, they have not found an audience: there is something both fey and labored about them.

Unlike those two poems, "The Woman at the Washington Zoo" has received much attention, and has even been adopted as a rallying point for the oppressed woman who wishes to speak, as does her sister in the poem, for liberation or "empowerment": "You know what I was, / You see what I am: change me, change me!" Part of the critical attention accorded the poem was given by Jarrell himself, who contributed an account of its origin and materials to a new edition of Brooks and Warren's *Understanding Poetry*. There he compares his heroine to those of "Cinderella" and "The End of the Rainbow," but also—and more significantly, I think—to the woman in "Seele im Raum," the impressive final poem from *The Seven-League Crutches*. In "Seele im Raum" (the title is out of Rilke, and two Rilke poems are a source for it), the woman in distress, in the midst of husband and children, creates, as symbol of her sickness, an eland ("the largest sort of African antelope," Jarrell tells us in a note). Her account of it is complicated, confusing:

> *I had seen it*
> *But not somehow—but this was like a dream—*
> *Not seen it so that I knew I saw it.*
> *It was as if I could not know I saw it*
> *Because I had never once in all my life*
> *Not seen it.*

The eland sits with them at table, the children and her husband joke about it, and its "great melting tearless eyes" mirror the woman's suffering. Then the eland is taken away from her, she is "cured," and she forgets about it until one morning, looking in a German dictionary, she comes across the word *elend* (meaning "wretched") and her consciousness is flooded with insight:

> —*It was worse than impossible, it was a joke.*
>
> *And yet when it was, I was—*
> *Even to think that I once thought*
> *That I could see it is to feel the sweat*
> *Like needles at my hair-roots, I am blind*
>
> —*It was not even a joke, not even a joke.*

She rises to eloquent apostrophe:

> *Yet how can I believe it? Or believe that I*
> *Owned it, a husband, children? Is my voice the voice*
> *Of that skin of being—of what owns, is owned*
> *In honor or dishonor, that is borne and bears—*
> *Or of that raw thing, the being inside it*
> *That has neither a wife, a husband, nor a child*
> *But goes at last as naked from this world*
> *As it was born into it—*
>
> *And the eland comes and grazes on its grave.*

Purposely, there is no resolution; instead the poem tries—as does "A Girl in a Library"—to put opposing feelings together and let them generate whatever intensity they can.

Jarrell was indebted to Rilke for the poem's soul-in-space aspect, its attempt to present a consciousness in which dream and reality, truth and lie, are all inadequate labels for something felt by "that raw thing." He was also indebted to Frost, particularly to the narratives in *North of Boston* in which women give vent to their resentments, suppressed desires, and wishes. When he interviewed

Frost in Washington in 1959, he seemed particularly, almost obsessively, concerned with "Home Burial" and "A Servant to Servants." "The woman always loses," Frost said to him in the interview, "but she loses in an interesting way. She pulls the whole thing down with her." Jarrell did not, however, follow Frost's example in "Home Burial" and write a poem in which a man and a woman confront one another in argument; he preferred rather to let the man—husband, father, employer, lover—be assumed as the unseen presence against which the woman mounts her case.

"The Woman at the Washington Zoo" is his most passionate instance of such a mounting, achieved in thirty lines notable for their economy and compression. If anything, the poem is too neatly executed, as if Jarrell had decided to strip away all the "and yets" with which his narratives usually abounded. The woman in her "dull null / Navy" dress feels herself in depressing contrast to the vivid saris that go by her "from the embassies"—Washington as the city of exotica—and finds herself thinking about her male employers, "my chief, / The Deputy Chief Assistant, nor his chief" (the wit is surely the poet's). They do not complain about her, true, but they do not praise her either. The only complaint is hers, as she admits that "this serviceable / Body that no sunlight dyes, no hand suffuses" is, like the animals in the zoo,

> *trapped*
> *As I am trapped but not, themselves, the trap,*
> *Aging, but without knowledge of their age,*
> *Kept safe here, knowing not of death, for death—*
> *Oh, bars of my own body, open, open!*

This is a long way from Frostian realism, where we participate in the illusion of a "real" woman speaking: Jarrell's colorless (so she tells us) servant to servants comes intensely to life when she uses words—note her expert turning about of "trapped" and "death," or the ease and quickness with which she makes use of her environment to express a metaphysical, soul-in-space situation. The poem is really rather high-tech stuff, as expertly, stylishly put together as the good cars Jarrell drove, the good leather coat he liked to wear.

Talking this way risks deprecating the poem, but it seems important to suggest the way its voice's power belies the woman's powerlessness and indicates the poet's shaping presence, a sound of strength and mastery rather than weakness and confusion. That sound grows more intense through the remainder of the poem:

> *The world goes by my cage and never sees me.*
> *And there come not to me, as come to these,*
> *The wild beasts, sparrows pecking the llamas' grain,*
> *Pigeons settling on the bears' bread, buzzards*
> *Tearing the meat the flies have clouded. . . .*
>   *Vulture,*
> *When you come for the white rat that the foxes left,*
>
> *Take off the red helmet of your head, the black*
> *Wings that have shadowed me, and step to me as man:*
> *The wild brother at whose feet the white wolves fawn,*
> *To whose hand of power the great lioness*
> *Stalks, purring. . . .*
>   *You know what I was,*
> *You see what I am: change me, change me!*

As a purely rhetorical performance this is striking and scary; whether there remains any conceivable woman to think about is more debatable. And, for that reason, it is possible to hold back from enthusiastic participation in that final cry to be changed. We must not ask, I think, changed into what?—nor does it help much to have in mind the oft-quoted final directive from Rilke's sonnet about the Archaic Torso of Apollo, who tells us, "You must change your life."

In fact, the notion of "change" as we meet it in Jarrell's poetry is difficult, perhaps impossible, to clarify. "It is like any other work of art. / It is and never can be changed," he wrote in "The Orient Express." The children who haunted the Carnegie Library, Juvenile Division, learned from the books they read "the knowledge for a life / But not the will to use it in our lives / That were always, somehow, so different from the books'." They learned "to understand, but not to change," and this seems to be all that human beings *can* learn, by their very imperfect natures. In fact, an ironic parody of this sought-after change is provided free of charge by the life that we live and that erodes us daily, which is what the "Grown One" in "Aging" sadly has to acknowledge. But the woman at the Washington Zoo is out for something else; or perhaps it is a measure of her desperation that she cries "change me, change me!" and then has no more to say, there at the end of her rope, the end of the poem. Near the very end of Jarrell's own life, he wrote a revealing letter to Robert Penn Warren, who had written expressing concern about Jarrell's illness. Home from the hospital after both manic and depressive fits, he now felt, he said, like his usual self, and he told Warren: "I've always wanted to change, but not to change into what you become when you're mentally ill." There is much mystery here, mainly having to do with the desire "to change" and what that might involve. In any case, the woman at the zoo was clearly not alone in her wish to be altered. Not until Jarrell wrote the poems that make up the personal, autobiographical segment of his final book, *The Lost World*, did he find the brilliantly adequate terms in which to explore change and the self.

T E N

The World Lost and Found

THE last five years of Jarrell's life, from the publication of *The Woman at the Washington Zoo* in September 1960 to his death in October 1965, are a mixture of triumph and tragedy. They contain feats of imaginative prowess like the children's stories and the dazzling lecture, "Fifty Years of American Poetry," he delivered at the National Poetry Festival in Washington in 1962. He continued to work on his translation of *Faust* and finished translating Chekhov's *Three Sisters* for a New York production in 1964. Above everything else stand the poems from his final book of poetry, *The Lost World*. These accomplishments took place against a background of difficulties—of physical and mental deterioration, then of domestic disturbance—beginning with his hospitalization for hepatitis at the beginning of 1962 and on through manic, mood-elevated highs to his hospitalization for depression and his attempted suicide in the spring of 1965. A few months after the suicide attempt came his sudden and fatal encounter with a car; the circumstances of that death remain unclear—although various people have expressed themselves strongly on the subject—and were probably not clear to Jarrell himself. What is clear is that, during these last years of his life, something in him gave way. The tightly strung, beautifully tuned instrument that had worked so well for so many years broke down as he turned fifty, and his and his wife's attempts to put it back together did not succeed. This sad story is made scarcely less so by the beauty and power of some of his last poems. A letter Lowell wrote to him in April of 1965, when Jarrell was in the hospital, contains a sentence that says everything one feels about his misfortunes: "Your courage, brilliance and generosity should have saved you from this, but of course all good qualities are unavailing"—an "of course" spoken by someone who had been there himself.

One of those unavailing good qualities that seems especially to mark these final years in Greensboro was the devotion and skill with which Jarrell continued to teach literature and writing to his students. He insisted that teaching was something he would pay to do, and he was no more able to keep it "in its place" than he could keep tennis or sports cars in theirs—like them, teaching was a consuming activity. The young women whom he taught have provided testimony to the memorableness of his classes. Whether he was giving a writing course or a course in modern poets (Frost, Eliot, and Hopkins were favorites), his method was unacademic, insofar as he did nothing more complicated—or more difficult— than to read poems and stories aloud and then discuss them with his students. He would point out felicities in a poem or story by interjecting, "Isn't that marvelous," or the like. His students were held by the look of his face and the sound of his voice; one student remembers:

> He was as passionate about a Chekhov story or a Lowell poem he'd known for years as a freshman just discovering Shakespeare, and he communicated this passion to the students who were open to it. He would lean over the table or podium, smile or laugh, always looking straight into the eyes of one person in the class, and become very animated as he related some enlightening anecdote.
>
> Anyway, his reading to us was strange and beautiful, and he read almost everything aloud at least once, even long stories.

276

Another student noted that "usually there was an animated, full-of-merriment expression on his face; but when he was touching on something in a poem or story that didn't quite work, his face would take on a pained expression as though he were suffering himself." That same student admired his disinterestedness, saying, "He never seemed to feel in competition with anyone, jealous of anyone, or unjustly critical of anyone. He could be truly objective about anyone's work: yours, his, Frost's." And another student recalls an interesting slip of the tongue her teacher made more than once: "Savoring a line from Frost's 'Home Burial' or pointing out a further treatment of symbol in *The Great Gatsby*, he might shake his head with excitement and confess, 'This is one of the two or three *very* best things I've ever WRITTEN.' Then, blushing and stammering, he'd make the correction. Or, sometimes, he'd be unaware of the mistake."

Jarrell began his classes by calling the roll, not so much for purposes of taking attendance as to say out loud the names of class members, establishing thereby some sort of contact. He would ask individuals what they thought of a poem or story, but was invariably gentle with the answer he received, making—as some good teachers can—the best case for what might have been a routine response. Classes were occasionally punctuated by pauses lasting for some minutes. The content of a course was not necessarily determined in advance. Once, at the beginning of a semester of modern poetry, he asked the class what they wanted to read, and when opinion divided between Frost and Eliot, Jarrell announced that they would read both. Another class never got beyond the Eliot with whom they had begun (a fact given credence by his extraordinarily marked-up copy of Eliot's *Complete Poems*, now in the university library at Greensboro). Good students—at least those who, in words quoted above, "were open to it"—had their lives as readers and writers changed utterly. One of the best of his students, the novelist Sylvia Wilkinson, said she took every course he offered and still feels gratitude for the caring intensity of his teaching and his encouragement of her writing: "I might have continued to write if I had never known him but it would have stayed walled up inside.

He broke down a fear I had had all my life. I have never known an adult who could feel so much so completely."

Two of Jarrell's comments about poems, jotted down by another of his best students, the writer Heather Ross Miller, indicate the quality of surprise and discovery that could occur in his classroom. Both were responses to Emily Dickinson poems: speaking about the line "I like a look of Agony," Jarrell ventured that it was like someone saying, "I've just been down to the stockyards. I love to see cows killed. Don't you?" As another way of suggesting how forcefully Dickinson must have struck her contemporary readers, he quoted the opening lines of another poem—"Because I could not stop for Death, / He kindly stopped for me"—and suggested that it was like someone saying, "We have a nice hotel room. The girl, myself, and the Sphinx." This sort of liveliness delighted many, though not all, of his students. One of the delighted noted that bad students—"particularly good-grade-making bad students"— were frustrated and mystified by him, as well they might have been. He may have put things, in the words of Frost's "Directive," "Under a spell so the wrong ones can't find it, / So can't get saved." But it does not appear that he was consciously exclusive toward his students, inviting the happy few into grace while leaving the rest outside. He loved teaching at Greensboro no less for the lack of a high-pressured, insistently demanding atmosphere. If the college was like Sleeping Beauty, rather than like Columbia or Harvard, he could love it for what it was. And the letters about his classes written years later by his students prove that they were listening, not sleeping. As for their importance to him, he remarked to Robert Penn Warren that his two years in Washington away from classes and students made him "want never to be without them again." Fittingly, Warren was chosen to address an audience of two thousand at a tribute to Jarrell in Chapel Hill, sponsored by the North Carolina Historical Society and the University of North Carolina Press.

That was in the fall of 1961; in February 1962, Jarrell entered the hospital to be treated for hepatitis. In March, he wrote Warren and Eleanor Clark that he'd been "extremely sick" that the hepatitis had been followed by "all sorts of duodenal and neuralgic complications," with the result that—except for teaching, which he had just resumed—"all I do is diet, take medicine, lie down, and wish I were well." Out of this experience came one poem, "The X-Ray Waiting Room in the Hospital"; but the year 1962 was an especially slim one so far as publishing poems was concerned. At the same time, and in a happy circumstance that would eventually have consequences for his own verse, Jarrell began his brief and sparkling career as a writer of children's stories.

The immediate cause of this new development was Michael di Capua, an editor of children's books at Macmillan, who admired Jarrell's poetry and conceived the idea that he would make a good translator for a volume of some stories by the brothers Grimm. Jarrell translated "Snow-White and the Seven Dwarfs," "The Fisherman and His Wife," and three other tales; di Capua was pleased with the result, and at his suggestion Jarrell that summer wrote one children's story, *The Gingerbread Rabbit*, and started a second—which would be his most popular—called *The Bat-Poet*. In retrospect, the conjunction of children's stories with the poet who wrote "Children Selecting Books in a Library" and "The Märchen" seems inevitable. In fact, and though he needed the push given him by di Capua, Jarrell's children's books developed out of an increasing involvement, over the past five or so years, with stories. The five collections of them for which he wrote introductions—first *The Anchor Book of Stories*, then three volumes of Kipling's tales and *Six Russian Short Novels*—combined with his courses in short fiction to make him think hard about the idea of story.

His introduction to *The Anchor Book of Stories* begins by quoting a dictionary definition in which "story" stands both for a narrative of what has occurred and for a fictitious narrative (something that didn't "really happen"). A story, then, Jarrell says, "tells the truth or a lie—is a wish, or a truth, or a wish modified by a truth." Already it's clear that he is less interested in laying down an accurate

279

definition of story than in opening things up so wide that no def-inition is of much use. As Frances Ferguson points out in her extended analysis of this introduction, it is more "a short story masquerading as a commentary on one man's anthology of great stories than a straightforward critical essay." "*Everything* suddenly seems to be a story," she concludes. What does it mean for Jarrell to say that a story is "a wish modified by a truth"? As an example, he provides us with what he calls "the first story":

A baby asleep but about to be waked by hunger sometimes makes little sucking motions: he is dreaming that he is being fed, and manages by virtue of the dream to stay asleep. He may even smile a little in satisfaction. But the smile cannot last for long—the dream fails, and he wakes.

The child in his "impotent omnipotence" is "like us readers, us writers, in ours." So, with this analogy, child, reader, and writer are brought together in their common wish—their attempt to stay asleep even as they are about to wake. Nothing less marvelous or primal, it seems, will do as a way of talking about such intimate and ultimate matters.

The Bat-Poet is a wish modified by a truth, a story about a bat who is different from his fellows, who likes to stay awake during the day when the rest go to sleep, who likes to look at and listen to daylight activities. The other bats think he's strange to be doing this, but even stranger when he starts putting words together to express what he's seen and heard. When the bat-poet recites his first poem for them, they interrupt after a few lines to disagree with his observations, question his metaphors, and generally cause him to lose track of his poem. Mildly shaken, he seeks out the mockingbird, whose prowess as a poet had inspired the bat to his own first attempts. The mockingbird consents to listen to his poem, even praises it, but in purely technical terms ("And it was clever of you to have that last line two feet short [   ] The next to the last line's iambic pentameter, and the last line's iambic trimeter"). Bewildered, having been treated to a lesson in scansion ("An iambic foot has one weak syllable and one strong syllable"), the bat-poet flies home, hangs upside down, and thinks, "The trouble isn't making poems, the trouble's finding somebody that will listen to them."

Having said as much, he finds someone who will listen to them, a chipmunk for whom he reads a poem about the owl from whose claws he has recently had a narrow escape. Whereas the mockingbird ignored the poem's content in favor of its construction ("What do I care how many feet it has?" thinks the bat. "The owl nearly kills me, and he says he likes the rhyme-scheme!"), the chipmunk shivers in sympathetic terror and says, "It's terrible, just terrible! Is there really something like that at night?" Pleased with this response, the bat proceeds to make up a poem about the chipmunk, putting into it—at the chipmunk's request—nuts, seeds, and "lots of holes." The chipmunk is delighted with the result, even to the extent of noting that "It all goes in and out, doesn't it?" In fact, the poem is an expert little performance:

> *In and out the bushes, up the ivy,*
> *Into the hole*
> *By the old oak stump, the chipmunk flashes.*
> *Up the pole*
>
> *To the feeder full of seeds he dashes,*
> *Stuffs his cheeks,*
> *The chickadee and titmouse scold him.*
> *Down he streaks.*

The Bat-Poet is a charming blend of ironic sophistication about the poet's vocation and intently observed, lovingly rendered bits of animal and natural lore. For example, the bat, hoping to write another poem, observes a cardinal cracking sunflower seeds in what seems an odd manner:

Instead of standing on them and hammering them open, like a titmouse, he'd turn them over and over in his beak—it gave him a thoughtful look—and all at once the seed would fall open, split in two. While the cardinal was cracking the seed his two babies stood underneath him on tiptoe, fluttering their wings and quivering all over, their mouths wide open. They were a beautiful soft bright brown—even their beaks were brown—and they were already as big as their father.

About writing like this—and it is the rule rather than the exception in *The Bat-Poet*—one feels as P. L. Travers did when she wrote (in regard to Jarrell's *The Animal Family*): "Someone, in love with an idea, has lovingly elaborated it simply to please himself—no ax to grind, making no requirements, just putting a pinch of salt on its tail—as one would with a poem—and setting it down in words." Why shouldn't a child enjoy it? Travers asked.

Mary Jarrell observes that, for her husband, she and Michael di Capua were "chipmunks": they were good, though—or perhaps even because—unprofessional non-poet listeners to someone else's poems. The someone else was preeminently Jarrell, who figured in his animal mythology as a bat; while Frost and Lowell were mockingbirds—imperious, exclusive, able to imitate and intimidate everyone. As the bat expresses it:

> *On the willow's highest branch, monopolizing*
> *Day and night, cheeping, squeaking, soaring,*
> *The mockingbird is imitating life.*

Bats, even the rather special one featured in this story, are less monopolistic creatures, and the tale ends with the bat-poet going to sleep, actually winter hibernation, soon after he has begun to recite one of his poems. Falling asleep in the middle of a poem is something the mockingbird would never do. The wish to become a poet, to have proper listeners who appreciate your poems, is modified in the bat by a truth of nature: there is a time and a place for poetry writing; life has its own demands and will sometimes prevail.

When di Capua received the manuscript of *The Bat-Poet*, he was already discussing with Maurice Sendak—who had just published the extremely successful *Nutshell Library*—the possibility of an illustrated edition of Grimm's tales. Garth Williams had illustrated *The Gingerbread Rabbit*, but Jarrell agreed with di Capua that Sendak was the right illustrator for *The Bat-Poet* because of his skill at producing "lyric or quiet or thoughtful or imaginative effects." Sendak, who would also illustrate Jarrell's other children's stories—*The Animal Family* and *Fly by Night*—developed great respect for his co-artist, calling him, later on, the most extraordinary writer he had ever worked with and praising especially his "graphic sense," his ability to conceive a book as a whole. Of the four children's books, *The Bat-Poet* and *The Animal Family* (which I will consider later) are triumphs; by comparison, *Fly by Night* seems relatively flat and not much fun, while *The Gingerbread Rabbit* is lots of fun but in no need of critical commentary.

With *The Gingerbread Rabbit* written and *The Bat-Poet* half completed, Jarrell turned his attention in the summer of 1962 to compiling one of his Kipling anthologies and to writing the long and rewarding introduction to *Six Russian Short Novels*. He was also preparing an address to be delivered in the fall at the first National Poetry Festival in Washington. Jarrell had been given pride of place at the festival; his was to be the first of three evening lectures. In accepting the invitation he promised to write a "little speech" that summer; it turned out to be nothing less than a long and memorable retrospective titled "Fifty Years of American Poetry," in which forty-seven poets—plus unnamed Beats and unnamed followers of Yvor Winters or Richard Wilbur—were referred to, a number of them discussed at some length. It is an astonishing performance, almost too much to read—and certainly to listen to—at a sitting (in print it runs to just under forty pages, and must have been an unleisurely sixty minutes' worth of talk). A quarter-century later, its descriptions and valuations still hold up more than well, their outstanding feature being the succinct, concentrated force—the force of wit—with which Jarrell marched the poets, one after another, up to the podium, there to receive their certificates of merit, or qualified merit, from the award master.

The speech-essay has an especially summary quality. It was the

283

end of the line for Jarrell as a critic of modern poets (he published nothing further about them in the final three years of his life), and by the time he came to deliver this retrospective, his mind was so fully made up that there was no room for change; its judgments were locked forever into place by the perfectly tuned sentences that framed them. There was nothing more to be said, or added. This self-enclosed quality is enhanced by Jarrell's having plundered, where appropriate, his previous writings, so that choice bits from essays on Frost or Stevens or Ransom are reused. The writing thus seems at one remove from direct perception; by quoting himself, Jarrell was in effect distancing the whole critical operation from the immediate present and memorializing his own apt formulations as much as commenting on the poet in question. Even when the material is new—most notably in the comments about Eliot—it strongly suggests the performance aspect of the address by "keynoting" the poetry festival in a manner that strives to be not merely the first words of the event but its last words also. Some sentences from the long paragraph on Eliot may illustrate what I mean. Jarrell comes to him after short, less than enthusiastic evaluations of Robinson, Masters, Sandburg, and Vachel Lindsay, followed by warmer appreciations of Frost, Pound (though with many reservations), Stevens, Williams, and Ransom.

At which point he clears his throat: "And then there is Eliot," a poet so famous and influential that "it seems almost absurd to write about him, especially when [. . .] all of you can read me your own articles about [him]." But the age's attitude toward this "combination of Lord Byron and Dr. Johnson" is different from what the future's will be:

Won't the future say to us in helpless astonishment: "But did you actually believe that all those things about objective correlatives, classicism, the tradition, applied to *his* poetry? Surely you must have seen that he was one of the most subjective and daemonic poets who ever lived, the victim and helpless beneficiary of his own inexorable compulsions, obsessions?

284

From a psychoanalytical point of view he was far and away the most interesting poet of your century. But for you, of course, after the first few years, his poetry existed undersea, thousands of feet below that deluge of exegesis, explication, source listing, scholarship, and criticism that overwhelmed it. And yet how bravely and personally it survived, its eyes neither coral nor mother-of-pearl but plainly human, full of human anguish!"

This was not at all an obvious or accepted way to talk about Eliot in 1962. Five years or so previously, Jarrell had more than once mentioned his having assembled a pile of notes for what was to be a long book on the psychoanalytic roots of Eliot's poetry, but all that came out of those notes was a paragraph, especially interesting for the form in which it is couched. Instead of pronouncing on Eliot's poetry, as he had on Frost's or Stevens's, he chose to quote what "the future" will say to us about Eliot's depths and richnesses. And since there is no arguing with the future, the form of this paragraph is an extreme case of the general form of Jarrell's speech at the festival. Never was there anything less meant to invite dispute or qualification from a listener or reader; before one can begin to pose a question, Jarrell is on to the next poet, shaping another neatly sweeping series of formulations.

Almost every paragraph puts its case so attractively that it commands our assent before we can consider it objectively. A few instances: on Sandburg—"It is marvelous to hear him say 'The People, Yes,' but it is not marvelous to read it as a poem"; on Lindsay—"He has the innocent, desperate eccentricity of the artist in a world with no room for, no patience with, artists; you could die for what you believed, Lindsay said, and no one would notice or care, but if you had the nerve to go broke time after time, they would notice"; on Pound—"Gertrude Stein was most unjust to Pound when she called that ecumenical alluder a village explainer: he can hardly *tell* you anything (unless you know it already), much less explain it. He makes notes on the margin of the universe; to

285

tell how just or unjust a note is, you must know that portion of the text yourself"; on Stevens—He "is full of the natural or Aristotelian virtues; he is, in the terms of Hopkins's poem, all windhover and no Jesuit [. . .] If he were an animal he would be, without a doubt, that rational, magnanimous, voluminous animal, the elephant"; on Williams—"The materials of Williams's unsuccessful poems have as much reality as the brick one stumbles over on the sidewalk; but how little has been done to them!—the poem is pieces or, worse still, a piece"; on Moore—"The poems say, sometimes, to the beasts: 'You reassure me and people don't, except when they are like you—but really they are always like you'; and it is wonderful to have it said so, and for a moment to forget, behind the animals of a darkening landscape, their dark companions."

What is the final thing to say about E. E. Cummings? "Many a writer has spent his life putting his favorite words in all the places they belong; but how many, like Cummings, have spent their lives putting their favorite words in all the places they don't belong, thus discovering many effects that no one had even realized were possible?" Or about Conrad Aiken, whom everyone conspired to forget? "He is a kind of Midas: everything that he touches turns to verse: so that reading his poems is like listening to Delius—one is experiencing an unending undifferentiating wash of lovely sounds." What did Richard Wilbur, present in the audience, think when he heard this ultimate truth about himself? "He obsessively sees, and shows, the bright underside of every dark thing [. . .] This compulsion limits his poems; and yet it is this compulsion, and not merely his greater talent and skill, that differentiates him so favorably from the controlled, accomplished, correct poets who are common nowadays."

Jarrell is just as memorable, and final, when he turns to recent American poetic movements, as when a paragraph on the school of Yvor Winters follows one on the Beats. The poetic theory of the Beats is characterized as "iron spontaneity." "Besides, their poems are as direct as true works of art are indirect [. . .] These bohemian public speeches make it impossible for the artist's unconscious to operate as it normally does in the process of producing a work of art." But this same "doctrinaire directness" can be noted in their opposite number, the followers of Winters, who in Jarrell's parable "met an enchanter who has said to them: 'You have all met an enchanter who has transformed you into obscure romantic animals, but you can become clear and classical and human again if you will only swallow these rules.' The poets swallow them, and from that moment they are all Henry Wadsworth Longfellow, a wax one."

In quoting without commentary as much as I have just done, I risk doing what with more justification Jarrell himself did when he quoted reams of Frost, then averred that, had he but the space to quote entire several of Frost's longer poems, "Pharisee and Philistine alike would tiptoe off hand in hand, their shamed eyes starry." But I think such quoting is a legitimate response to the especially concentrated, poetic force with which—in this last will and testament—he delivered the goods. The procession of tributes ended in the present with Lowell, about whom he said: "The awful depths, the plain absurdities of his own actual existence in the prosperous, developed, disastrous world he and we inhabit are there in the poems." Jarrell describes and praises "the pathos of the local color of the past" in *Life Studies*, also "his wonderful poem about Boston Common" (the only recently published "For the Union Dead"). Lowell is a poet who has developed rather than repeated himself: his poems have a "largeness and grandeur, exist on a scale that is unique today." And in the abrupt conclusion to "Fifty Years of American Poetry" he remarks of Lowell, "You feel before reading any new poem of his the uneasy expectation of perhaps encountering a masterpiece."

Ironically, the Poetry Festival coincided with the Cuban missile crisis. The day after Jarrell's talk, Mrs. Kennedy's sherry party was canceled, and as Mary Jarrell points out, some of the poet participants were distracted by the crisis, even to the point of packing their bags and heading home early. Not Jarrell, who was—as his wife put it—"inside his poetry bubble," and who wrote Warren afterward that all the poetry activities gave "one" no time to worry about Cuba and the Russians. There he spoke for himself—perhaps for himself only.

In June of the following year, Jarrell wrote enthusiastically to Michael di Capua about the five-month European trip on which he and Mary were about to embark:

> We're enchantingly flooded in maps, passports, steamer and airline tickets for us, a steamer ticket for the Jaguar, guidebooks, European picture books [. . .] We've got plans all made to see the paintings in London, Paris, the Belgian and Dutch cities, Munich and other German places, Florence, Venice, Rome, and other Italian places.

His letter was accompanied by the complete manuscript of *The Lost World*, several of whose best poems had been composed that spring during a period of extraordinary creativity. (This rush of poetry was stimulated by his mother's sending him the letters he had written her from Los Angeles when he was living with his grandparents in 1926–27.) The European trip was to be a second honeymoon, eleven years after the Jarrells' marriage, conducted in part as an homage to the paintings, the buildings, the operas they would see together. Near the end of the trip, he wrote two letters from the Albergo Berchielli in Florence which suggest that for the moment, there on the banks of the Arno, he had achieved a sanely poised acceptance of life and of his own investment in it, even as he was seven months away from his fiftieth birthday. In a long letter to Adrienne Rich, whose poems he admired and commented on to her in great detail, he set down some thoughts about the world provoked by lines from a new poem she had sent him ("Difficult and ordinary happiness, / No one nowadays believes in you"):

> If you believe in happiness and have ordinary good luck you really can be happy a lot of the time—but most people of our reading-and-writing sort have conscientious objections to any happiness, they'd far rather be right than happy. It *is* terrible

in our time to have the death of the world hanging over you, but, personally, it's something you disregard just as you disregard the regular misery of so much of the world, or your own regular personal aging and death.

Of course, such a disregard, at least as far as the "regular personal aging and death" part of it went, was precisely what—as the poet of loss—he could not afford to practice, since to lose "loss" would have been to lose his great subject.

The wisdom in the letter to Rich is not tragic wisdom but a cultivated disregard of the agony of others, and one's own, in favor of capturing some happiness. There is a bit of James's "will to believe" in it; also of Frost, who once wrote to Louis Untermeyer (apropos of the nervous breakdown of Frost's sister, Jeannie): "I suppose I am a brute in that my nature refuses to carry sympathy to the point of going crazy just because someone else goes crazy, or of dying just because someone else dies." And Frost was on Jarrell's mind at the time; having read Elizabeth Hardwick's essay on him in *The New York Review of Books*, he wrote to her and Lowell, saying that he had always regarded Frost (who had died the previous January) as "a unique natural phenomenon beyond good and evil." He told the Lowells that he, Jarrell, existed for Frost wholly as "the person who'd written those pieces about his poetry," and was thus regarded in a very special light:

> He felt I was an Indian who'd sold him, *given* him, Manhattan Island, and he was willing to keep me on a special little reservation in return. I felt that he talked more like poetry than anybody else I'd ever hear, that his voice made other voices sound a little high in comparison, so what did I care whether he was right or wrong? (He actually *said* that his writing had had all the success he wanted it to, so what did he care what happened with nuclear weapons?)

This absolute valuing of Frost's voice (compared to which all other voices sounded a bit "high"—an apt differentiation), to the point where it overrode matters of mere truth or falsity, was a tribute to

Frost's power. It may also have represented Jarrell's sense that among those voices that sounded, in comparison, "a little high" was his own high-pitched one. And in the little over a year between his return home from Europe and his breakdown and hospitalization in early 1965, that voice would increasingly rise to fever pitch as the demon of elatedness possessed it.

Yet in reading Jarrell's letters after his return from Europe in November 1963 (it coincided with Kennedy's assassination) until his death less than two years later, one is mainly struck by the absence of *any* voice. Of the 521 pages in Mary Jarrell's edition of the letters, only thirty-five document those two years, and most of them consist largely of her interpretive narration of his life. Many of these final letters are written to di Capua and are mainly concerned with business matters, book design, publishing dates, and the like. It is as if the real Jarrell had gone away somewhere —and perhaps, in a sense, that is what happened. The focus turns to his physical and psychic condition, beginning with his grief over Kennedy's death and his subsequent complaints about fatigue. (That his enervation could be a lingering residue from the hepatitis seems plausible.) His doctor in Greensboro prescribed more exercise and a bland diet—harmless but ineffective measures. (Mary brought him some pink and blue dumbbells for Christmas, 1963, called Glamor Belles.) As spring approached, he wrote di Capua that he was feeling better—"surely with spring I'll get all well"; but di Capua's sudden departure from Macmillan, after a serious disagreement with his superiors, was not calculated to improve Jarrell's condition.

He turned fifty in May, and when his friend Lucy Hooke made light of the event—"Fifty is nothing, Randall. You're making mountains out of molehills"—Jarrell tellingly replied, "When you're depressed, there *are* no molehills." A new physician diagnosed him as having what would soon come to be known as "mid-life crisis," and prescribed a moderate dosage of the mood elevating drug Elavil. But after a month on it he still felt (in his wife's words) "as listless and drowsy as ever," and resolved to visit the

Cincinnati psychiatrist he had been much impressed with when, in 1958, he spent some weeks there giving lectures. This psychiatrist increased Jarrell's dosage of the drug, lifted most of the dietary restrictions, and told him to call in every month and report on his progress. By August, in Jarrell's own testimony, he was feeling much better; he and Mary were living high in the mountains of Blowing Rock, North Carolina, and—from what he now was permitted to eat—deriving "a hopeful pleasure instead of a settled gloom."

Over the remaining months of 1964 and into the new year he continued to take what he now referred to as "magic pills" at the same high-dosage level, maintaining contact with the Cincinnati psychiatrist by phone, if at all. In October he gave a reading at the Guggenheim Museum of his own and Elizabeth Bishop's poems. Lowell, who introduced him, noted that Jarrell had shaved off his beard, an action which may have signaled his new, though precariously based, high spirits. To di Capua in October of 1964 he wrote: "I've been feeling so good I've worked hard on a lot of things and made plans for more." One of those things was an introduction to Christina Stead's novel *The Man Who Loved Children*, in which he praised Stead's "natural excess" while turning out an essay of almost fifty pages. In addition to various projects in stages of non-completion, his own excess involved him in a scheme to reform the English department of which he was a member. J. A. Bryant, Jr., was department chairman at that time and, in recognition of Jarrell's special distinction, had made it possible for him to teach what and when he wanted. Bryant also provided what he called "substitutes of sorts" whenever Jarrell wanted to be away, as increasingly he did. (Bryant notes that after the five months in Europe "he was away almost more often than he was here.") In addition to his schedule of Phi Beta Kappa readings and lectures, he made frequent trips to Nashville, visiting his mother—for the first time in years—when she became ill.

As the elevated mood persisted, it was evident that—in Bryant's words—"most dealings with Randall had become more or less delicate." On different occasions he proposed—to Robert Watson and Peter Taylor, both of whom demurred—that certain members of the English department be fired. At another point he presented Bryant with a curricular scheme which struck the chairman as a "fantastic program that reflected all his current interests (among them Russian literature), one which would have been impossible to put into effect without a complement of Jarrells to teach it." His classes tended to run overtime—he couldn't stop talking. When he introduced Hannah Arendt, who had come to Greensboro to lecture, he spoke for twenty minutes or so, giving a rambling account of meeting one of his heroes—the Baltimore Colts quarterback Johnny Unitas—on a plane. This performance prompted Arendt to suggest to Bryant that Jarrell sorely needed psychiatric help.

His relationship with Peter Taylor had become strained, and so increasingly—and understandably, considering his behavior—had things with his wife. Mary Jarrell reports that he would no longer think of going to bed before midnight, and would sleep only five or six hours. "I'm feeling calm but harried," he wrote oxymoronically to di Capua near the end of 1964, and perhaps those juxtaposed adjectives say volumes about the strange composition-decomposition of his personality at the time. On a visit to Nashville, he tipped a waitress with a $1,500 check. There were rumors of a young woman at Goucher College with whom he fancied himself in love, a fancy which doubtless contributed to his estrangement from Mary. A crisis point was reached in early 1965, when Bryant says he received a call from the Cincinnati psychiatrist informing him that Jarrell was on a "flying binge" in which he was using his American Express card unrestrictedly to fly from one place to another. On his return from his third visit (in two weeks) to Anna Regan in Nashville, his wife and Bryant arranged for the chancellor of the university and a campus policeman to meet Jarrell at the airport, from which he was taken—with his cooperation—to the hospital in Chapel Hill. "I *was* exhausted and I *was* elated," he wrote di Capua afterward from the South Wing of the North

Carolina Memorial Hospital, predicting also that he would be released in a week or ten days.

The same letter contained a terse announcement: "I don't know whether Mary has told you; but she and I are separated and will be divorced after a while." But Jarrell was moving faster in his mind than, this time, he could move in fact. His "magic pills" were discontinued and he was medicated with Thorazine, which not only made him feel depressed but made "thought and action so difficult for you that you can't be your real self." The Thorazine was discontinued, but the depression held on and deepened. Finally, in the latter part of April, when shock treatments were being considered, Jarrell—at home at the time—slashed his left wrist. This act may have been triggered by a brutal review of *The Lost World* he had read a few days before: in any case, Mary Jarrell notes that it seemed to release him from his depression. In a letter he wrote to her in May from the hospital, his tone no longer sounded like someone who wanted out of the relationship. He thanked her for the roses she brought him, and "all the other things [. . .] that for so long made me better and happier and kept something like this from happening to me earlier. You are the one big good real thing in my life," he said, concluding with a declaration of love. Gradually he was allowed to go home for short periods on weekends, and was released for good on July 1.

All in all, as he noted in a letter to Robert Penn Warren late that summer (Warren had inquired after his health), Jarrell had spent about four months in the hospital. At a party he and Mary gave for Bryant, who was leaving for Europe, Jarrell was (in Bryant's words) "amiable but subdued, almost as if he had been sedated." Certainly the "subdued" quality comes through movingly in two passages from letters he wrote that fall to Warren and to Maurice Sendak. To the former he said that he had not written any poems, but had "been thinking so much about the passage of time, and what it's like to live a certain number of years in the world, that I think it's sure to turn into some poems in the long run." One takes note of those last three words. To Sendak, whose father was seriously ill, he wrote:

> Our misery about such things is so hard to explain or bear—
> I guess all one can say is that we can't escape them, and that
> afterwards we know what matters most to us, what life really
> seems to us, and are better off in that way; we know that the
> surface that seemed to matter to us is just the surface, and
> that it doesn't matter compared to our real life and real self.

There is something in these words of Hamlet's tone near the end
of the play: "If it be now, 'tis not to come; if it be not to come, it
will be now; if it be not now, yet it will come: the readiness is all."
Hamlet is wittier, but Jarrell had spent his life being wittier than
anybody, and now he was, in a way, atoning for it.

He spent the summer at home, recuperating, and returned to
teaching in the fall; but his injured wrist had not healed properly
and in October he made an appointment at the Hand House of
the university medical school in Chapel Hill for physical therapy.
At the time of his checking into the hospital he was full of prospects.
He had just written a lively letter to Adrienne Rich (partly in
response to her praise of *The Animal Family*, of which she had seen
a pre-publication copy), which contained various reflections about
Wallace Stevens—whom he had been reading aloud to his wife—
Hardy, and Hopkins, and about how hard it was to write a really
good poem, the word "good" underlined. He told Rich that he
would be coming up, with Mary, to Boston, to give a reading later
that month at Simmons College and that he hoped to see her then.
When a space at the Hand House became available, however, the
reading was postponed until the following spring. Meanwhile, he
had accepted an invitation to be writer-in-residence at Smith College for the academic year 1966–67.

In what was to be his last class, he taught Hopkins's poem "Felix
Randal" ("Felix Randal the farrier, O is he dead then? my duty
all ended"), and one of his students remembers how, in her words,
he commented "on the cruel frustrations of a job which never

seemed fulfilled to the priest and the great grief he felt in failing the farrier." The student also noted that Jarrell's arm was in a sling and that his wife "followed him about to class":

> *This seeing the sick endears them to us, us too it endears.*
> *My tongue had taught thee comfort, touch had quenched thy tears,*
> *Thy tears that touched my heart, child, Felix, poor Felix Randal.*

His colleague Robert Watson drove him to the hospital, and on the way they discussed Hopkins's "The Wreck of the Deutschland," which Jarrell's students were reading for the class that Watson was going to teach while Jarrell was away. He brought along with him to the hospital a copy of Bishop's new book of poems, *Questions of Travel*, which he planned to review, and the Johnson three-volume edition of Emily Dickinson's poetry, just published, about which he also hoped to write. On Monday evening, October 11, he talked on the phone to his wife, requesting a heavy wool sports jacket and leather gloves for walking in the early evening. Three evenings later, on one of those walks along a highway near Chapel Hill, headed back to the hospital, he was struck and killed by an oncoming car.

When Lowell came to write one of his sonnets about Jarrell, he directed all his portentous rhetoric at that imagined moment:

> *Then the night of the caged squirrel on his wheel,*
> *lights, eyes, peering at you from the overpass;*
> *black-gloved, black-coated, you plod out stubbornly*
> *as if in lockstep to grasp your blank not-I*
> *at the foot of the tunnel . . . as if asleep, Child Randall,*
> *greeting the cars, and approving—your harsh luminosity.*

Lowell believed, as do Peter Taylor and his wife (Eleanor Taylor's poem "New Dust" portrays Jarrell as a suicide), that Jarrell had, in a moment of conviction, sudden oppression, or impulse, killed himself. One meets this assumption in many quarters today, and the biographer Jeffrey Meyers has devoted much energy to proving conclusively that the death *must* have been a suicide. On the other hand, Mary Jarrell has maintained over the years that it was an accident, and her commentary in the volume of letters should be noted. Because of his dark clothes and the lateness of the hour— about 7:30 p.m.—

> he was not visible to the car's driver until too late to be avoided, and in a split second he was sideswiped—"hit from the side," as the coroner said, "not the front, or the front wheels of the car."

Although the occupants of the car in question told the patrolmen who questioned them that Jarrell "seemed to whirl" and that "he appeared to lunge in the path of the car," Mary Jarrell points out that if he had actually "lunged" he would have been run over. She cites the newspaper's statement that "the impact spun Jarrell around and knocked him to the side, as would have happened since he was vertical." So spun around, she argues, all his injuries were to the left side of the body: "from the abrasions on his left cheek and the fatal blow at the left base of his skull (where, being vertical, he hit and damaged the doorpost and windshield of the car), to the contused left side, to the broken bones in the left foot, which was the only part of his body that came in contact with a wheel."

After a three-week investigation, the doctor in charge of the autopsy ruled in agreement with the coroner and the medical examiner that it was an accidental death, "reasonable doubt about its being a suicide" being present in their minds. In reviewing Jarrell's *Letters*, Christopher Benfey has noted the aptness, with respect to this matter, of lines from "90 North":

> *Here at the actual pole of my existence,*
> *Where all that I have done is meaningless,*
> *Where I die or live by accident alone—*

Was Jarrell's death an accident? The people nearest to him when it occurred were the two occupants of the car, who thought he "appeared to lunge" into its path. This statement was properly conjectural, given how difficult it is when driving on a dark road to gauge accurately the presence and motions of a pedestrian. From the pedestrian's point of view, such judgments are at least as difficult, though more hazardous. Jarrell was known to be a very fast, some felt reckless driver; and when on foot he could show great obliviousness of the close presence of speeding cars. The critic Robert Taylor, who heard him read at Wheaton College, Massachusetts, in the fall of 1964, walked with him afterward to the parking lot. Jarrell, caught up in praising something from Peter Taylor's fiction, "stopped in the middle of the street to expand upon his theme while traffic roared around us, and just how long we stood is a relative matter: to me it was an infinity."

But, more importantly, Jarrell's line "Where I die or live by accident alone" reminds us that he was indeed alone when he met his death. Not even his best friends, Lowell and Taylor, convinced that it was suicide, or his wife, at least as convinced that it was not, or Jeffrey Meyers, dedicated to "proving" suicide and linking Jarrell with Berryman and the "manic," self-destructive poets of their generation—none of them can, in the final analysis, move beyond conjecture. Nor could the medical authorities, in their "reasonable doubt" decision. In the face of the conjectural, one possible response—the one I find most appropriate—is that really it is not only impossible but also unimportant to "decide" about Jarrell's death by labeling it suicide or accident. To "die or live by accident alone" makes questions of motivation or impulse shift uneasily into one another, also makes us less certain about exactly what we have asserted, and how authoritative an assertion it is, when we say that a person did or did not do something. My own impulse is to believe that Jarrell's death was unintentional; that—however slowly—he was recovering from his madness of the previous spring; that his forward-looking plans, professional and artistic, revealed a will to live; that he was fundamentally too decent a person to involve other people—the occupants of the death car—in such a heedless manner; that, as a way of putting an end to oneself, lunging into a car is filled with possibilities for awkward miscarrying. Yet these arguments seem fragile and inconclusive when juxtaposed with the sudden and final meeting on the dark highway.

"Here at the actual pole of my existence, / Where all that I have done is meaningless": the strongest refutation of that bleak pronouncement is the two books Jarrell published in the final year of his life. In their frequent luminosity, their warmth, the hospitality and humor of their creative glow, *The Lost World* and *The Animal Family* provide the only satisfactory response to the confusion attendant on any attempt to make sense of the fact of his death. When Robert Watson reviewed *The Lost World* in March (Jarrell was then in the hospital), he compared the effect of the title poem on our lives as mid-century Americans to that of Wordsworth's poetry on his contemporaries. And we may recall that after Wordsworth died in 1850 his admirer Matthew Arnold's "Memorial Verses" asked unashamedly "who, ah! who, will make us feel?" Wordsworth, Arnold wrote, had helped us do just that, so that

> *Our foreheads felt the wind and rain.*
> *Our youth return'd; for there was shed*
> *On spirits that had long been dead,*
> *Spirits dried up and closely furl'd,*
> *The freshness of the early world.*

It does not seem to me fanciful to locate such freshness in certain poems from *The Lost World* and in *The Animal Family*; its presence in them makes us feel that Jarrell's life, even though it was cut short, had completed itself.

The Lost World includes twenty-two poems, one of them the three-part title poem, three of them extracted from *The Bat-Poet*. Unlike *The Woman at the Washington Zoo*, the volume contains no translations. Two of its poems, "A Hunt in the Black Forest" and "Woman," had appeared years previously in quite different form, and the revised "Woman" was one of the longer poems Jarrell had written. Otherwise, the poems were recent work. Beginning with the earliest reviews and continuing until the present, there has been sharp disagreement about the value of Jarrell's achievement in this, his last book of poems. On the one hand, his judgment possibly colored by Jarrell's death, Lowell called it his best book, while R. W. Flint said that it and the war poems were the two peaks of Jarrell's art. Denis Donoghue and John Crowe Ransom also wrote warmly about the volume, especially its title poem. Detractors of *The Lost World* often renamed as vices what others had thought virtues. Jarrell was charged with a prevailing flatness of idiom, with looseness of construction and self-indulgent sentiment, indeed sentimentality. Irvin Ehrenpreis spoke harshly of "the self-pity of a man who has put early innocence in the place of moral judgment"; and James Dickey lamented the poet's passivity before experience, his failure to work hard enough toward more complex and satisfying ways of speaking than his bewildered speakers can command: "He generally does not hold out long enough for the truly telling phrase, for the rhythm that matches most exactly the subject, the image, the voice."

But by all odds the loudest and most abusive of the early reviews was, unfortunately, the one which got into *The New York Times Book Review*—Joseph Bennett's short but crushing notice. Bennett singled out four poems, the only ones in the volume which he said showed clear craftsmanship (they were an odd foursome, but let that be), then hauled out his heavy artillery, speaking of Jarrell's "familiar, clanging vulgarity, corny clichés, cutenesses, and the intolerable self-indulgence of his tear-jerking, bourgeois sentimentality." (To be "bourgeois" is evidently the ultimate sin.) "Folksy, pathetic, affected—there is no depth to which he will not sink, if shown the hole." And Bennett managed other choice phrases, calling the book "trashy and thoroughly dated," and castigating its "doddering infantilism." There was no bit of verbal abuse Bennett was unwilling to descend to, and he did not even need to be shown the hole.

These charges will be countered here with a few references to what I think most readers have agreed are the best poems from the volume: "Next Day," "The Lost World," "The Lost Children," and "Thinking of the Lost World." But there are a number of interesting, even distinguished poems in other modes than that of the recollective psyche turned on itself—for example, "A Hunt in the Black Forest," "The House in the Wood," and the wholly original "Field and Forest" (this last the perfection of Jarrell's dark-mythy style). "In Galleries" and "The Old and the New Masters" convert his love of looking at pictures in museums into humane gestures of expressiveness. There is also the simple and charming "Well Water," as well as more satiric poems which—for me at least—show him at less than his best ("Three Bills," "In Montecito," and "A Well-to-Do Invalid"). But it is the domestic, autobiographical narratives that Lowell had in mind when he wrote the following, totally apt description of *The Lost World*:

> In his last and best book [. . .] he used subjects and methods he had been developing and improving for almost twenty years. [The poems'] themes, repeated with endless variations, are solitude, the solitude of the unmarried, the solitude of the married, the love, strife, dependency, and indifference of man and woman—how mortals age, and brood over their lost and raw childhood, only recapturable in memory and imagination. Above all, childhood! This subject for many a careless and tarnished cliché was for him what it was for his two favorite poets, Rilke and Wordsworth, a governing and transcendent vision. For shallower creatures, recollections of childhood and youth are drenched in a mist of plaintive pathos, or even bathos, but for Jarrell this was the divine glimpse, lifelong to be lived with, painfully and tenderly relived, transformed, matured—man with and against woman, child with and against adult.

This seems to me true both about Jarrell and about childhood. But sound as Lowell is on the subjects and precursors of these poems, his glowing language doesn't account for what makes them so good, and so different from the self-indulgent, tear-jerking displays Joseph Bennett would have us believe they are.

For whatever else these poems may be, they are performances, cunningly staged by an artist who knows how far to go in his rhetorical demands on a listening audience. Here Jarrell's master was Frost—not Wordsworth or Rilke—one of whose favorite metaphors was that of poetry as play, as a play, as performance. Frost was most explicit about the matter at the close of his essay on Edwin Arlington Robinson, when he placed the poet against a backdrop of "immedicable woes, woes flat and final" and then bid him perform his act: "And then to play. The play's the thing. Play's the thing. All virtue in 'as if.' " In some of Jarrell's poems, this metaphor of play is overtly proclaimed; but even when it's not, as in "Next Day"—the opening poem in the volume—it is present in the behavior of words:

> *Moving from Cheer to Joy, from Joy to All,*
> *I take a box*
> *And add it to my wild rice, my Cornish game hens.*
> *The slacked or shorted, basketed, identical*
> *Food-gathering flocks*
> *Are selves I overlook. Wisdom, said William James,*
>
> *Is learning what to overlook. And I am wise*
> *If that is wisdom.*

The play with the names of household detergents is both delightful and an indication that we're in the presence of something other than a "real housewife" in a supermarket. In fact, this woman is about as clever as Randall Jarrell; she has bits of William James in her quotation box and turns one to advantage by pivoting on her own word, "overlook." She has a remarkably detached, humorously confident, and verbally packed way of summing up and pronouncing upon her companions in the market, those "shorted, basketed, identical / Food-gathering flocks."

The poem is about how, in fact, she can't "overlook" them, since they are "identical" to her in a less dismissible way. Indeed, as the boy carries out her groceries and loads them into her car, she realizes that he is overlooking her, patting her dog instead ("It bewilders me he doesn't see me"), and she is thrown into a sense of loss—her husband at work, her children away at school, her own life ("The last mistaken, / Ecstatic, accidental bliss") misplaced back there someplace ("back in some Gay / Twenties, Nineties, I don't know . . ."). Just recently she has lost, for good, the woman—a friend—whose funeral she attended the previous day (thus the poem's title, "Next Day"). Seeing her own face in the rearview mirror, she regards it with hatred, since it tells her she is old; then she thinks of her friend's "cold made-up face, granite among its flowers":

> Her undressed, operated-on, dressed body
> Were my face and body.
> As I think of her I hear her telling me
>
> How young I seem; I am *exceptional;*
> I think of all I have.
> But really no one is exceptional,
> No one has anything, I'm anybody,
> I stand beside my grave
> Confused with my life, that is commonplace and solitary.

Moments like these in Jarrell's last poems must be what provoke the charges of sentimentality, self-indulgence, and banal flatness of idiom. In this connection we may recall I. A. Richards's previously noted discussion of sentimentality as a response "inappropriate to the situation that calls it forth." But Richards goes on to suggest that, with respect to the poems he had asked his students to comment on, many of them were "afraid of free expansive emotion, even when the situation warrants it." This tendency, he said, led them "to suspect and avoid situations that may awaken strong and simple feeling."

In fact, the feelings created and explored by the best poems in

The Lost World are—to use Richards's adjectives—"strong" but not "simple." In writing about them, Jarrell succeeds in clarifying something felt, rather than reveling in its simplicity. I have in mind William James's distinction between simplicity and clearness in his essay "The Sentiment of Rationality." We are all subject, James says, to these two cravings; we want to reduce the multiplicity and confusion of things by running threads of order through them— we want to discover the One in the Many. But there exists a "sister passion" to simplicity, a passion for clearness which shows loyalty to "particulars in their full completeness," and is willing to live with "any amount of incoherence, abruptness, and fragmentariness" as long as "the separate facts" can be saved. Such a loyalty to particulars is what keeps Jarrell in his best poems from making them "illustrations" of a supposedly more important abstraction. The refusal of simplicity gives the poems solidity and, for all the pathos often attendant upon their situations, a tough graininess.

Consider a sequence from "The Lost Children" in which a mother is visited by her married daughter and son-in-law. They are looking through old photographs of the daughter and the daughter's sister, who is dead, and as they sit there in the mother's living room, the husband agreeably enjoying and making fun of the pictures, the mother has an experience of recovery in which the past is recaptured:

> *I look too*
> *And I realize the girl in the matching blue*
> *Mother-and-daughter dress, the fair one carrying*
> *The tin lunch box with the half-pint thermos bottle*
> *Or training her pet duck to go down the slide*
> *Is lost just as the dark one, who is dead, is lost.*
> *But the world in which the two wear their flared coats*
> *And the hats that match, exists so uncannily*
> *That, after I've seen its pictures for an hour,*
> *I believe in it: the bandage coming loose*
> *One has in the picture of the other's birthday,*

> *The castles they are building, at the beach for asthma.*
> *I look at them and all the old sure knowledge*
> *Floods over me, when I put the album down*
> *I keep saying inside: "I did know those children.*
> *I braided those braids. I was driving the car*
> *The day that she stepped in the can of grease*
> *We were taking to the butcher for our ration points.*
> *I know those children. I know all about them.*
> *Where are they?"*

James Dickey's accusation—"He does not search diligently enough for the thing that is his own beyond the thing that is owned both by him and all those aging housewives [. . .] those lost children" —can be countered by reminding ourselves that it is the poet who has shaped and animated the woman's voice here, giving it rising conviction and power as the remembered, wholly authentic "pictures" pile up, until the modest but firm insistence ("I *did* know those children") strikes a chord of true feeling. Or so I read the poem, and especially the final certification of knowledge given by that stepped-in can of grease, on the way to the butcher and the cherished ration points. The slightly awkward syntax of some of the particulars—"the bandage coming loose / One has in the picture of the other's birthday"—actually guards against slickness, keeps the voice from becoming sentimental. "I *know* those children. I know all about them. / Where are they?" She knows everything about them except where they are; this formulation has the force of wit, even as it registers just about as much as can be said about our relations to our children, to our pasts. To be able to speak about things in this way, with fullness and completeness, while admitting (in James's words) abruptness, fragmentariness, incoherence as the past floods over her—this is to effect a clarity of feeling.

Jarrell's strength as a poet had seldom lain in his rendering of situations: the speakers in his poems often talked on for too long, sometimes too airily, with not enough regard for the audience they were presumably addressing or for the scene about which they presumed to speak. The arguable sentimentality of poems like "The Night Before the Night Before Christmas," or "The End of the Rainbow," or the egregiously overlong "Hope" (from *The Lost World*) stems partly from their amorphous, unconvincing sense of place and character. They lack as well a narrative eye that discriminates and a voice that speaks with nuance and modulation. In his final paragraph about sentimentality, I. A. Richards—perhaps with D. H. Lawrence's poem "Piano" in mind (one of the poems his students disliked for its perceived sentimentality)—made the following attempt at a formulation:

> The only safe cure for a mawkish attachment to an illusory childhood heaven, for example, is to take the distorted sentiment and work it into close and living relation with some scene concretely and truthfully realised, which may act as a standard of reality and awaken the dream-infected object of the sentiment into actuality.

This recommendation bears noting in relation to the title poem of *The Lost World*, since it is there that those critics who deplore Jarrell's sentimentality should find its culmination—in the "mawkish attachment to an illusory childhood heaven" that he found during those months when he lived with his grandparents in Los Angeles.

Without subjecting the notion of "concretely and truthfully realised" to analysis (What is "concretely"? How is "truthfully" determined? and so forth), I appeal rather to the experience of reading a typical sequence from "The Lost World," this one chosen from the first section, "Children's Arms," in which the controlling metaphor is Virgil's, revised into a hymn to arms and the child, in Jarrell's phrase "this first Rome / Of childhood, so absolute in every habit." At dinner with his grandparents and great-grandmother, the boy receives a phone call:

> *The phone rings: Mrs. Mercer wonders if I'd care*
> *To go to the library. That would be ideal,*

I say when Mama lets me. I comb my hair
And find the four books I have out: The Food
Of the Gods *was best. Liking that world where*
The children eat, and grow giant and good,
I swear as I've often sworn: "I'll never forget
What it's like, when I've grown up." A prelude
By Chopin, hammered note by note, like alphabet
Blocks, comes from next door. It's played with real feeling,
The feeling of being indoors practicing. "And yet
It's not as if—" a gray electric, stealing
To the curb on silent wheels, has come; and I
See on the back seat (sight more appealing
Than any human sight!) my own friend Lucky,
Half wolf, half police-dog. And he can play the piano—
Play that he does, that is—and jump so high
For a ball that he turns a somersault. "Hello,"
I say to the lady, and hug Lucky . . . In my
Talk with the world, in which it tells me what I know
And I tell it, "I know—" how strange that I
Know nothing, and yet it tells me what I know!

The rhyming cement, the terza rima that holds the poem together, is probably the last thing one notices here, and its very unobtrusiveness suggests how hard Jarrell worked (as can be seen from the work sheets for "The Lost World") to elicit rhymes that would not announce themselves too proudly. At least as important is the colloquial ease of its pace: the sequence is as well written as good prose. The contemporary poet Douglas Dunn has accurately noted that the poem is "stringently colloquial, almost invisibly rhymed as if to forbid sloppiness rather than be formally elegant." But if sloppiness is forbidden, neither is sentimentality courted; the encounter between boy and dog is something other than an episode from *Lassie Come Home.* This is a dog, after all, who plays at playing the piano—just as Jarrell did; but the real play in the sequence involves the humorous double consciousness of the boy's promise, entertained ruefully by the man looking back, that "*I'll* never forget / What it's like, when *I've* grown up." The "ideal" boyish accent is there, but balanced by the adult ironist, a critic famous for his putdowns who can play with the notion of playing Chopin—as the child is forced to do—with "real feeling, / The feeling of being indoors practicing." We had not thought of *that* brand of real feeling before, nor had we previously gone on the little excursion in the final lines about the boy's "Talk with the world," as they playfully shuttle between telling and knowing while bringing out the strangeness involved in any attempt to think about big things in ultimate child-world terms.

The situation or "scene" that is concretely and truthfully realized here is made so by combining a sympathetic feeling for the child's arms, put on in order to "know" the world, with the humorously affectionate understanding of a man who knows the "feeling of being indoors practicing." Jarrell's balanced, supple style of discourse tells us no more than it can enact through line-by-line performance, one which shows those "feats of association"—though in a relatively low-keyed, modest way—which Frost called the essence of poetic prowess. But this particularly satisfying moment—the boy's happiness as he rides in Mrs. Mercer's electric car, Lucky at his side—has to be seen against other, less benign aspects of the child's experience. Irvin Ehrenpreis's severe verdict on Jarrell—"the self-pity of a man who has put early innocence in the place of moral judgment"—might have some point (though it totally misses the humor in the writing) if "The Lost World" contained nothing but idyllic, self-enclosed vignettes like the one about going to the library. But the most memorable and the darkest sequence in the poem comes in its third part—"A Street off Sunset"—when the boy's grandmother kills the chicken:

> *Mama comes out and takes in the clothes*
> *From the clothesline. She looks with righteous love*
> *At all of us, her spare face half a girl's.*
> *She enters a chicken coop, and the hens shove*

> *And flap and squawk, in fear; the whole flock whirls*
> *Into the farthest corner. She chooses one,*
> *Comes out, and wrings its neck. The body hurls*
> *Itself out—lunging, reeling, it begins to run*
> *Away from Something, to fly away from Something*
> *In great flopping circles. Mama stands like a nun*
> *In the center of each awful, anguished ring.*
> *The thudding and scrambling go on, go on—then they fade.*

This is disturbing enough, to the reader as well as to the horrified boy looking on. But the writing is taut; inventive in its verbs, participles, and adjectives; metaphorically alive and energetic in its evocation of the "Something" from which the poor "it" tries to run. The concluding reflection, recollected in non-tranquillity, is strong and final:

> *And whenever*
> *I see her, there in that dark infinite,*
> *Standing like Judith, with the hen's head in her hand,*
> *I explain it away, in vain—a hypocrite,*
> *Like all who love.*

Back there with Mrs. Mercer and Lucky in the electric car, things were—in the child's words—"So *agreeable*," as the glass enclosed him in "a womanish and childish / And doggish universe." By the end of the three-part poem, shocks to the enclosed system have been registered, as the womanish universe complicates itself.

In putting a case for why "The Lost World" resists the sentimentality it so obviously risks, I may be overly defensive, or needlessly arguing a case whose merits readers don't need convincing of. Yet, in the minds of some critics, Jarrell is guilty of softness and a cloying excess about childhood in ways his contemporaries Lowell and Berryman are not. My own sense is that, compared to those contemporaries, Jarrell worked out of a richer vein of nostalgia than either of them possessed. Yet nostalgia is not sentimentality. "In those days everything was better," concluded the speaker of "In Those Days," but the flat statement in context was qualified, prefaced by "And yet after so long one thinks." Jarrell's nostalgia was powerful enough, as expressed in words, to make us see why "after so long" one might think that way about the past.

His last word on the subject, as it were, is the ending to the final poem in *The Lost World*. "Thinking of the Lost World" returns, courtesy of a Proustian spoonful of chocolate tapioca pudding, to a scene from childhood, as the man travels back to "that calm country / Through which the stream of my life first meandered." But the California trees—the orange groves—have all been cut down; smog covers everything, and "Lucky's electric" car, along with other relics from the child's arms, cannot be found. "All of them are gone / Except for me; and for me nothing is gone," says the protagonist, and on that note concludes his dealings—his deal, really—with the lost world. Now, in a different automobile from the celebrated electric one, he takes inventory of his stock:

> When my hand drops to the wheel,
> It is brown and spotted, and its nails are ridged
> Like Mama's. Where's my own hand? My smooth
> White bitten-fingernailed one? I seem to see
> A shape in tennis shoes and khaki riding-pants
> Standing there empty-handed; I reach out to it
> Empty-handed, my hand comes back empty,
> And yet my emptiness is traded for its emptiness,
> I have found that Lost World in the Lost and Found
> Columns whose gray illegible advertisements
> My soul has memorized world after world:
> LOST—NOTHING. STRAYED FROM NOWHERE.
>   NO REWARD.
> I hold in my own hands, in happiness,
> Nothing: the nothing for which there's no reward.

Ransom, who admired the poem, said in his memorial tribute to his old student that he had at first thought this a tragic ending, then upon reflection had changed his mind. Certainly there is as much a comic tinge to these musings as there is anything "tragic" about them (one reaches, if for anything, for "tragicomic"). The boy has turned not only into a man but into his grandmother, as he contemplates his "spotted" hand with its ridged nails. "Where's my own hand?" he asks, with something other than melodramatic inflection, proceeding then to produce the empty hand reaching out and coming back with an acceptable exchange. The tragic possibilities of a world lost are humorously twisted—partly by the capital letters—into something as homely as the Lost and Found columns with their seemingly untempting message, NO RE-WARD. With the poem's work of excavation and evocation of the past now ended—as indeed the whole book has come to its end —the last two lines put the minimum and the maximum case for what has been found:

> *I hold in my own hands, in happiness,*
> *Nothing: the nothing for which there's no reward.*

To contradict King Lear, nothing has somehow been made out of nothing. There is no need to cry out, like the woman at the Washington Zoo, "Change me!" since the change is apparent: rueful acceptance mixed with real elation at what imagining the past has made available. It is a great moment of recovery, and surely no life could ever quite live up to it or fulfill its promise.

Perhaps the deepest impulse in "Thinking of the Lost World" and in the other poems Jarrell wrote near the end of his life was the will to believe that there was more to life than the disillusionment granted the child-grownup in "90 North":

> *I see at last that all the knowledge*
>
> *I wrung from the darkness—that the darkness flung me—*
> *Is worthless as ignorance: nothing comes from nothing,*
> *The darkness from the darkness. Pain comes from the darkness*
> *And we call it wisdom. It is pain.*

"The nothing for which there's no reward" is, on the other hand, something else again. When these last poems are seen as the end of a poetic career that began with the grim vision of things held out by "90 North," their moments of affirmation seem more hard won than a capitulation to thoughtless make-believe. Sometimes the achieved moment of recovery brings with it recognition and forgiveness of one's past, and Jarrell's troubled relations with his parents were ripe for such recognition. The last successful poem he finished (in the summer of 1964, says Mary Jarrell) was "The Player Piano," in the concluding stanzas of which an aging woman—once again Jarrell under a not very elaborate disguise—comes to terms with her dead parents:

> *Here are Mother and Father in a photograph,*
> *Father's holding me. . . . They both look so young.*
> *I'm so much older than they are. Look at them,*
> *Two babies with their baby. I don't blame you,*
> *You weren't old enough to know any better;*
>
> *If I could I'd go back, sit down by you both,*
> *And sign our true armistice: you weren't to blame.*
> *I shut my eyes and there's our living room.*
> *The piano's playing something by Chopin,*
> *And Mother and Father and their little girl*
>
> *Listen. Look, the keys go down by themselves!*
> *I go over, hold my hands out, play I play—*
> *If only, somehow, I had learned to live!*
> *The three of us sit watching, as my waltz*
> *Plays itself out a half-inch from my fingers.*

By now a familiar one, the metaphor of play is given new life even as the last line plays itself out before us. In finding metaphors for the parents ("Two babies with their baby") and signing the "true armistice" (as opposed to that false one which didn't end World

War I), an "as if" moment of play has occurred, at which point the living room appears and the magical piano does its playing.

Mawkishness is of course risked, even courted, by a lyric voice that speaks so affectingly about itself, its memories and desires, with no protective armor beyond the extravagances of improvisation played over a language Jarrell trusts will yield to his charms. Perhaps the most luminous instance of such a risk taken and triumphed over is found in the rapturous conclusion to "A Man Meets a Woman in the Street." Like "The Player Piano," Jarrell kept it back for inclusion in the book he hoped would follow *The Lost World*. The scene is New York City, where a man finds himself following a woman as she walks along Fifth Avenue. Her body and her aura are described in various extravagant ways; she triggers in his musings reminiscences and anecdotes about Jarrell favorites like Richard Strauss, Proust, Greta Garbo. The man remembers that when he woke up that morning in his country "forest / At dawn" before flying to New York:

> *I wished as men wish: "May this day be different!"*
> *The birds were wishing, as birds wish—over and over,*
> *With a last firmness, intensity, reality—*
> *"May this day be the same!"*

He silently implores the woman to turn to him and confess that she is his—only then will his wish come true. But as the narrative proceeds, he confesses that he has been playing a game, and—stepping up and touching the back of the woman's neck—he acknowledges that she is in fact his wife. They kiss, and walk arm in arm, "Through the sunlight that's much too good for New York, / The sunlight of our own house in the forest." The poem concludes with this summary of things:

> *After so many changes made and joys repeated,*
> *Our first bewildered, transcending recognition*
> *Is pure acceptance. We can't tell our life*
> *From our wish. Really I began the day*

Not with a man's wish: "May this day be different,"
But with the birds' wish: "May this day
Be the same day, the day of my life."

The case for "acceptance" has not, to my eyes, been made any more beautifully or eloquently than here at the end of "A Man Meets a Woman in the Street."

Lowell once wrote to Elizabeth Bishop, after having visited Jarrell at Dennis on Cape Cod in 1955:

Saw Randall [. . .] brown, knotted, and with a great black beard with a white splash in the center. He blows hot and cold on one, and both moods are disturbing. Now he is chilly, and I think of him as a fencer who has defeated and scarred all his opponents so that the sport has come to be almost abandoned, and Randall stands leaning on his foil, one shoulder a little lower than the other, unchallenged, invulnerable, deadly, salt marsh and deserted tennis court stretching below him.

In other letters to Bishop, Lowell kept returning to what he perceived as Jarrell's isolation, sometimes finding it maddening, at other times noble or sad. What makes the children's story published a month after his death so affecting is a similar quality of isolation and the storyteller's attempt to mitigate it, indeed transform it into community. The protagonist of *The Animal Family* is a bearded hunter who lives alone in a one-room house by the ocean. He lies in his bed, listening to the sound of the waves, and the sound is like that of his mother's singing. But his mother and father are dead; he is alone. Into his aloneness come, one by one, creatures to people it and make it a family: first a mermaid, whose singing reminds him of his mother's; then a bear, a lynx, and finally a little boy. Nothing more happens in the book than the fulfilling of the hunter's dream, a recurring one which disturbs him and which the mermaid finally explains to him: "I know what your dream means. It means you want a boy to live with us. Then you'll be your father's

313

shadow, and I'll be your mother's, and the boy will be yourself the way you used to be—it will all be the way it used to be." If this sounds like the setup for an ironic reversal, nothing could be further removed from the tone of *The Animal Family*. Instead, the hunter gets what he wishes for, when, discovered by the lynx and with the bear's assistance, a boy is rescued from the boat that holds him and his dead mother and is incorporated into the family. One is reminded of the close of Jarrell's "Windows," where the speaker is taken in by an unidentified "they" who live in the house into which he has been peering; as if in a dream, the "I" looks up speechlessly into an "it" that "blurs, and there is drawn across my face / As my eyes close, a hand's slow fire-warmed flesh." In *The Animal Family* the hunter smooths the sleeping boy's hair, then goes away; returning later, "his face looked absent and remembering, as if he were back with his own mother and father."

Lowell was less than enthusiastic about Jarrell's children's stories, calling them a "nice idyllic thing to do," but wishing he had bitten off something more dangerous and daring—something, perhaps, more like the hair-raising lyrics he himself was producing in the early 1960s. He also found, after Jarrell shaved off his beard in the fall of 1964, that without it his friend looked "strangely malleable and boyish." Jarrell might not have minded those adjectives; one of the loveliest moments in *The Animal Family* occurs after the boy has grown accustomed to living with the hunter and the other occupants of the house:

> The boy was happy, and yet he didn't know that he was happy, exactly: he couldn't remember having been unhappy. If one day as he played at the edge of the forest some talking bird had flown down and asked him: "Do you like your life?" he would not have known what to say, but would have asked the bird: "Can you not like it?"

It is like the resolution set forth near the conclusion of "A Man Meets a Woman in the Street": "We can't tell our life / From our wish." These were "nice idyllic" things to write, no doubt, and they are vulnerable to the criticism expressed in grimmer versions of the human condition, such as those found in the work of his old friend Lowell. But there is at least a measure of boldness involved in the effort to imagine what happiness might be like, even how or whether it might conceivably exist. Memorably embodied in the figures of a poem and a story, coming at the end of Jarrell's career and written against the backdrop of his last, unidyllic months—such glimpsed possibilities of joy, of life, have their resonance, indeed their permanence.

NOTES

The numerals at the left refer to page numbers in this book and the words that follow indicate the beginning of the annotated phrase or passage. I have not duplicated information already in the text.

The following abbreviations of books by and about Jarrell are used:

Kipling *Kipling, Auden & Co.: Essays and Reviews 1935–1964*. New York: Farrar, Straus and Giroux, 1980.

PA *Poetry and the Age*. New York: Ecco Press, 1980; first published 1953.

RJ *Randall Jarrell: 1914–1965*, eds. Robert Lowell, Peter Taylor, and Robert Penn Warren. New York: Farrar, Straus and Giroux, 1967.

L *Randall Jarrell's Letters*, ed. Mary Jarrell. Boston: Houghton Mifflin Company, 1985.

Third Book *The Third Book of Criticism*. New York: Farrar, Straus and Giroux, 1969.

INTRODUCTION

PAGE

4   "put his genius": *Part of Nature, Part of Us* (Cambridge, Mass.: Harvard University Press, 1980), p. 111.

5   "were sentimental": Anatole Broyard, "Cool Stories, Inflamed Poets," *The New York Times Book Review*, December 13, 1987.

5   Jarrell's career as a poet: Suzanne Ferguson, *The Poetry of Randall Jarrell* (Baton Rouge: Louisiana State University Press, 1971); J. A. Bryant, Jr., *Understanding Randall Jarrell* (Columbia: University of South Carolina Press, 1986).

5   "Rilke certainly is": *L*, p. 217.

PAGE   7 "either corrected, ignored": Lowell to Bishop, August 20, 1949 (Vassar College Library).

8 "His body was a little ghostly": *RJ*, p. 102.

8 "Me for Queen Victoria": *L*, p. 323.

8 "I want to say": Ibid., p. 506.

8 "this poet is now": *Kipling*, p. 141.

8 "he couldn't lie to you": Ibid., p. 257.

8 "in something nearer to madness": *RJ*, p. 64.

ONE EARLY LIFE AND WRITING

Much of my account of Jarrell's early years through high school, and especially the 1926–27 visit to his grandparents in California, is taken from an unpublished "Synopsis" by Mary Jarrell. I am indebted to her for allowing me to quote from it and from Jarrell's letters from California (included in "Synopsis") to his mother back in Nashville.

12 "obtained the healthy color": Mary Jarrell, "Synopsis."

14 "I've lived all over": *L*, p. 64.

15 "They had real gifts": Mary Jarrell, "The Group of Two," *RJ*, p. 285.

15 "She was young, and slender": Untitled talk on libraries (Jarrell archive, Berg Collection, New York Public Library).

16 "She was right": *RJ*, p. 286.

20 " 'How I cried' ": Ibid., p. 285.

21 "the craft and lore": Ibid., p. 73. See also Jeffrey Meyers, "The Tennis of Poetry," *London Magazine*, July 1985, pp. 47–56.

21 "a proper nonchalance": This and further quotations are from newspaper reviews of the plays, and from the *Hume-Fogg Echo*, March 1929 and March 1930.

23 "She was so pretty": Mary Jarrell, "Synopsis."

23 Little by little, Warren recalled: Interview with Robert Penn Warren, August 23, 1985.

23 "insistent and almost overbearing": *RJ*, p. 155.

24 Lanier recalls him: Letters from Lyle H. Lanier, August 14 and September 15, 1986.

25 "We have never been able": *Vanderbilt Masquerader*, November 1934.

PAGE 27 "jolly Jewish dinners": *L*, p. 1.

28 "It's all true about the growing up": Ibid., p. 64.

29 Cecile Starr, six years younger: Interview with Cecile Starr Boyajian, January 21, 1986.

30 Zaro Starr's words: Interview with Zaro Starr, February 15, 1986.

32 as Elizabeth Petway Moses recalled: Letter from Elizabeth Petway Moses, February 19, 1986.

35 "I've won all the matches": *L*, pp. 2–3.

36 Warren wrote Jarrell: Robert Penn Warren to Randall Jarrell, May 17, 1935 (Beinecke Library, Yale University).

37 "Brooks and I want": Ibid.

39 "I am grading some": Jarrell to Warren, November 1936 (Beinecke).

40 "to some extent it will be well": Brooks to Jarrell, August 11, 1935 (Beinecke).

41 "The author has the habit of quoting": This and following quotations are from "Ten Books," *Kipling*, pp. 3–15.

42 "really [knew] Auden's poetry": *L*, p. 3.

44 "universal perspective": Bruce Bawer, *The Middle Generation* (Hamden, Conn.: Archon Books, 1986), pp. 80–89.

Two ACADEMICAL

46 "very good chance": *L*. p. 7.

47 "a prodigy of a child": "The Rugged Way of Genius," *RJ*, p. 178.

47 "Randall was announcing": Ibid., p. 181.

47 "I've seen Mr. Ransom": *L*, p. 4.

48 "Mr. Ransom, who is well": Ibid., p. 7.

49 "pretty good company": *Selected Letters of John Crowe Ransom*, eds. Thomas Daniel Young and George Core (Baton Rouge: Louisiana State University Press, 1985), p. 226.

49 "So advanced in his thought": Ibid., p. 240.

49 "as a teacher he's extremely": Ibid, p. 241.

50 "I don't believe that": Interview with Warren.

51 "I can see and hear": *RJ*, p. 102.

51 "The two of them were looking": Ibid., pp. 224–45.

PAGE 52 "read more books": *Alumni News* of the University of North Carolina at Greensboro, Spring 1966.

52 "Gambier is rather like Siberia": *L*, p. 11.

52 "for sheep and for sports": Jarrell to Warren, March 20, 1938 (Beinecke).

52 "I feel just like an angel": Quoted by Lowell in *RJ*, p. 102.

53 "the tone is formal enough": *L*, p. 17.

53 A more impressive contribution: "The Morality of Mr. Winters," *Kipling*, pp. 16–19.

56 "Its casualness, finality": Ibid., p. 22.

58 "I feel very frivolous and unconcerned": *L*, p. 19.

59 "the whole of Existentialism": *The Tyrants* (New York: Anchor Press / Doubleday, 1982), p. 127.

60 "What you say about 'On the Railway Platform' ": *L*, p. 66.

62 "the general rhythmical structure": Warren to Jarrell, March 30, 1938 (Beinecke).

62 its rhythm was "purposely broken": Jarrell to Warren, March 1938 (Beinecke).

62 "an occupational risk": *L*, p. 30.

THREE MAKING A REPUTATION

64 "Texas is lovely": *L*, p. 23.

65 "*one* of them": Ibid., p. 38.

65 "at eighteen, has read": Ibid., p. 24.

65 "I confess that if Texas": Ibid., p. 52

65 "cold as a corpse": Ibid., p. 53.

65 "it would really have more effect": Ibid., p. 51.

66 "Select well, O Allen": Ibid., p. 57.

67 "For an inscrutable reason": *RJ*, p. 232.

67 "gifted, self-adulating little twerp": Tate to Arthur Mizener, October 25, 1967.

67 "somebody with judgment": *L*, p. 26.

67 "Mackie's latest game": Ibid., p. 39

68 "I was interrupted": Ibid., p. 45.

68 "couldn't tell a screwdriver": Interview with Herschel and Barbara Baker, July 24, 1985.

PAGE   69   "He is very intelligent": *L*, pp. 293–94.

69   "I think I'll wait": Ibid., p. 25.

70   "I look like a bear": "A Note on Poetry," *Kipling*, p. 47.

70   "Very interesting language": Ibid., p. 49.

71   developed by critics like: see Frank Kermode, *Romantic Image* (London: Routledge, 1957), and John Bayley, *The Romantic Survival* (London: Constable, 1957).

72   "How can poems be written" (and quotations following): *Kipling*, pp. 81–83.

74   "surprising anonymity in style": Ferguson, p. 8.

74   "a happily or unhappily": *L*, p. 14.

75   "I've been writing stuff": Ibid., p. 48.

75   "My nose has been bleeding": Ibid., p. 62.

77   "*said* (like a speech from a play)": Ibid., p. 26.

77   "We become cultivated": Jarrell archive, Berg Collection.

81   "anyone who writes": *L*, p. 34.

82   "While ailing in Syria": These and following quotations from "Poetry in a Dry Season" are in *Kipling*, pp. 33–35.

83   "I felt as if I had been run over": *RJ*, p. 199.

83   "a sort of bobby-soxer's *Mauberley*": *Kipling*, p. 151.

83   "a lot of respect for Jarrell": *L*, p. 41.

83   "the dullest and prosiest poetry": This and following quotations are from "Poets: Old, New, and Aging," *Kipling*, pp. 41–46.

84   "clever and entertaining": *The New Republic*, February 17, 1941.

84   a piece titled "Poets as Reviewers": *The New Republic*, February 24, 1941.

84   "I am so flattered": *L*, p. 41.

85   "laugh unbelievingly when I think": Ibid., p. 43.

86   "skillfully dispatched the fifteen remaining poets": *The New Republic*, March 17, 1941.

86   "It was neither a success": *L*, p. 35.

86   "Good criticism, which points out badness": "Contemporary Poetry Criticism," *Kipling*, pp. 58–64.

87   "to make up for that": *L*, p. 35.

89   He separates Auden: The essay on Auden from which the following quotations are taken can be found in *Third Book*, pp. 115–50.

93   "In Mexico, after the first week": Jarrell to Tate (Princeton University Library).

PAGE   93   "The most amusing thing": *L*, p. 49.

93   "We got so sick of Mexico": Ibid., p. 67.

93   "I have the impression that": Jarrell to Tate (Princeton).

94   writing to Wilson: *L*, p. 49.

94   "and I can't even turn over": Jarrell to Brooks (Beinecke).

94   "very sick for about seven weeks": Jarrell to Tate (Princeton).

94   "sick or dopey": *L*, p. 62.

94   "is, very often, roughly dialectical": Ibid., p. 60.

95   Vladimir Nabokov was also visiting Wilson: Letter from Mary McCarthy, July 10, 1986.

95   The most intelligently critical: "First Blood," *The New Republic*, November 30, 1942, pp. 281–82.

FOUR IN SERVICE

97   These letters give: I have not provided specific references for passages quoted from the war letters, and indeed the dates of many of them, as is usual with Jarrell's letters, can be ascertained only roughly. The relevant section of *L* is pp. 71–111. In addition, and with Mary Jarrell's permission, I have quoted from other letters to Mackie Jarrell not included in the volume.

97   "For to write what you can": *L*, p. 65.

98   "with how (relatively) cheerful": Ibid., p. 273.

98   "For about two months": Ibid., p. 100.

106   "What I do is run a tower": Ibid., p. 121.

109   Flint reminded himself: *RJ*, pp. 76–85.

110   "She does not understand": *Kipling*, p. 129.

111   "silly anthology": *L*, p. 132.

112   James Dickey's 1955 dialogue-review: *RJ*, pp. 33–48.

113   "Unless you're vain or silly": *L*, p. 151.

114   "a quiet poem": Ibid.

118   "A ground tone of swaying iambics": *Kipling*, p. 80.

119   "the portentous ending of a tiny poem": "Nightmares and Irresponsibilities," *The New Republic*, December 26, 1960, pp. 18–19.

122   a "heavy bomber training-field": *L*, p. 132.

122   "merely a vehicle of presentation": Ibid.

124   "What he saw and what he felt": *Kipling*, p. 113.

PAGE 124 "a victory of the deepest moral feeling": Ibid., p. 120.

125 James Dickey was enamored: "The G.I. Can of Beets, The Fox in the Wave, and The Hammers Over Open Ground," in *Night Hurdling* (Columbia, S.C.: Bruccoli Clark, 1983), pp. 124–40.

127 "I felt so strongly about everything": *L*, p. 120.

FIVE NEW YORK AND *THE NATION*

128 it received intelligent and appreciative commentary: Schwartz's review is in *RJ*, pp. 184–87; Spencer's is in *The Saturday Review of Literature*, January 5, 1946, p. 7.

131 "the Society for the Scientific Diet": "Freud to Paul: The Stages of Auden's Ideology," *Third Book*, pp. 186–87.

132 "Saturday I had to go to a border jail": *L*, p. 142.

134 "I believe that my tastes": Ibid., p. 153.

135 "will grieve and bother me": Ibid., p. 157.

135 "with great quantities of philosophy": Ibid., p. 153.

138 "the national anthem of my own particular war": Ibid., p. 105.

138 Mary Jarrell writes entertainingly: "Randall Jarrell and Music" (unpublished essay by Mary Jarrell).

139 Haggin remembered that Jarrell: Interview with B. H. Haggin, July 23, 1985.

139 "a sort of exemplary monster": *Kipling*, p. 154.

140 "Gee, gee! I almost died of bliss": Letter to Mary von Schrader Jarrell, *L*, p. 308.

140 "I am going to do something rather notably absurd": *L*, p. 251.

140 "small, expensive, with ingeniously": Letter to Margaret Marshall, Ibid., p. 165.

140 "the worst place to live": Ibid., p. 168.

141 "a whole new world of sound": *RJ*, p. 4.

142 "a shy, sincere, serious schoolgirl": *L*, p. 246.

142 "too dignified for you": Ibid., p. 163.

142 "and that was very amazing": *RJ*, p. 15.

143 "a terror as a reviewer": Ibid.

143 "blazing with ambition": *We Dream of Honour: John Berryman's Letters to His Mother*, ed. Richard J. Kelly (New York: W. W. Norton, 1968), p. 230.

PAGE 144   "To say that he had been": *RJ*, p. 77.

144   "the new generation of American poets": Dudley Fitts, *The New York Times Book Review*, March 28, 1948.

145   "a serious, objective": *Kipling*, p. 134.

146   "I had rather read your poems": *L*, p. 127.

146   "I think it's terribly important": Ibid., p. 139. In "Randall Jarrell and Robert Lowell," Bruce Michelson shows how "Jarrell's splendid balance of trenchancy and circumspection" was evidenced by his criticisms of the *Lord Weary* poems. (*Robert Lowell*, ed. Harold Bloom. New York: Chelsea House, 1987, pp. 139–61.)

147   "who could make other writers feel": *RJ*, p. 106.

148   "I think you write more": *L*, p. 139.

148   invariably met with disbelief: Interview with Peter Taylor, July 28, 1987.

148   "Inside its elaborate stanzas": *PA*, pp. 215–16.

149   David Kalstone put the matter: *The New Republic*, June 3, 1985, pp. 32–36.

149   "the world and everything in it": *L*, pp. 116.

150   "beauty, delicacy, and intelligence": *PA*, p. 226.

150   "wonderful and unlikely": Ibid., p. 233.

151   "She is morally so attractive": Ibid., p. 235.

152   "just wonderful": *L*, p. 218.

152   "The most important thing": *PA*, p. 248.

153   before appointing visiting "novelist-teachers": Letter from Harold Taylor, September 4, 1986.

154   "the very advanced, very experimental": *RJ*, p. 248.

154   "But," he concluded: *L*, p. 173.

Six   A COUNTRY LIFE

156   "We ought to be moving": *L*, p. 177.

156   "a tremendous modernist house": Ibid., p. 175.

156   a "cottage in the country": Ibid., p. 39.

157   "Greensboro leaves one alone": Ibid., p. 185.

157   "ensconced on the couch": *RJ*, p. 234.

157   "The first day one of them": *L*, p. 180.

PAGE 157 "the average North Carolina girl": Ibid., p. 219.

158 "and now amuse myself": Ibid., p. 218.

158 "distinctive in its way": "Randall Jarrell's Landscape," *The Nation*, May 1, 1948, p. 476.

158 Graham felt that Jarrell's name: "Jarrell's *Losses*: A Controversy," *Poetry*, September 1948, pp. 302–7.

160 "the Farmer-Poet": *PA*, p. 28.

160 Jarrell wrote mockingly to Lowell: *L*, p. 188.

160 "by having irregular line lengths": Ibid., p. 191.

166 "very dramatic, very emotional": *The Function of Criticism* (The Swallow Press, Chicago, 1957), p. 87.

167 "Frost's seriousness and honesty": *PA*, p. 31.

170 Leslie Fiedler taxed Jarrell: "Some Uses and Failures of Feeling," *Partisan Review*, August 1948, p. 926.

172 "It wasn't our Leopoldskron": *L*, p. 207.

172 "a talented Viennese ceramist": Ibid., p. 195.

173 "Nothing but the army": Ibid., p. 201.

173 "Europe had about as much effect": Ibid., p. 203.

173 "My reaction to Europe": Ibid., p. 204.

173 "I can't be anyone's husband": Ibid., p. 197.

174 "They compared me to Rilke": Ibid., p. 207.

174 "My mouth is wide-open": Ibid., p. 198.

174 "I'm writing you": Ibid., p. 202.

175 "You're wasted, and the ocean's": Ibid., p. 203.

175 "I lead an odd, independent": Ibid., pp. 204–5.

176 "made me behave very badly": Ibid., p. 212.

176 "and forgive me": Ibid., p. 245.

177 "full of Faustian yearnings": Ibid., p. 201.

179 "Rilke certainly is": Ibid., p. 217.

180 "Among the new poems": *RJ*, p. 115.

182 embodies Jarrell's most extensive: Ferguson, p. 146.

184 "the child's redreaming": *L*, p. 303.

185 "one of the most mature": "The Dramatic Lyrism of Randall Jarrell," *Poetry*, March 1952, pp. 335–46.

185 "The same Oedipal love-hate": *The Black Goddess: A Study of the Archetypal Feminine in the Poetry of Randall Jarrell* (Bern: Francke Verlag, 1975).

SEVEN THE LIFE OF CRITICISM

PAGE 187 "Oh, oh, OHH!": *L*, p. 274.

188 "whose newspapers and magazines": *PA*, p. 18.

189 "Any American poet": Ibid., p. 10.

190 "a tremendous philippic": Lowell to Bishop, September 18, 1950 (Vassar).

191 "Then this man": *PA*, p. 15.

191 "*Why, he'd say anything*": Ibid., p. 238.

192 "I've never been funnier": *L.*, p. 257.

194 "transcendental, all too transcendental": *Third Book*, p. 64.

195 "allows himself to waver": "Through the Looking Glass," *The Threepenny Review*, Spring 1984, p. 11.

198 "perhaps best uses both": *RJ*, p. 116.

200 "No-no-no! Re-dikkl-us!": *L*, p. 254.

200 "more and more different": Ibid., p. 275.

200 "She more and more disapproved": (Houghton Library, Harvard University).

201 "Living has never been at all": *L*, p. 258.

201 "O star, sister, breathe on me!": Ibid., p. 258. Jarrell's letters to Mary from Princeton may be found in *L*, pp. 263–352. I have not provided specific page references for passages quoted from them in this and the following chapter.

202 "I am living": Ibid., p. 281.

202 "awfully broke": Ibid., p. 285.

202 "I can cook": Ibid., p. 298.

203 Eileen Simpson . . . remembers him: Interview with Eileen Simpson, January 22, 1986.

203 "my extraordinarily messed-up": *L*, p. 284.

205 "His is the kind of egotism": *Selected Letters of Robert Frost*, ed. Lawrance Thompson (New York: Holt, Rinehart and Winston, 1964), p. 123.

205 In reviewing Jarrell's *Letters*: "Poet in the Sun Belt," *The New York Review of Books*, May 9, 1985, pp. 29–31.

206 "There is no doubt about the words": "Examples of Wallace Stevens," in *Form and Value in Modern Poetry* (1957), p. 188.

207 "Here and there a drunken": *PA*, pp. 137–38.

PAGE 207 "In *Auroras of Autumn* one sees": Ibid., p. 145.

208 "Whatever is wrong with the poems": *Third Book*, p. 65.

208 "He can never forget": *PA*, p. 90.

210 "He is like one of those": Ibid., p. 253.

210 "It is too much a succession": Ibid., p. 258.

211 "Yet he takes Credit": Ibid., p. 263.

212 "one needs simply to quote": Ibid., p. 114.

212 "One has an immediate vision": Ibid., p. 117.

213 "In the last lines of this quotation": Ibid., p. 127.

214 "there is something essentially ridiculous": Ibid., p. 132.

215 "But when one writes": Ibid., p. 39.

215 "Pharisee and Philistine": Ibid., p. 63.

216 "The tone of the phrase": Ibid., p. 47.

218 "the public figure's": Ibid., p. 33.

218 "things made out of lives": Ibid., p. 68.

Eight CRITICIZING THE INSTITUTIONS

220 He wrote Elizabeth Bishop: *L*, p. 298.

221 "Criticism *does* exist": *PA*, p. 72.

222 "But if you wanted to talk": Ibid., p. 79–80.

224 "Readers, real readers": Ibid., p. 80.

225 "resolutely unsystematic": *RJ*, p. 64.

225 "needs to care more for stories": *PA*, p. 94.

229 The lectures have never been published: The manuscript of these lectures is part of the Jarrell archive in the Berg Collection at the New York Public Library.

232 "He told it entirely seriously": *L*, p. 356.

232 "extravagantly mechanical and verbose": Ibid., p. 357.

232 "the possibilities of the new": Ibid., p. 360.

233 "how lonely you are when": Ibid., p. 359.

234 "which I would like to claim": Ibid., p. 301.

234 "an odd book's an odd problem": Ibid., p. 334.

241 "sees also good in the beings": "To Benton, with Love and Judg-

ment: Jarrell's *Pictures from an Institution.*" (In *Critical Essays on Randall Jarrell*, ed. Suzanne Ferguson. Boston: G. K. Hall & Co., 1983, p. 274.)

241 "that paragon of virtue": "The Tender and the 'Tough,' " *The Sewanee Review*, Winter 1955, p. 142.

243 "rooted in humaneness": Agee's comment, from a lost letter to Jarrell, was used as publicity material for *Pictures* (see *L*, p. 394).

243 "not at all a wearing *job*": *L*, p. 378.

243 "in which the main structure": Ibid., p. 399.

244 "Man is the animal": Ibid., p. 265.

244 "Your poems seem really": Ibid., p. 422.

NINE THE GROUP OF TWO

246 "fine, bright, smog-free": *RJ*, p. 277.

246 "dazzling skill, individuality": "The Little Cars," *Kipling*, p. 199.

247 "Like birds, they run": Ibid., p. 197.

247 "nearer than anything else": *RJ*, p. 276.

247 "To be married to Randall": Ibid., p. 278.

248 "ideal father": Beatrice Hofer, in conversation.

250 "Why of course!": *RJ*, p. 281.

250 Robert Watson . . . remembers: Ibid., p. 258.

250 "books, or paintings": Ibid., p. 263.

251 Friedlaender . . . recalls: Interview with Marc Friedlaender, July 29, 1986.

251 "I've written a fair amount": *L*, p. 394.

252 "that Indian Summer": *A Sad Heart at the Supermarket* (New York: Atheneum, 1962), p. 16.

254 Donald Hall, reviewing it: *The New Republic*, December 26, 1960, pp. 18–19.

254 a response "inappropriate to the situation": *Practical Criticism* (New York: Harvest / Harcourt, Brace and World, 1968), p. 246.

256 "lost either in his subject": *PA*, p. 250.

256 "the world of the younger poets": *L*, p. 413.

257 "When I look in the mirror": Ibid., p. 399.

257 "predicted the Alexandrianism": *RJ*, p. 203.

PAGE 258 "The readers of America": To Philip Vaudrin and Harry Ford, *L*, p. 401.

258 "we really are going to buy": Ibid., p. 397.

259 "unlike our smooth younger poets": October 11, 1957 (Houghton Library).

259 (as John Bayley has suggested): *The Uses of Division* (New York: Viking, 1976), pp. 171–82.

262 "a world in which everything": *Third Book*, p. 60.

263 Jarrell was invited to serve: See William McGuire's history of the consultantship in poetry at the Library of Congress, *Poetry's Catbird Seat* (Washington: Library of Congress, 1988), pp. 193–206.

264 "lots of newspaper and radio things": *L*, p. 414.

266 *"A nice soft wife"*: *Kipling*, p. 253.

266 "When I wear it and Mary": Ibid., p. 283.

267 "depressed about the United States": Unpublished letter, October 1957.

269 (Mary Jarrell's account): *L*, pp. 417–18.

274 "I've always wanted to change": Ibid., p. 515.

TEN THE WORLD LOST AND FOUND

276 "Your courage, brilliance and generosity": Quoted in *L*, p. 510.

278 "want never to be without them again": Ibid., p. 461.

279 "all sorts of duodenal": Ibid., p. 454.

280 "a short story masquerading": "Randall Jarrell and the Flotations of Voice," *Georgia Review*, Fall 1974, pp. 423–39.

282 "Someone, in love with an idea": *Critical Essays on Randall Jarrell*, p. 57.

283 "lyric or quiet or thoughtful": *L*, p. 461.

284 "Won't the future say to us": These and other quotations from the lecture may be found in *Third Book*, pp. 295–334.

288 "We're enchantingly flooded": *L*, p. 472–73.

288 "If you believe in happiness": Ibid., pp. 480–81.

289 "I suppose I am a brute": *The Letters of Robert Frost to Louis Untermeyer* (New York: Holt, Rinehart and Winston, 1963), p. 103.

289 "He felt I was an Indian": *L*, p. 483.

Notes

PAGE 290   Of the 521 pages in Mary Jarrell's edition: Unless otherwise specified, references and quotations in the following pages draw heavily
upon *L*, pp. 486–521.

291   Bryant also provided: This and further quotations are from Bryant's
account of his relations with Jarrell, 1961–65. (Letter from J. A.
Bryant, Jr., January 30, 1987.)

295   the biographer Jeffrey Meyers: See "The Death of Randall Jarrell,"
The Virginia Quarterly Review, Summer 1982, pp. 450–67.

296   "he was not visible": *L*, p. 520.

296   "seemed to whirl": Ibid.

297   "stopped in the middle of the street": Letter from Robert Taylor,
July 17, 1985.

299   "the self-pity of a man": "Poetry Without Despair," *The Virginia
Quarterly Review*, Winter 1966, pp. 165–67.

299   "He generally does not hold": "Orientations," *The American
Scholar*, Autumn 1965, pp. 646–48.

299   "familiar, clanging vulgarity": "Utterances, Entertainment and
Symbols," *The New York Times Book Review*, April 18, 1965, p. 24.

300   "In his last and best book": *RJ*, p. 109.

302   "inappropriate to the situation": "Sentimentality and Inhibition,"
in *Practical Criticism*, pp. 241–54.

304   "He does not search diligently enough": Dickey, p. 648.

305   "The only safe cure": *Practical Criticism*, p. 254.

306   "stringently colloquial": "An Affable Misery: On Randall Jarrell,"
Encounter, October 1972, p. 47.

313   "Saw Randall . . . brown, knotted": April 3, 1964 (Vassar).

314   "nice idyllic thing to do": Lowell to Bishop, April 6, 1964 (Vassar).

314   "strangely malleable and boyish": Lowell to Bishop, November
16, 1964 (Vassar).

INDEX